CISSP® Exam Prep

Questions, Answers & Explanations

CISSP® Exam Prep

Questions, Answers & Explanations

SSI Logic Publishing

Published by SSI Logic
PO Box 39038
Washington, DC 20016

Looking for more CISSP exam prep?
Visit us online at www.cisspexampractice.com

ISBN-10: 0982576846
ISBN-13: 978-0982576847

All inquiries should be addressed via email to:
support@ssilogic.com

or by mail post to:
SSI Solutions, INC
PO Box 39038
Washington, DC 20016

CISSP® is a registered certification mark, and (ISC)² is a service mark of the International Information Systems Security Certification Consortium, Inc. in the United States and other countries.

Table of Contents

Additional Resources

INTRODUCTION

Welcome

Thank you for selecting SSI Logic's *CISSP® Exam Prep – Questions, Answers, and Explanations* for your CISSP study needs. The goal of this book is to provide condensed mock exams and practice tests which allow you to become comfortable with the pace, subject matter, and difficulty of the Certified Information Systems Security Professional (CISSP) certification exam.

The content in this book is designed to optimize the time you spend studying in multiple ways.

1. Practice exams in this book are condensed to be completed in one hour; allowing you to balance your time between practice tests and offline study.

2. Passing score requirements in this book are slightly higher than the real exam; allowing you to naturally adjust to a higher test score requirement.

3. Practice exams included in this book cover the entire scope of the CISSP exam, while shorter quizzes focus only on specific CISSP Common Body of Knowledge (CBK) Domains.

The practice exam content in this book is structured into two general types of exam preparation:

- "Lite" Mock Exams, which allow you to test your knowledge across condensed versions of the CISSP exam; designed to be completed within one hour.

- Domain Area Quizzes, which reflect brief practice tests focused on specific CBK® Domain Areas; designed to be completed in 15 to 30 minutes, depending on the exercise.

We wish you the best of luck in your pursuit to become a certified CISSP.

CISSP® Exam Overview

The CISSP practice questions in this book reflect the Domain areas presented in the official CISSP Common Body of Knowledge (CBK).

About the Certified Information Systems Security Professional (CISSP) Certification

The CISSP certification is managed by the International Information Systems Security Certification Consortium (ISC)² and reflects (ISC)² 's CISSP Common Body of Knowledge (CBK). The CISSP program is the first IT certification to be an ANSI ISO/IEC Standard 17024:2003 accreditation; an accreditation achieved in June 2004.

As of January 2010, the CISSP certification has been acquired by more than 60,000 individuals worldwide. The CISSP certification is a globally recognized credential, with individuals certified in more than 130 countries. On average, salaries associated with CISSP certified professionals are consistently ranked high among the IT industry, with an average salary of $94,070 per year.

The minimum requirements in attaining the CISSP certification:

- Work experience: A minimum of five years of security work experience in two or more CISSP domains; or four years of work experience with an applicable degree or certification
- Accept the CISSP Code of Ethics and attest to the truth of your professional experience
- Answer four questions regarding criminal history and related background
- Have your qualifications endorsed by another (ISC)² certified professional
- **Pass the CISSP Exam**

CISSP Exam Details

The CISSP exam is designed to objectively assess and measure Information Security knowledge. Concepts covered in the CISSP exam are directly derived from the ten Domains of the CISSP Common Body of Knowledge (CBK).

The actual CISSP exam is offered via proctored, paper-based exams; with computer based testing (CBT) expected by 2013. A summary of the exam structure and passing requirements are as follows:

- There are 250 total multiple choice questions which make up the CISSP exam
- Individuals have 6 hours to complete the exam
- The passing grade required is a scaled score of 700 out of a possible 1000 points

The Ten CBK Domains

The ten CBK® Domains covered by the CISSP exam are listed below.

- Information Security and Risk Management
- Access Control
- Security Architecture and Design
- Telecommunications and Network Security
- Business Continuity and Disaster Recovery Planning
- Software Development Security
- Cryptography
- Legal, Regulations, Compliance and Investigations
- Physical (Environmental) Security
- Security Operations

The CISSP certification is a globally recognized credential, and must be renewed every three years. The certification can be renewed through Continuing Professional Education (CPE) credits, or by retaking the CISSP exam.

About the International Information Systems Security Certification Consortium (ISC)²

The (ISC)² is a not-for-profit organization headquartered in the U.S.A, most widely known for its CISSP certification. The (ISC)² develops and maintains the (ISC)² Common Body of Knowledge (CBK), upon which a common framework of terms and principles in the Information Security field are based. In addition to the CISSP certification, the (ISC)² also credentials the SSCP, CAP, and CSSLP certifications.

PRACTICE EXAMS AND QUIZZES

CISSP Mock Exam (Baseline) Practice Questions

Test Name: CISSP Mock Exam (Baseline)
Total Questions: 40
Correct Answers Needed to Pass: 30 (75.00%)
Time Allowed: 60 Minutes

Test Description

This is a cumulative CISSP Mock Exam which used as a baseline score for your CISSP aptitude. This practice test includes questions from all ten domains of the CISSP CBK.

Test Questions

1. Separation of duties is an important aspect of Security Operations. Which of the following scenarios does not violate the separation of duties principle?

   A. A computer user is allowed to install software and also to modify her security profile.

   B. A development team performs unit testing and quality assurance testing.

   C. A security administrator is allowed to view and delete audit logs.

   D. A computer user is allowed to install software and alter desktop configurations.

2. A security administrator completed the configuration of an antivirus software. She was however concerned about how the system would behave when an actual virus was encountered. Which of the following will help her in resolving this?

   A. An ICE test

   B. A self-test

   C. An EICAR test

   D. A script test

3. The IT team in a company with a poor security policy uses a mechanism by which they are able to access code without any security checks. This is likely to be a:

   A. Database program

   B. Maintenance hook

   C. Security bypasser

D. Administrator hook

4. During development of a software product, the development team performed unit testing on the code during the coding phase. Subsequently a different team performed formal testing on the product. This is in accordance with what principle?

  ✓ **A.** Separation of duties

  B. Division of labor

  C. Generally accepted testing principles (GATP)

  D. Agile methodology

5. A user logged into an online banking system using a secure connection and performed certain online transactions. She left her desk for about 5 minutes and then returned to continue a transaction on the online banking system. At this time, the online banking system required her to login again. Which of the following is a reason this could happen?

  A. This is most likely a bug in the online banking software and the user needs to register a formal complaint.

B. When a web session is idle for a period of time, the internet connection gets timed out. Hence the user needs to login again into the online banking system.

C. All secure connections are setup such that they timeout automatically after 5 minutes. Hence it is important to ensure that a periodic refresh is done every 5 minutes so that the web server doesn't log the user out.

  ✓ **D.** When a web session is idle for a specified period of time, the connection is closed out since the web server does not receive a cookie from the session. The cookie has a timestamp and as a result the session gets timed out.

6. A high security system was found to have a high level of electromagnetic emanation. Which of these standards is likely to have been violated?

  A. Ampere

  B. Tropic

  C. Faraday

  D. Tempest

7. Although the terms event and incident are often used

interchangeably, they are different. Which of the following statements is incorrect in this context?

A. An event is a negative occurrence that can be observed, verified and documented.

B. An incident may have a positive or a negative impact on the company.

EVENT IS ALWAYS NEGATIVE

C. A terrorist attack is a type of incident.

D. An insider attack is a type of incident.

8. A security officer developed a security program to handle the security requirements of an organization. The first three stages of the life cycle of the security program were (a) Plan, (b) Implement and (c) Operate. Select a choice from the following which best represents the next activity to be done as part of the Security Program.

A. Restart the planning process

B. Assess business drivers

C. Assign roles and responsibilities

D. Monitor the program

9. In the context of an IT environment, what does asset identification and management refer to?

A. Asset management involves knowing and keeping up-to-date the complete inventory of software in the department including operating systems, applications and individual libraries.

B. Asset management involves knowing and keeping up-to-date the complete inventory of hardware, including the names of the manufacturers.

C. Asset management involves knowing and keeping up-to-date the hardware, software, firmware, operating systems, and applications.

D. Asset management involves knowing and keeping up-to-date the complete inventory of hardware including laptops and printers.

10. A bank is planning to implement a security model which allows for dynamic changing of access controls to prevent conflict of interest. Which of the following would fit this requirement?

A. Biba model

B. Brewer and Nash model

C. The Access Control Matrix model

D. Clark and Wilson model

11. Two sets of computers are communicating with each other. One set of computers uses session keys while the other set of computers uses static symmetric keys. Which of the two is preferable to provide better protection?

A. Static symmetric keys provide better protection than session keys since they are valid only for one session.

B. Both session keys and static symmetric keys provide equal protection since they are valid only for one session.

C. Both session keys and static symmetric keys provide equal protection since they are valid only for multiple sessions.

D. Session keys provide better protection than static symmetric keys since they are valid only for one session.

12. Which of the following types of plans establishes personnel safety and evacuation procedures?

A. IT contingency plan

B. Cyber incident emergency plan

C. Business resumption plan

D. Occupant emergency plan

13. Lighting in buildings is often controlled such that lights in different parts of the building turn on and off at different times. This gives potential intruders the impression that there are people at work in different parts of the building. What is this called?

A. Standby lighting

B. Bypass lighting

C. Standoff lighting

D. Controlled lighting

14. Which of the following proxy firewalls does not operate at the network layer of the OSI model?

A. Stateful proxy

B. Packet filtering

C. Stateless proxy

D. Kernel proxy

15. Clustering refers to a fault-tolerant server technology similar to redundant servers with the difference that each server takes part in processing services that are requested. Which of the following statements about clustering is incorrect?

   A. Clustering helps in load balancing where each system takes a part of the processing load.

   B. Clustering offers poor scalability.

   C. Clustering provides failover such that other systems continue to work if one fails.

   D. Clustering provides for availability

16. A vandal stole a hardcopy of a list of credit card numbers and typed these into a spreadsheet on his computer. However, he was arrested by the police and his computer was seized. What category of computer crime law would apply?

   A. Computer-assisted crime

   B. Computer-induced crime

   C. Computer is incidental crime

   D. Computer-targeted crime

17. A frame relay is a WAN solution that allows multiple companies and networks to share a WAN media. In this context, what is the equipment used at the company-end (such as a router or a switch) called?

   A. Data Circuit-Terminating Equipment (DCE)

   B. Data Broadcasting Equipment (DBE)

   C. Data Terminal Equipment (DTE)

   D. Data Circuit Equipment (DCE)

18. A software company developed an encryption software that eventually became very popular. A competitor of the company bought a copy of the software and took it apart to understand its functionality. The competitor then came out with a product that performed a similar type of encryption. What is this known as?

   A. Decryption

   B. Research and development

   C. Reverse analysis

   D. Reverse engineering

19. Which of the following represents the correct sequence of activities in the event of a disaster?

A. Disaster, Alternate operations, Continuity operations, Normal operations

B. Disaster, Interim operations, Alternate operations, Normal operations

C. Disaster, Recovery operations, Emergency response, Normal operations.

D. Disaster, Backup operations, Salvage operations, Normal operations

20. An important objective of threat assessment as part of BCP is to evaluate existing organizational controls and procedures to determine the likelihood of a potential interruption of services. Which of the following is not a type of threat assessment?

A. Environmental security assessment

B. Information security assessment

C. Futuristic assessment

D. Physical and personnel security assessment

21. Key management is a very challenging aspect of cryptography. If a key is not securely stored/transmitted, the strength of the algorithm becomes immaterial. What is the recommended period to change cryptographic keys?

A. It depends on the level of security required by the data.

B. Every month

C. Every day.

D. Every week

22. A company decided to use combination locks on the doors of its data processing center. Once the combination has been set, what is the usual guideline followed to change it?

A. Every year and when an employee who knows the code leaves the company

B. Every week and when an employee who knows the code leaves the company

C. Every six months and when an employee who knows the code leaves the company

D. Every month

D. Smoke-activated detectors

23. At a generic level, evidence of a crime needs to be relevant to the case at hand and meet the criteria of the five rules of evidence. These rules states that:

   A. Evidence must be authentic, complete, convincing, admissible and unaltered.

   B. Evidence must be authentic, irrefutable, complete, convincing and admissible.

   C. Evidence must be authentic, accurate, complete, convincing and admissible.

   D. Evidence must be authentic, accurate, convincing, admissible and clear.

24. A security officer would like to ensure that an early warning is received in case a fire breaks out. The early warning can then be used to sound a warning alarm to start off evacuation procedures. Which of these may be used as an early-warning device?

   A. Fixed-temperature sensors

   B. Heat-activated detectors

   C. Fire suppressors

25. Which of these is not a best practice for physical security in organizations?

   A. Limit the number of entry points to a facility

   B. Encourage placement of trees close to the facility to deter intruders

   C. Force all guests to go to a front desk and sign in before entering a facility

   D. Encourage employees to question strangers

26. A disgruntled employee had to be terminated due to certain security violations. Which of these is the best way to terminate the employee?

   A. Give the employee a day's notice, disable his accounts at the end of the day, and have a security guard escort the employee out of the facility after the necessary exit formalities have been completed.

   B. Give the employee a month's notice, disable his accounts at the end of 30 days, and have a security guard escort the employee out of the facility after the necessary exit formalities have been completed.

C. Give the employee a week's notice, disable his accounts at the end of 7 days, and have a security guard escort the employee out of the facility after the necessary exit formalities have been completed.

D. Disable the employee's accounts right away and have a security guard escort the employee out of the facility after the necessary exit formalities have been completed.

27. Privacy is a serious issue as the world relies more and more on technology and the user of computers / digital information. What law protects US citizens' sensitive information collected by government agencies?

A. HIPAA

B. Computer fraud and abuse act

C. The Federal privacy act

D. Graham-Leach-Bliley act

28. Companies normally have an acceptable use policy which indicates what software users can install. What type of controls should be put in place to prevent unauthorized users

from being able to install unauthorized software?

A. Administrative controls

B. Technical controls

C. Hardware controls

D. Physical controls

29. A network administrator wants to minimize the number of public IP addresses that his organization purchases. Which of the following implementations will help him achieve this?

A. Static mapping

B. This is not possible. The company will need to purchase IP addresses corresponding to each computer that needs to connect to the Internet.

C. Port address translation (PAT)

D. Hidden address translation (HAT)

30. Grid computing is a load-balanced parallel means of massive computation. Which of these statements about grid computing is not correct?

A. In grid computing the nodes do not trust each other.

B. In grid computing, the excess CPU processing power of loosely coupled systems combined.

C. In grid computing, the grid members are of variable capacity.

D. Grid computing is ideal for processing sensitive data due to the high capacity available.

31. A BCP / DRP team came up with an exhaustive set of procedures to be implemented in case of a disaster. How should the team proceed to test these?

A. Include only a small group of people as part of its first test exercise.

B. Include all employees as part of its first test exercise.

C. Include all employees in the most critical operations as part of its first exercise.

D. Include employees in the least critical operations as part of its exercise.

32. Which of the following is not an instance of a computer-targeted crime?

A. Carrying out hacktivism by defacing a government's website

B. Installing rootkits and sniffers.

C. Capturing passwords and sensitive data

D. Carrying out a DDos attack.

33. The Clark-Wilson model establishes a system of subject-program-object bindings so that the subject does not have direct access to the object any more. Each data item is defined and changes are allowed only by a limited set of programs. Which of these is not a defined item?

A. Integrity verification procedure (IVP)

B. Hidden data element (HDE)

C. Constrained data item (CDI)

D. Transformation procedure (TP)

34. In order to support auditing of implemented security controls, a number of frameworks have been created. Which of the following ISO standards specifies requirements for a documented information security management system?

A. ISO 31000

B. ISO/IEC 27001

C. ISO 9000

D. ISO 14001

35. A company recognized the need to have a business continuity plan in place. Which of the following guidelines will help the company in this process?

    A. NIST 900-34

    B. ISO 800-34

    C. ISO 9000:34

    ✓ **D.** NIST 800-34

36. In which type of operating system do all of the operating system's functionality work in ring 0 and in privileged or supervisory mode?

    A. Virtual machines

    B. Layered operating systems

    ✓ **C.** Monolithic operating systems

    D. Polylithic operating systems

37. Critical data needs to be protected from accidental or malicious changes. Such data needs to be accessed through properly formatted requests. Which of the following concepts does not use such a methodology?

    A. Data hiding

    B. Layering

    C. Protection domains

    D. Polymorphism

38. Which of the following is a simple method used in symmetric key cryptography to ensure message integrity?

    A. Message digest

    B. Diffie-Hellmann algorithm

    ✓ **C.** Checksums

    D. HAVAL

39. A company had sensitive data stored in a database. It wanted to ensure that certain data was not available to lower-level users. The company created a table containing multiple tuples with the same primary keys and each instance was distinguished by a security level. The data for the lower-levels was changed to some arbitrary values. Hence, lower-level users who accessed the data received

a fake view of the data. What is this called?

A. Views

B. Polyinstantiation

C. Polymorphism

D. Multi-tuple security

40. Data in a database is structured in many ways depending on the type of information stored. Which of these is not a valid database management model?

A. Hierarchical database management model

B. Network database management model

C. Ordered database management model

D. Relational database management model

CISSP Mock Exam (Baseline)
Answer Key and Explanations

1. D - A computer user may be allowed to set an initial password, install software and alter desktop configurations. In this case, there is no breach of the separation of duties principle. However, the user must not be allowed to modify his/her security profile. [Security Operations]

2. C - After an antivirus software has been installed, an EICAR test can be performed. In this test a string that all antivirus products recognize as hostile is used. Antivirus products have an EICAR.com file and a signature matches this file. This allows an administrator to test the reaction of the anti-virus system when a virus is encountered. [Software Development Security]

3. B - This is likely to be a maintenance hook. Maintenance hooks are a type of backdoor and refer to code within software to which the developers have access. They allow the developers to bypass usual security procedures. They are prone to attack by malicious hackers. [Security Architecture and Design]

4. A - Unit testing can be performed during the development cycle by the programmers developing the code. However, when formal testing is required, it is usually done by a different team to ensure separation of duties. This enhances the chance that bugs will be found. In general, a programmer should not develop, test and release software. [Software Development Security]

5. D - Online banking software uses secure connections. They use cookies with timestamps on them and the web server periodically requests the cookie to ensure that the session has not been hijacked. When the system is inactive for a period of time, the web server does not receive the cookie when it requests for it. Hence it times out the user's session and requires a re-login. [Cryptography]

6. D - Tempest is a standard that outlines how countermeasures can be developed to control spurious electrical signals that radiate from electrical equipment. Equipment that needs to be highly secure should prevent or control this type of radiation and adhere to the Tempest standards. [Access Control]

7. B - An event is a negative occurrence that can be observed / verified / documented whereas an incident is a series of events that negatively affects the company. Virus, insider and terrorist attacks are incidents. [Legal, Regulations, Compliance and Investigations]

8. D - The next step in the process would be to monitor and evaluate the program. This would include

reviewing logs, audit results, and service level agreements. This would also include development of improvements to the program. [Information Security and Risk Management]

9. C - Asset management in an IT environment is typically an automated solution and involves knowing everything that exists in the environment. This includes hardware, firmware, operating systems, applications, individual libraries and other run time components. Just having the list of inventory may not help. Interdependencies also need to be known. [Security Operations]

10. B - The Brewer and Nash model allows access controls that can change dynamically depending on the actions of a user. It ensures that conflict of interest is protected. [Security Architecture and Design]

11. D - Session keys provide better protection than static symmetric keys since they are valid only for one session. Hence if an attacker were to capture a session key it would no longer be valid for the next session and the window of opportunity available to the attacker is very limited. [Cryptography]

12. D - Organizations usually have various types of recovery plans. The Occupant emergency plan specifically establishes personnel safety and evacuation procedures. As a general principle, human life is given the highest priority in the event of a disaster. [Business Continuity and Disaster Recovery Planning]

13. A - This is referred to as standby lighting. It is similar to a technique used in residential homes where certain gadgets can be configured to turn lighting on or off at pre-determined times. This gives the illusion that the house is occupied. The same technique is used in companies and security guards can configure the times that lights turn on and off. [Physical (Environmental) Security]

14. D - In a kernel proxy firewall, all the inspection and processing takes place in the kernel and does not need to be passed up to a higher software layer for processing. The other three firewall proxies work in the network layer. [Telecommunications and Network Security]

15. B - Clustering offers good scalability since a group of servers can be viewed logically as a single server to users and can be managed as a single logical system. [Security Operations]

16. C - This is an example of a 'computer is incidental' type of crime. It is incidental that the hacker stored the list of credit card numbers in his computer. He may as well have

retained the hard copy in which case it would have just been a case of theft. [Legal, Regulations, Compliance and Investigations]

17. C - The equipment used at the company's end is called Data Terminal Equipment (DTE). It could be a router or a switch and provides connectivity between the company's own network and the frame relay network. DCE is the equipment used by the service provider. [Telecommunications and Network Security]

18. D - This is known as reverse engineering. There could be legal issues associated with this activity but it is used by many companies to understand how their competitor's products work and to improve upon features in their products. [Cryptography]

19. B - Once a disaster strikes, Interim operations kick in. These include emergency responses and situational assessments. This is then followed by alternate operations during which recovery and restoration operations are performed. This then allows the company to recover back to normal operations. [Business Continuity and Disaster Recovery Planning]

20. C - Futuristic assessment is not a specific type of threat assessment. The other three are valid types of threat assessments and cover a large number of areas such as loss of key personnel, physical control weaknesses, emergency plan assessment, telecommunications availability, continuity planning etc. [Business Continuity and Disaster Recovery Planning]

21. A - The necessary level of security required and the frequency of use of a cryptographic key determine how often the key should be changed. For example, a small retail store may only change its keys once a month whereas a military establishment may change them every day. [Cryptography]

22. C - The combinations need to be changed at least every six months. Changing them every week may be too much of an overhead. Additionally they also need to be changed whenever an employee who know the combination leaves the company. [Physical (Environmental) Security]

23. C - At a generic level, evidence in a computer crime needs to be relevant to the case at hand. The five rules of evidence are that it should be authentic, accurate, complete, convincing and admissible. [Legal, Regulations, Compliance and Investigations]

24. D - Smoke-activated detectors are very useful as early-warning devices. They operate using photo-electric

devices, which detect variations in light intensity. If the beam of light produced by the device is obstructed due to smoke, an alarm sounds and this can be used to kick-off evacuation and other procedures. [Physical (Environmental) Security]

25. B - Having trees very close to a facility may be a security hazard since they will enable intruders to gain access to upper-story windows / balconies / skylights. This needs to be balanced with the objective of concealing a facility. [Physical (Environmental) Security]

26. D - Although it may seem harsh to do so, it is best to ensure that the termination happens quickly and in such a manner that the disgruntled employee cannot cause any harm prior to his/her exit. The company's HR policies will dictate the actual procedure but in case of disgruntled employees, their accounts / accesses should be disabled right away and they should be escorted out of the facility by security guards or supervisor after complying with necessary exit formalities. [Information Security and Risk Management]

27. C - The Federal privacy act protects US citizens' sensitive information that is collected by government agencies. It states that data must be collected in a fair and lawful manner. The data must be held for a reasonable amount of time and used only for the purpose for which it was collected. [Legal, Regulations, Compliance and Investigations]

28. B - Technical controls need to be in place to ensure that unauthorized users are not able to install unauthorized software in the environment. These consist of password and resource management, identification and authentication methods, configuration of the infrastructure etc. [Security Operations]

29. C - Port Address Translation (PAT) is an NAT implementation where the company can use only one public IP address for multiple computers that communicate with the Internet. This is achieved by the NAT device which changes the header information and maps internal addresses to the public IP address, but with a different port number. [Telecommunications and Network Security]

30. D - In grid computing, the secrecy of the contents of a workload unit allocated to a grid member cannot be guaranteed. Hence, it is not suitable for processing sensitive data even though massive computational power is available. [Security Operations]

31. A - Once written plans have been developed, they need to be tested for specific weaknesses. Companies cannot afford to have any impact to normal operations. Hence the tests should be carried using a small group of people from various departments until each learns his / her responsibility. Testing on all employees may actually disrupt operations as also may testing on the most critical department. On the other hand testing on the least critical department may not yield useful results. [Business Continuity and Disaster Recovery Planning]

32. A - A computer-assisted crime is one in which a computer is a tool used to carry out a crime. A computer-targeted crime is one in which a computer is the victim of an attack to harm it. Hence, hacktivism, which involves protesting a government's activities by defacing their websites is not a computer-targeted crime. [Legal, Regulations, Compliance and Investigations]

33. B - A hidden data element (HDE) is not one of the items defined by the Clark-Wilson model. The other three are defined by the model. Additionally, an unconstrained data item is used to define data not controlled by the Clark-Wilson model. [Security Architecture and Design]

34. B - ISO / IEC 27001 specifies the requirements for establishing, implementing, operating, monitoring, reviewing, maintaining and improving a documented information security management system.

ISO 9001 deals with quality management, ISO 14001 deals with environment management and ISO 31000 deals with risk management. [Information Security and Risk Management]

35. D - The National Institute of Standards and Technology (NIST) has put together a set of best practices and documented them as a series of steps in the NIST 800-34 document. Although this specifically deals with IT contingency plans, the steps are the same while creating enterprise-wide BCPs. [Business Continuity and Disaster Recovery Planning]

36. C - In a monolithic operating system, all of the kernel's activity takes place in privileged or supervisory mode. Hence, all the functionality is in ring 0. This improves performance but causes a security risk since more code runs in privileged mode and can be exploited by attackers. [Security Architecture and Design]

37. D - Data hiding, layering and protection domains are different terms used to describe the same concept. The methodology used by them is that the secure data cannot be accessed except via a set of properly formatted requests sent to system APIs. Polymorphism is not used in this context. [Security Architecture and Design]

38. C - Checksums are simple error detecting codes and are used in symmetric key cryptography to ensure message integrity. The checksum is created and appended to a message. The receiver will decrypt the message and generate their own checksum to verify the integrity of the message. [Cryptography]

39. B - This is known as polyinstantiation and is used for very sensitive data. A simpler strategy would be to simply deny access when a lower-level user accesses a higher-level object. However, this indirectly gives the lower-level user information that sensitive data exists at that level. Polyinstantiation overcomes this issue. [Software Development Security]

40. C - The ordered database management model is not a valid one. The other three choices are valid. Of the three types, the hierarchical database model is the oldest. [Software Development Security]

CISSP Mock Exam (LITE) - 1
Practice Questions

Test Name:
CISSP Mock Exam (LITE) - 1
Total Questions: 40
Correct Answers Needed to Pass:
30 (75.00%)
Time Allowed: 60 Minutes

Test Description

This is a cumulative CISSP Mock Exam which can be used as a benchmark for your CISSP aptitude. This practice test includes questions from all ten domains of the CISSP CBK.

Test Questions

1. An Internet Service Provider adds a large generator and battery bank to its infrastructure. Which of the following needs to be added to the list of operational procedures?

   A. Monthly testing of the generator and annual testing of the batteries

   B. Annual testing of the generator and monthly testing of the Batteries

   C. Annual testing of the generator and the batteries

TESTED AT SAME TIME

   D. Monthly testing of the generator and the batteries

2. A new software with many vulnerabilities was installed. As a result, it is likely that the system is no longer providing its necessary minimum level of protection. This minimum level is referred to as:

   A. A requirement

   B. A start-up

   C. A guideline

   ✓ **D.** A baseline

3. Although less common today, phreakers are special class of hackers who manipulate telephone systems to receive free services. Which of the following is NOT used by phreakers?

   A. Red Box

   B. Blue Box

   C. Black Box

   D. Teal Box

4. A lawyer serves notice on a business entity for a civil wrong against a

business entity that he represents. This would be dealt with under:

A. Criminal law

B. Administrative law

✓ **C.** Tort law

D. Cyber Law

5. The most important goal for the results of any computer forensics should be which of the following?

A. Equipment Redeployment

B. Retaliation and Redress

✓ **C.** Admissibility in Court

D. Cost-Savings where possible

6. A company uses asymmetric cryptography and a public key system. The private key will be known only to the company while the public key will be known to everyone. In such a public key system:

A. Only the public key can be used to encrypt data but the data can be decrypted with either the private or public keys

B. Both the public key and the private key can be used to

encrypt and decrypt data. Data encrypted with the private key can be decrypted with either the private or public keys.

✓ **C.** Both the public key and the private key can be used to encrypt and decrypt data. Data encrypted with the private key requires the public key to be decrypted.

D. Only the public key can be used to encrypt data and the private key is required to decrypt it.

7. Rob is writing up a detailed set of procedural security measures. He plans to follow this up with a series of educational programs to educate employees within the company. This would be the best way to minimize:

A. Malicious threats

✓ **B.** Accidental threats

C. Environmental threats

D. External threats

8. Which of the following is not a preventive measure against static electricity in a data center?

A. Ensure that static-free carpets are used.

B. Ensure proper grounding for electrical wiring.

C. Ensure that people use antistatic bands while working on computers.

D. Ensure that humidity is as low as possible.

9. A company hires an accounting firm to audit finances. Because of certain contractual obligations, the accountants may not be allowed to view the names of customers in the General Ledger database. However, it is appropriate that they see invoice numbers and all other data. Which of the following solutions requires the least effort to implement?

A. Custom Database View

B. Redacted Printouts

C. Sanitized Data Mirror

D. Custom Web Interface

10. A problem in Software Development Security is that some developers build in methods to bypass security. They usually do this for testing and efficient development purposes. What is this practice termed as?

A. Viruses

B. Spyware

C. Rootkits

D. Backdoors

11. The AIC triad is made up of three main principles of information security: availability, integrity and confidentiality. Which of the following threats can compromise availability?

A. Password leak

B. Social engineering

C. Dumpster diving

D. Denial-of-Service attack

12. While setting up measures for handling fire hazards, you are concerned that activation of sprinklers, immediately following the detection of a fire may interfere with evacuation activities. Which of the following may be a good option to pursue in such a case?

A. Use of a low-pressure sprinkler system

B. Use of a dry pipe system.

C. Use of a wet pipe system.

D. Use of a manually controlled sprinkler system.

13. John is a web developer. What would be the best way for him to connect to a database without exposing its physical location and passwords used to connect to it?

A. Use a Restricted Source Name (RSN)

B. Use a Data Source Node (DSN)

C. Use a Data Source Name (DSN)

D. Use a Restricted Source Node (RSN)

14. A fire broke out due to a leak in the diesel tank of a back-up power generator. Which of the following should not be used to put out such a fire?

A. Carbon di-oxide

B. Water

C. Monoammonimum phosphate

D. Sodium bi-carbonate

15. Which of the following is the cause of most information breaches in email?

A. System errors

B. Spam

C. Long chains of forwards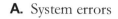

D. Intentional abuse

16. What classification of gate is designed to secure an industrial yard where only authorized individuals are permitted entry and which is not expected to serve the general public?

A. Class I

B. Class IV

C. Class II

D. Class III

17. When two different keys generate the same output for the same message, what is it called?

A. Wardialing

B. Polyinstantiation

C. Collision

D. CORBA

18. Ray wants to ensure that a message he sends to Ron is not altered in any way. He encrypts the message's value and includes it with his message (he does this by digitally signing his message). What does Ron have to do to ensure the message came from Ray?

A. Ron needs to perform the hashing function on the message and come up with a hash value. Ron will then decrypt the hash value sent in the message using Ray's public key and compare with the hash value he obtained. If they are the same, it indicates the message was not altered.

B. Ron needs to perform the hashing function on the message and come up with a hash value. Ron will then decrypt the hash value sent in the message using Ray's private key and compare with the hash value he obtained. If they are the same, it indicates the message was not altered.

C. Ron needs to perform the hashing function on the message and come up with a hash value. Ron will then decrypt the hash value sent in the message using his public key and compare with the hash value he obtained. If they are the same, it indicates the message was not altered.

D. Ron needs to perform the hashing function on the message and come up with a hash value. Ron will then decrypt the hash

value sent in the message using his private key and compare with the hash value he obtained. If they are the same, it indicates the message was not altered.

19. Karen is in charge of her company's Internet security. She decides to implement a fake DMZ that hosts a specialized server. This server holds no data, but answers any scan or hack attempt with positive results. The purpose is to trick an attacker into wasting enough time on this system so that detection possibilities are increased. This type of system is commonly known as:

A. Honeypot

B. Hobgoblin

C. Tarbaby

D. Pitfall

20. During a security audit, an external auditor finds several unlocked electrical panels in common areas. She writes this up as a potential security issue. Which of the following groups of people is most likely to cause a potential security hazard by taking advantage of the unsecured panels?

A. Auditors

B. Hackers

C. Administrators

D. Disgruntled Employees

21. Which of the following teams is responsible for starting recovery of the original site in the aftermath of a disaster?

A. Restoration team

B. Backup team

C. Assessment team

D. Salvage team

22. Because of the size of Alex's company, it has been decided that rotation of duties is not practical. Which of the following is another good way to detect fraudulent activity?

A. Criminal Background Checks

B. Wire Sniffers

C. Mandatory Vacations

D. Video Surveillance

23. What type of virus infects both the boot sector and executable files?

A. Polymorphic

B. Self-garbling

C. Multipart

D. Meme

24. As part of the planning to implement an antivirus software, Jim is considering implementing a program which will work proactively and detect malware. This technique is called:

A. Immunization

B. Heuristic detection

C. Signature-based detection

D. Fingerprint detection

25. Which of the following options best describes mature procedures and processes?

A. Well-documented

B. Well-known

C. Ad-Hoc

D. Obsolete

26. A systems analyst designs an access control software application such that the authentication and authorization processes are independent ones that happen sequentially. Which of the following vulnerabilities can a hacker use to break into such a system?

A. Code jam

B. Strength of the wireless network

C. Two-factor authentication

D. Race condition

27. A hacker attempts to perform a replay attack by capturing traffic from a legitimate session and using the information to authenticate his session. This type of attack can be avoided by:

A. Use of session variables

B. Use of time-stamp validation.

C. Use of SSL

D. Use of cryptic parameters

28. As network administrator, you have a requirement to split up a network into collision domains and broadcast domains. Which of the following networking devices should you use?

A. A router

B. A hub

C. A repeater

D. A bridge

29. Two mechanisms by which malicious code may be detected are via _____ for known viruses and _____ for unknown viruses.

A. Patches and Updates / Filtering

B. Testing / Code execution prevention

C. Heuristics / Port blocking

D. Signatures / Heuristics

30. Intrusion detection systems are used to determine if attacks are occurring on a network. You have been asked to implement an intrusion detection system that uses predefined knowledge about attacks to determine if an attack is occurring. Which one of the following would you consider?

A. Statistical anomaly-based intrusion detection

B. Protocol anomaly-based intrusion detection

C. Least-privilege-based intrusion detection system

✓ **D.** Signature-based   intrusion detection

31. Which of the following physical security controls are preventative rather than detective?

    A. Guard Dogs

    B. Logging

    C. Motion Sensors

✓   **D.** Padlocks

32. Company A hires Company B to develop an application. Company B only does business on a licensing model, and therefore will not provide a copy of the application's source code to Company A. However, Company A wants to be protected in case Company B ceases to exist. What is a good option for Company A?

    A. Safety-Deposit Box

    B. 24-bit Encryption

    C. Software Escrow

    D. Non-Disclosure Agreement

33. As a network administrator in a large-sized company, you understand that government regulations require you to maintain a record of your company's email for seven years. This would be a large amount of data. A very good option would be to:

✓   **A.** Use a SAN.

    B. Use RAIT

    C. Use RAID

    D. Use RAIL

34. Data leakage can cause huge losses to the company depending on the criticality of the data. Companies can look at publicly available data to understand the channels from which data is lost and plug potential security loopholes. Which of the following are the top two (in that order) causes for loss of data?

    A. Internet, Emails

    B. Internet, Mobile Devices

    C. Emails, Internet

    D. Mobile devices, Internet

35. Software Development Security is often a balancing act between:

    A. Process and Procedure

B. Developers and Administrators

✓ **C.** Functionality and Security

D. Client and Server

36. Due to recent security breaches, the security administrator of a large financial institution has mandated that all critical data infrastructure be secured by three-factor authentication. Which of the following choices best meets the requirement?

A. Use of a fingerprint Scanner, *ARE* Smart Card, PIN Number *HAVE* *KNOW*

B. Use of a smart Card, PIN Number, Password

C. Use of a hardware Token, PIN Number, Password

D. Use of a fingerprint Scanner, Password, PIN Number

37. A company uses a particular combination of a word, name, shape, color, sound, symbol as their corporate "signature." These are registered to prevent copying by others. What is this known as?

A. Copyright

✓ **B.** Trademark

C. Trade Secret

D. Corporation

38. Which type of attack introduces fake packets into the data stream so that the session can be hijacked?

A. Sniffer Attack

B. TCP Sequence Number Attack

C. DNS Poisoning

D. Ping of Death Attack

39. Company guidelines have required you to use a biometric system as one of the authentication methods. You are okay with a situation where authorized users are rejected, but would like to ensure that the system rejects unauthorized users to a high degree of accuracy. Which of the following error rates are you more likely to prefer?

A. 1% Type I errors, 25% Type II errors

B. 25% Type I errors, 10% Type II errors

C. 10% Type I errors, 25% Type II errors

D. 25% Type I errors and 1% Type II errors

AUTHORIZED ARE DENIED

STUDY

40. What term refers to the creation, administration/maintenance and deactivation of user objects and attributes?

A. Revisioning

B. Authorization

C. Authentication

D. Provisioning

CISSP Mock Exam (LITE) - 1
Answer Key and Explanations

1. D - A backup power system must be tested end-to-end even though it is intended to be used only for emergencies. Hence both the generator and the battery need to be tested. Monthly testing is the preferred option. Annual testing for such a backup system is inadequate. [Physical (Environmental) Security]

2. D - Baselines are used to define the minimum level of protection required. By establishing, documenting, and adhering to the requirements, a company will be implementing a baseline of protection. [Information Security and Risk Management]

3. D - A blue box simulates a particular calling tone, enabling the theft of long-distance service. A red box simulates the alert tones of coins being deposited into a pay phone. A black box manipulates line voltage to enable toll-free calling. [Legal, Regulations, Compliance and Investigations]

4. C - A civil wrong against a company or business entity would normally be dealt with under tort law. [Legal, Regulations, Compliance and Investigations]

5. C - A clear chain-of-custody and excellent forensic methods are the end goal. Poor forensics will destroy the best evidence in a criminal case. [Legal, Regulations, Compliance and Investigations]

6. C - A common misunderstanding is that a public key is used only to encrypt and the private key is only used to decrypt. Either of the keys can be used to encrypt data. However, data encrypted with a public key will require the private key for decryption and vice-versa. [Cryptography]

7. B - A commonly accepted security principle is that more than three-fourths of all security violations attributed to insiders of a company are accidental in nature. These are best avoided by a good set of educational programs and by strong procedural security measures. [Physical (Environmental) Security]

8. D - Low humidity conditions are conducive for static electricity which can damage computer equipment. On the other hand, high humidity causes corrosion. Hence the humidity needs to be optimally controlled. [Physical (Environmental) Security]

9. A - A database view is a custom subset of data based upon a query. It is easy and effective because it runs against live data and only

returns selected data sets. All of the other options require significant effort and expense. [Software Development Security]

10. D - When a developer creates a shortcut into a system, it is usually called a backdoor or trapdoor. This type of practice is generally frowned upon and has become less common in modern development environments. [Software Development Security]

11. D - A DoS attack attempts to disrupt or totally disable client access to one or more systems. This results in systems not being available. The other three options listed may impact integrity / confidentiality. [Information Security and Risk Management]

12. B - A dry pipe system may be used in such a case. Typically, the valve which needs to be activated by the smoke/fire sensor is activated in a delayed manner. The delay allows evacuation activities to take place without interference due to the sprinklers. [Physical (Environmental) Security]

13. C - A Data Source Name (DSN) is a logical name for the data store and does not use the drive letter or directory location of the database. This can be used when programming using Open Database Connectivity

interface (ODBC). [Software Development Security]

14. B - A fire due to a diesel leak is classified as a class B fire, which includes fires due to petroleum products and coolants. Water should not be used in trying to put out such a fire. [Physical (Environmental) Security]

15. C - A long chain of forwards is often the culprit when private information is breached. An email, with private information, circulated between departments internal to the organization, could get forwarded to an external party without the entire contents of the message being checked. This then results in loss of private information. [Legal, Regulations, Compliance and Investigations]

16. D - A gate is the movable part of a barrier that is designed to control physical access. There are four main classifications for vehicular gates. A Class III gate is designated for industrial usage, and is not intended to be accessed by the general public. [Physical (Environmental) Security]

17. C - A good hash function should never produce identical hash values. Doing so is called a collision. Collision is the basis of hash cracking techniques. [Cryptography]

18. A - A hash value that was encrypted with a sender's private key is called a digital signature. Since Ray has encrypted the hash value with his private key, Ron will have to decrypt the message with Ray's public key and compare it to the hash value that he got when he performed the hashing function on the message. [Cryptography]

19. A - A honeypot is a system that attempts to lure attackers away from real information and data assets. Multiple honeypots can act together and it would be called a honeynet. [Telecommunications and Network Security]

20. D - An unlocked electric panel can easily be misused by disgruntled employees. Hackers may not have access to unlocked electrical panels and auditors / administrators are unlikely to target unlocked electric panels. [Physical (Environmental) Security]

21. D - The salvage team is responsible for starting work on the recovery of the original site. This team (like a restoration team) needs to know how to do many tasks such as installing operating systems, handling wiring requirements, setting up workstations , servers etc. [Business Continuity and Disaster Recovery Planning]

22. C - A mandatory vacation is a policy that requires employees to take a full weeks or even two full weeks of vacation at a time each year. The theory is that any fraudulent behavior will be caught by others during that time. Criminal background checks only give a historical perspective. Snuffers and cameras are usually not sufficient to catch fraud. [Security Operations]

23. C - A multipart virus first finds its way into system memory, and then infects the boot sector of the hard drive. It then infects the entire system. [Business Continuity and Disaster Recovery Planning]

24. B - A proactive technique that can detect malware is called Heuristic detection. This is in contrast to signature-based detection (fingerprint detection), which can not do this. [Software Development Security]

25. A - Mature procedures or processes are usually well-documented. The documentation should continue to be updated as the process changes or grows more efficient. [Security Operations]

26. D - A race condition is a situation where two or more processes use a shared resource and perform their operations in an incorrect order due to non-availability of the resource. If authentication and authorization are split as separate functions, there is a possibility that an attacker uses a race condition to have the authorization step completed before authentication. This will allow access into the system. [Access Control]

27. B - A replay attack involves an attacker grabbing traffic from a valid, legitimate session, and then 'replaying' it, giving the impression that it is valid traffic, and authenticating his session. The counter to this is to use some mechanism of a time-based (or timestamp) validation so that the information grabbed by the attacker is no longer "current". [Software Development Security]

28. A - A router is used when there is requirement to split up a network into collision domains and broadcast domains. A bridge can do simple filtering to separate collision domains but not broadcast domains. A repeater can do neither. A hub is a multi-port repeater. [Telecommunications and Network Security]

29. D - Signatures are sequences of code extracted from malware by antivirus vendors. The anti-virus software has an engine that uses these signatures to identify malware. Heuristics attempt to catch unexpected behavior that is malicious even for unknown viruses and zero-day

attacks. [Software Development Security]

30. D - A signature-based intrusion detection system uses accumulated knowledge to determine if an attack is being made. Models of known attacks are developed and these are called signatures. When an attack matches the information within a signature, the intrusion detection system takes the required action to protect the network or system. [Access Control]

31. D - A simple padlock is preventative - although it may not necessarily be very effective by itself. The other choices are all detective. [Physical (Environmental) Security]

32. C - A Software Escrow is a third party who is entrusted with the final source code as a protection to both the development entity and the purchasing entity. No other choice offers a complete solution. [Software Development Security]

33. A - A Storage Area Network (SAN) is used in large-sized companies that need to handle large volumes of data. SANs provide the necessary redundancy and fault-tolerance apart from being extremely reliable. RAID and RAIT cannot be used for such a requirement. [Security Operations]

34. D - A survey of various types of data leaks has revealed that mobile

devices head the list, followed by the Internet as the single largest causes. [Security Operations]

35. C - A system that offers the best functionality and ease of use is one that usually has little security in place. In contrast a completely secure system is one that almost none can use. In practice, a trade-off is achieved between the two extremes, based on what is acceptable. [Software Development Security]

36. A - Three-factor authentication combines something you know (a PIN number), something you have (smartcard), and something you are (your fingerprint). This provides strong authentication. [Access Control]

37. B - A trademark can be a combination of a word, name, shape, color, sound or symbol. These can be registered to ensure that they are unique. [Legal, Regulations, Compliance and Investigations]

38. B - A Transmission Control Protocol (TCP) Sequence Number Attack exploits the communication session that is created between two hosts. An attacker eavesdrops on the traffic and then predicts the correct sequence numbers. He then introduces fake data packets with the correct sequence numbers. This then allows the attacker to hijack the session. [Telecommunications and Network Security]

39. D - A Type I error occurs when authorized users are rejected by the biometric system whereas Type II errors occur when unauthorized users are accepted by the system. In an ideal scenario, both types of errors should tend to zero. Since the intent is to have a highly secure system even at the cost of higher Type I errors, the correct answer is 25% Type I errors and 1% Type II errors. [Access Control]

40. D - Provisioning is the term used to refer to the creation, administration / maintenance and deactivation of users objects and permissions / attributes. [Access Control]

Domain Area Test: Information Security and Risk Management Practice Questions

Test Name:
Domain Area Test: Information Security and Risk Management
Total Questions: 15
Correct Answers Needed to Pass: 11 (73.33%)
Time Allowed: 25 Minutes

Test Description

This practice test specifically targets your knowledge of the Information Security and Risk Management domain area.

Test Questions

1. One of the primary steps in a quantitative risk analysis is to determine the annualized loss expectancy (ALE). How is the ALE calculated?

   A. Single loss expectancy / Frequency per year

   B. Asset value x 2.8

   C. Single loss expectancy X Frequency per year *(ANNUAL RATE OF OCCURANCE)*

   D. Asset value + (Single loss expectancy / Frequency per year)

2. An Electrical provider must maintain documentation of their electronic security perimeter in precisely the way set forth in the North American Energy Reliability Corporation (NERC) Critical Infrastructure Protection documents, particularly CIP-005-1, or face significantly daily fines. What is this an example of?

   A. Standards

   B. Baselines

   C. Practices

   D. Policies

3. Which of the following terms refers to a security hole that could result in an attack on a system?

   A. Risk

   B. Exposure

   C. Threat

   D. Vulnerability

4. Before Joan can begin work at her new job, she must undergo a Criminal Background Check and participate in Security Awareness Training. What type of control are these preventative measures?

A. Technical Controls

B. Administrative Controls

C. Physical Controls

D. Resident Controls

5. After risks are mitigated, what is the amount of risk remaining called?

    A. Annualized Loss Expectancy

    B. Single Loss Expectancy

    C. Residual Risk

    D. Exposure Factor

6. Which of the following has the highest potential to be a security hazard to a company that has well-defined security procedures.

    A. An employee who performs critical duties is fired.

    B. The Information Security Officer falls ill.

    C. Grid power is lost for 3 hours

    D. A web server containing employee performance data crashes.

7. Senior management plans to implement a security policy that outlines what can and cannot be done with employees' e-mail for monitoring purposes and to address privacy issues. What would such a security policy be called?

    A. Advisory

    B. Issue-specific

    C. System-specific

    D. Organizational

8. Which of the following denotes the magnitude of potential losses due to a threat?

    A. Risk

    B. Exposure

    C. Vulnerability

    D. Loss

9. Which of the following contains general approaches that also provide the necessary flexibility in the event of unforeseen circumstances?

    A. Policies

    B. Standards

    C. Procedures

D. Guidelines

10. Non-enforced password management on servers and workstations would be defined as a:

A. Risk

B. Threat Agent

C. Vulnerability

D. Threat

11. Information such as data that is critical to a company needs to be properly identified and classified. In general, what are the guidelines to classify data?

A. Classify all data irrespective of format (digital, audio, video) excluding paper.

B. Classify only data that is digital in nature and exists on the company servers.

C. Classify all data irrespective of the format it exists in (paper, digital, audio, video)

D. Classify only data that is digital in nature and exists on the company servers, desktops and all computers in the company.

12. In a secure network, personnel play a key role in the maintenance and promotion of security procedures. Which of the following roles is responsible for ensuring that the company complies with software license agreements?

A. Product-line manager

B. Process owner

C. Solution provider

D. Data analyst

13. Once risk assessment of a company is performed, threats and vulnerabilities are identified and the total / residual risk is determined. Which of the following is not one of the ways in which risk is handled?

A. Risk Inference

B. Risk Mitigation

C. Risk Acceptance

D. Risk Avoidance

14. Steve is doing risk analysis as part of his company's Information Risk Management. He ends up with a calculation that the annualized loss expectancy (ALE) due to a virus attack on the company's network is $

25000. He also calculates that the single loss expectancy (SLE) due to this event would be $ 25000. What can you say about the annualized rate of occurrence (ARO)?

A. The ARO will be greater than 1.0

B. The ARO will be less than 1.0

C. The ARO cannot be calculated in this case.

D. The ARO equals 1.0

15. Which of the following statements is not true with respect to the relationships between threat, vulnerability, exposure, countermeasure and risk?

A. A threat agent takes advantage of a vulnerability.

B. The probability of a fire causing damage is a risk.

C. A countermeasure can mitigate a vulnerability. NO. IT CAN MITIGATE A RISK

D. A vulnerability can expose a system to possible damage YES

Domain Area Test: Information Security and Risk Management Answer Key and Explanations

1. C - A quantitative risk analysis calculates the ALE, which is the annual loss of an asset if expected threats are realized. This value allows the company to evaluate the financial implications of potential threats. ALE is calculated as the product of Single Life Expectancy (SLE) and the Frequency per year, also known as Annual Rate of Occurrence (ARO). [Information Security and Risk Management]

2. A - A Standard is non-negotiable. It must be followed to the fullest extent. A Baseline is a minimum configuration that is required across all of an organization's technology. [Information Security and Risk Management]

3. D - A 'vulnerability' refers to a security hole that can potentially be tapped, resulting in an attack. It is not that an attack has been made, just that the possibility exists. If an attacker uses a vulnerability then it is said to have been "exploited." [Information Security and Risk Management]

4. B - Administrative controls are preventative in nature and include background checks, drug testing, security training on the Human Resources side, and also include policies, procedures, and data classification. [Information Security and Risk Management]

5. C - After a Risk Analysis is performed, controls may be implemented. The risk that remains and is not mitigated by the controls is called Residual Risk. [Information Security and Risk Management]

6. A - Among these choices, the greatest risk is from an employee performing critical duties being fired. He may be in a position to compromise the security if he is disgruntled and wants to 'get back'. The other situations will be handled well since the company has a well-defined security procedures in place. [Information Security and Risk Management]

7. B - Issue-specific policies are also called functional implementing policies. They address specific issues that management feels needs more explanation and attention. [Information Security and Risk Management]

8. B - Exposure is the magnitude of losses a potential vulnerability may cost an entity, if exploited by an agent of threat. [Information Security and Risk Management]

9. D - Guidelines are general approaches and provide the

necessary flexibility to handle emergencies. Guidelines may also be certain recommended approaches / actions to handle certain scenarios. [Information Security and Risk Management]

10. C - A vulnerability is a S/W, hardware, or procedural weakness that could be easily exploited by an attacker. Non-enforced password management on servers and workstations is a vulnerability. [Information Security and Risk Management]

11. C - It might appear that one only needs to classify "digital data". However, all data needs to be classified, irrespective of the format in which it exists. [Information Security and Risk Management]

12. A - Product-line managers are responsible for ensuring that license agreements are complied with. They are also responsible for translating business objectives and specifications for the developer of a product or solution. [Information Security and Risk Management]

13. A - Risk Inference is not a valid way to handle Risk. Risks are usually dealt with in four ways - risk mitigation, risk avoidance, risk transference and risk acceptance. [Information Security and Risk Management]

14. D - The annualized loss expectancy is obtained by the product of the single loss expectancy and the annualized rate of occurrence. In this instance, the ALE equals the SLE, hence the ARO equals 1.0 [Information Security and Risk Management]

15. C - A countermeasure usually mitigates a risk and not a vulnerability. A vulnerability is just the potential possibility that a risk may occur. [Information Security and Risk Management]

CISSP Mock Exam (LITE) - 2
Practice Questions

Test Name:
CISSP Mock Exam (LITE) - 2
Total Questions: 40
Correct Answers Needed to Pass:
30 (75.00%)
Time Allowed: 60 Minutes

Test Description

This is a cumulative CISSP Mock Exam which can be used as a benchmark for your CISSP aptitude. This practice test includes questions from all ten domains of the CISSP CBK.

Test Questions

1. Which of the following choices is an easy and less expensive way to improve physical security?

   A. Surveillance Cameras

   B. Man Traps

   C. Bunkering

   D. Additional Lighting

2. With regard to finding a network address, _____ knows the IP address and broadcasts to find the matching MAC address; whereas _____ knows the MAC address and broadcasts to find the matching IP address.

   A. ARP / DNS

   B. ARP / RARP

   C. RARP / DNS

   D. DNS / ARP

3. Security policies can be categorized as regulatory, advisory or informative. What is true of an advisory policy?

   A. An advisory policy may not describe how confidential information will be processed.

   B. An advisory policy may describe the consequences of not abiding by the rules and procedures.

   C. An advisory policy cannot be enforced.

   D. An advisory policy is designed for educational purposes.

4. A Microsoft Exchange email server uses the X.400 protocol internally to exchange email with Outlook clients within the network. What standard protocol does it use to send mail to other servers on the Internet?

A. IMAP4

B. X.400

C. SMTP

D. POP3

5. How would you distinguish S-HTTP from HTTPS?

A. S-HTTP is used to protect the communication channel between two computers while HTTPS protects a message that is sent from one computer to another.

B. S-HTTP is SSL over HTTP whereas HTTPS uses encryption.

C. HTTPS is the same as S-HTTP and both protect the communication channel between two computers.

D. HTTPS is used to protect the communication channel between two computers while S-HTTP protects a message that is sent from one computer to another.

6. Kerberos is a very effective authentication mechanism. One of its weaknesses is that:

A. Denial-of-service attacks can easily be launched and these

severely compromise the Kerberos server.

B. The encryption processes are based on passwords and traditional password-cracking attacks can compromise the system.

C. The realm key used for initial trusted communications is easily hacked.

D. The ticket-granting ticket granted by the Ticket Granting Server to a requesting resource is susceptible to interception.

7. Which of the following locations would be the least useful in keeping a copy of a business continuity and disaster recovery plan?

A. An offsite location.

B. A backup location.

C. The BCP coordinator's home.

D. The primary location

8. Data on a server has been compromised due to a hack into the system. A forensic investigator needs to copy the data on a hard disk on the server. Which of these will be the first step to be performed as part of the process?

A. Use a file copy method to make sure that all files (including hidden and system files) are copied.

B. Create an image of the hard disk onto the new media.

C. Ensure that a bit-level copy is performed sector by sector, using a specialized tool.

D. Ensure that the new media into which the hard disk is being copied is properly purged.

9. Which of these is not a characteristic of an Intrusion Detection System?

A. Intrusion Detection Systems should have a fail-safe configuration.

B. Intrusion Detection Systems are relatively inexpensive.

C. Intrusion Detection Systems should detect tampering.

D. Intrusion Detection Systems require human intervention to respond to alarms.

10. A company has implemented an HTTP/HTTPS proxy server for the purpose of filtering World Wide Web content. Administrators place the proxy server so that it physically resides on the local area network. They assign it an IP address and the internal interface of the border firewall is then configured to only accept port 80/443 requests from the IP address. What is this an example of?

A. AD

B. DAC

C. ACL

D. RBAC

11. When an attacker is considering attacking a networked target, what is the first thing he or she does?

A. Inject bad packets

B. Hijack a session

C. Run exploitation scripts

D. A port scan

12. What is a method by which a malicious user can use a weakness in an application, operating system, protocol, or network stack called?

A. Bug

B. Vulnerability

C. Exploit

 D. Worm

13. Samantha works for an accounting firm with the responsibility of traveling to client sites to assist in SOX compliance checking. Which of the following accurately describes this work?

A. External Audit

B. Blackbox Penetration Testing

C. Whitebox Penetration Testing

D. Internal Audit

14. Jeremy is hired by a publicly traded company to perform SOX compliance checking. Which of the following accurately describes this work?

A. Blackbox Penetration Testing

B. External Audit

C. Internal Audit

D. Whitebox Penetration Testing

15. Senior management plans to implement a security policy that outlines what can and cannot be done with employees' e-mail for monitoring purposes and to address privacy issues. What would such a security policy be called?

A. Advisory

B. Issue-specific

C. Organizational

D. System-specific

16. A hospital is setting up a Magnetic Resonance Imaging (MRI) center. You are called in to advise the hospital during the planning phase. Which type of cabling would you advise the hospital to use for this center, given that cost is not a major concern?

A. UTP

 **B.** Fiber-optic cabling

C. Copper cables

D. STP

17. Concurrency issues within a database due to improper table locking can cause tables to be over-written with stale information. What sort of an issue is this?

A. Confidentiality

B. Relativity

C. Availability

D. Integrity

18. Which of the following mechanisms ensures the integrity of data held within a database?

A. Multi-level commit

B. Four-phase commit

C. Single-phase commit

D. Two-phase commit

19. What kind of a policy would a large organization typically enforce during a 15-day period prior to New Year's day?

A. Apply a restriction on emails and ensure that no executable file attachments are allowed entry or exit the company.

B. Apply a minimal restriction on emails and ensure that no image attachments (ex: jpg, gif files) are allowed in email.

C. Regulate all email traffic and apply a restriction on the kinds of attachments that can be allowed via email.

D. Apply a restriction and ban use of email for personal purposes.

20. Evaluation Assurance Levels (EALs) are assigned under the Common Criteria Model, and give an indication of the thoroughness of testing. A formally verified system design would be classified as:

A. EAL5

B. EAL7

C. EAL1

D. EAL6

21. Which of the following is not true about cable media?

A. Cables that are not in use should be disconnected from networking devices.

B. UTP and fiber-optic cables are common types of cable media.

C. All cable media should be periodically checked for tampering.

D. UTP cables are very safe and cannot be tapped.

22. The process by which the credentials of one entity is established to

another utilizing credentials such as passwords, one-time tokens, or PIN numbers is known as:

A. Authentication

B. Accountability

C. Administration

D. Authorization

23. A key logger and remote admin tool was used to harvest passwords and the digital signature of a senior officer of a brokerage firm. Several orders to sell were then issued without approval, all signed by the firm's digital signature. What basic goal of cryptosystems has been compromised?

A. Secrecy

B. Integrity

C. Confidentiality

D. Authenticity

24. The process of granting privileges to an entity based upon the time of day, group membership, network address, or verification of its credentials is known as:

A. Authorization

B. Administration

C. Authentication

D. Accounting

25. An important tool used in risk management is risk analysis. Which statement about risk analysis is not true?

A. Threats are given an exposure rating in a qualitative risk analysis

B. The Delphi technique can be used in a qualitative risk analysis.

C. A risk analysis must be directed by senior management.

D. The Herzberg principle applies to qualitative risk analysis.

26. Which of the following access controls is based on the sensitivity of the data?

A. Sensitivity-dependent access control

B. Content-dependent access control

C. Context-dependent access control

D. Data-independent access control

27. This early security model was constructed mainly for the purpose of preserving the confidentiality of data. It is characterized by the concepts of "cannot read up" and "cannot write down". Which of the following security models does this most likely refer to?

A. Bell-LaPadula Model

B. Clark-Wilson Model

C. Brewer and Nash Model

D. Biba Model

28. Biometric devices are among the most accurate and secure methods of authentication available. However, some users find them obtrusive and are therefore reluctant to use them. What biometric recognition system is the most widely accepted and implemented?

A. Iris patterns based

B. Retinal pattern based

C. Facial features based

D. Fingerprint based

29. If asked to select a fast and relatively unbreakable algorithm amongst the choices of DES, Double DES, Blowfish and Triple DES, which one would you choose?

A. DES

B. Blowfish

C. Triple DES

D. Double DES

30. This security model was developed to prevent potential conflicts of interest. It employs dynamic access controls that change depending on a subject's access history. Which of the following security models does this describe?

A. Biba Model

B. Brewer and Nash Model

C. Clark-Wilson Model

D. Bell-LaPadula Model

31. When a graph of the error rate in a biometric system is plotted against its sensitivity, the point where the false accept rate intersects the false reject rate curve is known as:

A. DMZ

B. FRR

C. CER

D. FAR

32. You are currently doing a comprehensive technical evaluation on the security components within your organization. What does this refer to?

   A. Affirmation

   B. Accreditation

   C. Hallmark

   D. Certification

33. In change control, _____ requires comprehensive testing and assessment of a system's security, while _____ requires management to formally accept the system at the documented security level.

   A. Accreditation, Authorization

   B. Certification, Accreditation

   C. Auditing, Authorization

   D. Auditing, Certification

34. Which of the following is not part of the current state assessment phase for BCP/DRP?

A. Business impact assessment (BIA)

B. Benchmark / Peer Review

C. Threat analysis

D. Design initial acceptance testing of plans

35. What type of iris lens would typically be used in an area that has fixed lighting?

   A. Manual

   B. Annuciator

   C. Automatic

   D. Charged-coupled

36. An employee of a company attempted to steal a CD disk containing confidential information. He was caught in the act by a security guard. Which of these types of evidences would be the strongest in a legal prosecution against the employee?

   A. Corroborative evidence of the employee's action

   B. Best evidence of the employee's action

C. Conclusive evidence of the employee's action

D. Direct evidence of the employee's action

37. A company encrypts a file with AES encryption. It is sent to the intended recipient via email with the password in the body of the message. If the email is intercepted, which basic goal of a cryptosystem has been compromised?

A. Nonrepudiation

B. Integrity

C. Confidentiality

D. Authenticity

38. A purchasing agent is placing an order using a credit card account. The account number is on the order form. Which of the following ways would be the least secure method to complete this transaction?

A. HTTPS

B. Courier Service

C. Fax

D. Postal Mail

39. A security professional has been invited to be on the panel during the planning phase of constructing and setting up a data center. Which of these would be a good suggestion from her?

A. Construct the data center as multiple rooms to minimize risk.

B. Construct the data center as a single room at ground level.

C. Construct the data center as a single room in the basement.

D. Construct the data center as a single room on the highest floor of the building to avoid break-ins.

40. The AIC triad is made up of three main principles of information security: availability, integrity and confidentiality. Which of the following threats can compromise data integrity?

A. Viruses

B. Social engineering

C. Denial-of-Service (DoS) attack

D. Dumpster diving

CISSP Mock Exam (LITE) - 2
Answer Key and Explanations

1. D - Adding lights is a simple and cost-effective way to prevent physical security breaches. Bright lights generally deter intruders. Mantraps, camera systems, and bunkers are comparatively expensive solutions and require much more administrative effort. [Physical (Environmental) Security]

2. B - Address Resolution Protocol (ARP) knows the IP address, but needs to match it with a hardware (MAC) address. In contrast, the Reverse Address Resolution Protocol (RARP) knows the hardware (MAC) address but needs to find the IP address. [Telecommunications and Network Security]

3. B - Advisory policies explain to employees the actions and conduct that should and should not take place within the company. These policies also describe the consequences of failing to follow the organization's rules and procedures. [Information Security and Risk Management]

4. C - SMTP is an Internet standard for email transmission between email servers. A client may read mail received through one of the other protocols. However, this question revolves around how one mail server can send messages to another mail server. [Security Operations]

5. D - Although both HTTPS and S-HTTP sound very similar, they are different in that, HTTPS is used to protect the communication channel between two computers while S-HTTP protects a message that is sent from one computer to the other. [Cryptography]

6. B - Although Kerberos is by itself a very robust authentication mechanism, its weak link lies in the fact that it uses passwords for encryption and these can be subject to traditional attacks. [Access Control]

7. D - Among the choices listed, the primary facility is the least effective for storage of the business continuity and disaster recovery plans. This is because in case of a disaster striking the facility, it may not be possible to retrieve the plans. The other choices, including keeping a copy of the plan in the BCP coordinator's home will serve the purpose. [Business Continuity and Disaster Recovery Planning]

8. D - Among the given choices, the first step to be performed is to purge the new media completely before copying the hard disk contents. There have been instances where the media has contained prior

information and was considered inadmissible in courts. [Legal, Regulations, Compliance and Investigations]

9. B - Intrusion Detection Systems are quite expensive. The other choices listed are valid characteristics of IDSs. [Physical (Environmental) Security]

10. C - An Access Control List (ACL) is a filter that can be configured, in this case, to drop packets that do not come from a particular source. This configuration is sometimes referred to as a "Proxy on a Stick," and can be more stable than a multi-homed proxy system. [Access Control]

11. D - An attacker will first need to know what ports are open on a system so that the attack strategy can be built from that knowledge. An attacker can also run exploitation scripts but they will take much longer and may be of no use if a web server is not running on the target machine. [Security Operations]

12. C - An exploit is a way by which a system can be altered or used without authorization for purposes other than those of the owner. A vulnerability is the possibility that exploitation might take place A bug is a flaw in software that might cause a vulnerability to exist. [Software Development Security]

13. A - An external auditor is hired to assist an organization. This can take the form of an on-going contractor engagement, or a brief spot-check. [Security Operations]

14. C - An internal auditor works for the organization. While some auditors can also perform penetration testing, it is usually not their main job function. [Security Operations]

15. B - Issue-specific policies are also called functional implementing policies. They address specific issues that management feels needs more explanation and attention. [Information Security and Risk Management]

16. B - An MRI center will likely be subject to high electromagnetic emission. Hence, only fiber-optic cabling and STP are options that can be used here among the choices given. Since cost is not a consideration, fiber-optic cabling is the preferred solution. [Telecommunications and Network Security]

17. D - When data becomes inconsistent or untrustworthy, the integrity of the data is said to be compromised. Neither availability nor confidentiality is not an issue here. [Software Development Security]

18. D - A two-phase commit mechanism is a control used in databases that

ensures the integrity of the data held within the database. The other choices are not valid. [Software Development Security]

19. C - As a trend, it has been found that a number of new viruses are released during the holiday season prior to New Year. The vulnerability that is exploited is that many emails with attachments (not only executables) that are carriers of viruses get exchanged during the holiday season. Having a restrictive email attachment policy helps control this to some extent. [Software Development Security]

20. B - As the assurance levels increase, the thoroughness and testing performed increases. Thus the package where system design is verified and tested is the highest level EAL7 [Security Architecture and Design]

21. D - UTP cables are not necessarily safe. It is possible to tap into the middle of UTP cables and use sniffers to capture network traffic. [Security Operations]

22. A - Authentication verifies that the credentials submitted by an entity match its stored information. Authentication does not track usage or actions (accountability) or prevent / deny access to resources (authorization). Often, multifactor authentication is used for better

authentication. This is a combination of something you know (password / PIN), something you have (smartcard/token), and/or something you are (biometrics). [Access Control]

23. D - Authenticity means that the sender is validated and identified. In this case, the messages were all properly sent and executed using the firm's digital signature but they were not authentic. [Cryptography]

24. A - Authorization allows users access to resources. It ensures that an entity has been given the necessary rights and privileges to perform requested actions. [Access Control]

25. D - The Herzberg principle is not related to risk analysis. The other three are valid statements. [Information Security and Risk Management]

26. B - Content-dependent access control is based on the sensitivity of the data. The more sensitive the data, the lesser the number of individuals who will have access to it. [Software Development Security]

27. A - Bell-LaPadula was created for the U.S. Military in the 1970s for to protect secret information from leaking on multi-user and time-share mainframes. In such a system a subject cannot read information at a higher security level, or cannot read "up." At the same time, to prevent declassifying data inappropriately, a subject cannot save data to a lower security level, or cannot write "down." [Security Architecture and Design]

28. D - Biometrics is the science of measuring and statistically analyzing human biological characteristics. Biometric devices use a unique, measurable feature of an individual to authenticate their identity. Fingerprint scanning is widely accepted as a reliable means of human recognition and authentication, and is considered less obtrusive than other systems. [Physical (Environmental) Security]

29. B - Blowfish is considered almost unbreakable considering today's computing standards. The other algorithms were considered unbreakable when they first came up. However, increase in computing power has now rendered them breakable. [Cryptography]

30. B - Brewer and Nash was created to prevent conflicts of interest. For instance, an accounting firm has financial data from two companies that compete. An accountant who accesses the records of one is automatically locked away from accessing the records of the other. This method is significantly different from Bell-LaPadula, Biba, and Clark-Wilson in that the privileges

dynamically adjust based upon activity. [Security Architecture and Design]

31. C - CER, or the Crossover Error Rate is the point at which the FAR (False Accept Rate) crosses the FRR (False Reject Rate). A DMZ is a demilitarized zone and is a networking concept. [Access Control]

32. D - Certification is a process that involves a comprehensive technical evaluation on the components within your organization. The overall evaluations would involve risk analysis, safeguards, verification, auditing, and other tests that are able to assess the components in question. The end goal of the certification process should be to ensure that the products, systems, or components meet the overall security requirements of the organization. [Security Architecture and Design]

33. B - Certification is the process by which security components are evaluated technically for compliance to an applicable standard or policy. Accreditation is the formal acceptance by management that the system's security and functionality is adequate. [Software Development Security]

34. D - Design initial acceptance testing of plans is done in the design and development phase of the

BCP/DRP. The other three activities listed are done during the current state assessment phase. [Business Continuity and Disaster Recovery Planning]

35. A - Closed-circuit TV (CCTV) systems have many components, which include cameras, transmitters, receivers, recording systems, and monitors. The camera used in a CCTV system has many characteristics that need to be taken into account. One of these characteristics is the lens. There are two kinds of irises used in camera lenses in CCTV systems - automatic and manual. Manual lenses would be used in areas with fixed lighting and automatic lenses are used in areas where the light changes from time to time. [Physical (Environmental) Security]

36. C - Conclusive evidence would be the strongest and would not require any corroboration. [Legal, Regulations, Compliance and Investigations]

37. C - Confidentiality means that unauthorized users cannot access the protected information. This is not a breach in authenticity because the source was never in question. [Cryptography]

38. C - Courier Services can be bonded. There are many laws that make tampering with U.S. Mail a federal

offense. HTTPS is a relatively secure asynchronously encrypted transmission. However, there is no guarantee that a fax will be picked up from the machine by the intended recipient. [Security Operations]

39. B - Data centers should typically be at ground level so that they can be easily accessed by emergency crew. They should also be constructed as a single room which makes it easier to secure. The other options listed are not preferred ones. [Physical (Environmental) Security]

40. A - Data integrity is compromised when it is modified by an unauthorized person or program and the accuracy of the data is no longer certain. Since a virus is able to alter system files and data, it can compromise data integrity. [Information Security and Risk Management]

Domain Area Test: Access Control Practice Questions

Test Name:
Domain Area Test: Access Control
Total Questions: 15
Correct Answers Needed to Pass:
11 (73.33%)
Time Allowed: 25 Minutes

Test Description

This practice test specifically targets your knowledge of the Access Control domain area.

Test Questions

1. Which of the following is an example of a brute force attack?

    A. A program that captures UserID / password values as they are entered by the user

    B. A program that uses a predefined list of values and compares it to captured values

    C. A program that uses every possible input combination to try to determine a password

    D. A program that sniffs the network and captures packets

2. What type of access control does a stateful firewall use?

    A. Content-dependent access control

    B. Rule-based access control

    C. Context-dependent access control

    D. Access control grid

3. You use an access card to access specific rooms within a building. In the context of three-factor authentication, which of the following does the access card represent?

    A. Something you have

    B. Something you validate

    C. Something you are

    D. Something you know

4. Randy has worked in an organization for fifteen years. He has been granted accesses to various systems and they have never been revoked. If the company has to be compliant with Sarbanes-Oxley (SOX) regulations, at a minimum, how often does Randy's manager need to review his access permissions?

A. Annually

B. Every month

C. Every six months

D. Every two years

5. Greg is a security professional and wants to ensure that users do not access the company's HR database between 10 PM and 5 AM. Which of the following access control mechanisms might he employ?

   A. Trust based Access Control

   B. Smart Cards

   C. Time of Day Access Control

   D. Off-hours Access Control

6. Alison is responsible for the security of a group of infrastructure devices. She discovers that an external attacker is using an automated password search program to try and break into the company systems. What is a simple yet effective strategy that is used to mitigate this type of attack?

   A. Password Aging

   B. One-time password

   C. Limit Logon Attempts

D. Password Checkers

7. Which of these access control models is most likely to be used by the United States military?

   A. DAC

   B. MAC

   C. AAA

   D. RBAC

8. In which of the following access control models does the owner of a file have the maximum flexibility to grant another user access to a file?

   A. Administrative access control

   B. Mandatory access control

   C. Role Based access control

   D. Discretionary access control

9. When a biometrics system incorrectly accepts an impostor who should not actually be granted access, what type of error is it called?

   A. Type II Error

   B. Type I Error

C. Type IV Error

D. Type III Error

10. A hacker managed to hack into a computer system and stole some financial information related to the profitability of a company. Such information would normally be classified as:

A. Public

B. Secret

C. Unclassified

D. Sensitive

11. In a system governed by a multi-level security policy, a subject can access an object only when:

A. The security level of the subject is at level zero

B. The security level of the subject is equal to or greater than that of the object's classification

C. The security level of the object is at level zero.

D. The security level of the subject is lesser than that of the object's classification

12. A network administrator in a company finds that employees in the company clog the network by exchange of music and movie files. Employee A shares his directory and enables Employee B to copy the files across the network, thus using up valuable bandwidth. What kind of access control permits this to happen?

A. Role Based Access Control

B. This is a problem related to HR policies and not access control.

C. Discretionary Access Control

D. Mandatory Access Control

13. A security professional is evaluating biometric solutions for access control to a critical facility. If she is given a set of cross-over rates (CERs) to choose from, which of these should she prefer?

A. CER of 90

B. CER of 3

C. CER of 10

D. CER of 97

14. The junior manager of a finance department was granted access privileges to all files on the company server including employee performance details, employee payroll details, client feedback reports. This is a situation that should best be avoided and is termed as:

A. Access creep

B. Authorization creep

C. Excessive privileges

D. Excessive read

15. You are trying to book a holiday package through a website on the internet. You log in to the holiday resort's website and are automatically able to make your airline and car rental reservations on different websites without needing to sign in again. This would be possible through:

A. Digital sign-on

B. Password synchronization

X C. Single Sign-on

o D. Federation TRUSTING AN OUTSIDE DOMAIN.

Domain Area Test: Access Control Answer Key and Explanations

1. C - A brute force attack is designed to use every possible combination when determining the correct value. The attack keeps occurring until a combination is found. For example, if the beginning of the password is known, such as 'pass' for 'password', then the attacker will try every other possible value for the remaining values that are missing. This could include: pass1, pass2, passaa, passAA, etc. [Access Control]

2. C - A stateful firewall uses context-dependent access control. Context-dependent access control involves using a collection of information for making access decisions. Instead of allowing access based on the sensitivity of the data, as with content-dependent access control, a stateful firewall using context-dependent access control will review a TCP connection and ensure that all of the correct steps are followed before allowing any packets to be transmitted through the firewall. [Access Control]

3. A - Access cards, keys, swipe cards, and badges are all examples of something you have. They are physical devices that you carry on your person so that you can be authenticated when you wish to access something. [Access Control]

4. A - As per Sarbanes-Oxley regulations, managers need to review their employees' access permissions at least once a year. [Access Control]

5. C - Greg could use time-of-day access control. Since the HR data is confidential, placing an access restriction will ensure that most users cannot access the HR database between 10 PM and 4 AM. Off-hours and trust based access control do not exist. Smart cards will not serve the purpose here. [Access Control]

6. C - Limiting logon attempts provides protection against dictionary and exhaustive attacks. A threshold is set to allow only a limited number of logon attempts. Once this is exceeded, a user's account will be locked out. Password aging is to keep passwords fresh. It will not help against such attacks. Password checkers are used to test the strength of users' passwords so they will not help prevent attacks. A one-time password does not serve the purpose here. [Access Control]

7. B - In a Mandatory Access Control (MAC) system, users and data are given a security clearance such as confidential, top secret etc. The operating system makes the final decision about fulfilling a user request to access data. The MAC model is specifically used in the military where confidentiality and classification of information are very important. [Access Control]

8. D - In the discretionary access control model, a user is the owner of a file if he creates it. Such a system will allow the owner to specify which other users can access the file. In other access control methods, the owner of a file does not have as much flexibility to specify who can access the file. [Access Control]

9. A - Mistaken authentication by a biometric system is called a Type II Error (false acceptance). A Type I Error occurs when a biometric system rejects an authorized individual (called false rejection). [Access Control]

10. D - Financial information is usually classified as sensitive. This type of information requires special precautions to ensure the confidentiality and integrity of the data. [Access Control]

11. B - Multilevel security policies prevent information flow from a higher to a lower security level. Hence these policies permit a subject to access an object only if its security level classification is equal to or greater than that of the object. [Access Control]

12. C - Such a situation can arise in a discretionary model. Employee A

will have the necessary permissions to share a directory or file with Employee B. Employee B then tries to access and copy the file(s) over the network, resulting in excess traffic. In the other access control models, users do not have as much freedom to permit other users to access their files. [Access Control]

13. B - The biometric system with a crossover error rate (CER) of 3 is the most accurate system. The CER represents the point at which the false rejection rate (authorized individuals are rejected) equals the false acceptance rate (unauthorized individuals are accepted). A lower value indicates a more accurate system. CERs of 90 and 97 will not occur in practice. [Access Control]

14. C - This is a situation called Excessive Privileges and is quite hard to control in larger organizations. In general, an employee should only be given access to as much data as he/she needs to access. [Access Control]

15. D - This is possible through federation which allows a federated identity to be portable across businesses and allows the user to be authenticated across different systems and businesses. [Access Control]

CISSP Mock Exam (LITE) - 3
Practice Questions

Test Name:
CISSP Mock Exam (LITE) - 3
Total Questions: 40
Correct Answers Needed to Pass:
30 (75.00%)
Time Allowed: 60 Minutes

Test Description

This is a cumulative CISSP Mock Exam which can be used as a benchmark for your CISSP aptitude. This practice test includes questions from all ten domains of the CISSP CBK.

Test Questions

1. Which of the following uses asymmetric-key encryption encryption?

   A. RC4

   B. Diffie-Hellman

   C. 3DES

   D. DES

2. Which of the following is NOT useful for Encryption?

   A. AES

   B. Digital Signature Algorithm

   C. RSA

   D. DES

3. In running a backup on a system, what should the first step be?

   A. Run a differential backup

   B. Run an incremental backup

   C. Run a full backup

   D. Run both a differential and an incremental backup

4. The company's database server contains multiple tables with customer orders. If a disaster results in the server going offline the company would start to lose significant amounts of money after about 24 hours. What category of maximum tolerable downtime (MTD) should the server be placed in?

   A. Normal

   B. Urgent

   C. Critical

   D. Nonessential

5. An information systems security professional enforces separation of duties with the intention of reducing frauds and errors. However, this results in inflexible operations. What could the professional do to ease things?

    A. Implement static separation of duties

    B. Implement conditional separation of duties

    C. Implement job rotation instead

    D. Implement dynamic separation of duties

6. Users have been complaining that they have to enter too many userids and passwords to access systems. You are looking at a solution to help them out. Each of the following technologies may assist in this except:

    A. Password synchronization

    B. Password network

    C. SSO

    D. Federation

7. Which Common Criteria Evaluation Assurance Level (EAL) involves

semiformal design and testing of systems?

    A. EAL 5

    B. EAL 7

    C. EAL 1

    D. EAL 3

8. Which of the following is not a countermeasure to eavesdropping on a network?

    A. Use of routers

    B. Encryption of network traffic

    C. Traffic padding

    D. Rerouting of information

9. Which of the following memory technologies is most commonly used to store computer BIOS microcode?

    A. DRAM

    B. ROM

    C. EEPROM

    D. RAM

10. In the context of cryptography, which of the following is incorrect?

A. A message can be digitally signed and this provides nonrepudiation

B. A message can be hashed and this provides integrity

C. A message can be digitally signed and this provides authentication

D. A message can be encrypted and this provides integrity

11. When IPSec is used in transport mode, what is the only part of the message that is encrypted?

A. Payload

B. Authentication Header

C. Routing Header

D. Symmetric Public Payload

12. What is the most common security issue for faced by companies?

A. DoS attacks

B. Data diddling

C. Excessive privileges

D. IP spoofing attacks

13. A security professional is performing a Failure Modes and Effects Analysis (FMEA). Which of the following is correct about FMEA?

A. Failure Modes and Effects Analysis is only useful while analyzing single sub-systems.

B. Failure Modes and Effects Analysis cannot be applied to determine where exactly a failure is likely to occur.

C. Failure Modes and Effects Analysis is very theoretical in nature and does not have practical application.

D. Failure Modes and Effects Analysis can be applied to determine where exactly a failure is likely to occur.

14. A junior network technician has approached you and asked for your opinion on what would be the most secure cable to implement within the organization. What should you tell her?

A. Shielded Twisted Pair (STP)

B. Unshielded Twisted Pair (UTP)

C. Fiber-optic

D. Coaxial

15. The ICMP protocol is intended to send status messages. However, attackers have figured out how to insert data inside an ICMP packet to communicate with a compromised system. This is done by setting up a backdoor on systems. Which of the following is a well-known attack which uses this method to target systems?

    A. Ping of death

    B. Router attack

    C. Loki attack

    D. Longdale attack

16. In access control terminology, an account username is _____ and the password is _____.

    A. Authorization, Identification

    B. Identification, Authentication

    C. Authentication, Authorization

    D. Accountability, Authentication

17. A diagnostic program called ping is used to determine if a specified host is on a network. What is the ping of death?

    A. A ping works by sending an ICMP echo packet to the target host. If this is greater than a legal packet size of 65,636 bytes, the operating system crashes or becomes unstable.

    B. A ping works by sending an IKE echo packet to the target host. If this is greater than a legal packet size of 32,768 bytes, the operating systems crash or become unstable.

    C. A ping works by sending an ICMP echo packet to the target host. If this is greater than a legal packet size of 32,768 bytes, the operating systems crash or become unstable.

    D. A ping works by sending an IKE echo packet to the target host. If this is greater than a legal packet size of 65,636 bytes, the operating systems crash or become unstable.

18. Todd evaluates an enterprise software that will be installed on the company's network. This software will also be accessible through the web. Which of the following features would be a bad practice, and grounds for rejecting the software?

    A. The need to use a secureID card for all web accesses.

B. A feature such as user access through a WAP-enabled mobile device.

C. A feature such as user access through a VPN interface.

D. A feature such as administrative access through a web-based interface.

19. An organization is evaluating the pros and cons of using a hardware cryptography system versus a software cryptography system. If the organizations wants a high speed cryptography solution, which option would it prefer?

A. A software solution provides the fastest throughput.

B. The best option would be to use a VPN connection that avoids the need for cryptography.

C. A combination of hardware and software will be the most effective solution.

D. A hardware solution will be the best option and function at a higher speed.

20. Which of these options is not a presentation layer standard?

A. MPEG

B. JPEG

C. TIFF

D. HTTP

21. Use of SSL over HTTP technology, also known as HTTPS, helps prevent which of the following attacks?

A. Teardrop

B. Man-in-the-middle

C. Smurf

D. Fraggle

22. Of the protection rings used by operating system security, in which of the following would applications such as web browsers, email, and word processors reside?

A. Ring 0

B. Ring 2

C. Ring 1

D. Ring 3

23. The continuity planning project team (CPPT) is facing challenges in getting various units of the organization to participate in the Disaster Recovery and Continuity Planning process. This is very likely because of:

A. Poor communication.

B. Lack of management support

ALWAYS MGMT

C. Lack of understanding of the disaster recovery planning process.

D. A poorly prepared business impact assessment.

24. Camille is works for an accounting firm in a remote lab, away from the main offices. Her main job is to perform security checks against client websites. To do this, she is provided only a web address. Which of the following accurately describes this work?

A. Blackbox Penetration Testing

B. External Audit

C. Whitebox Penetration Testing

D. Internal Audit

25. Gerald works for an accounting firm as a part of a tiger team. He has received all of the Rules of Engagement documentation for the current project. Included in the documents is information about specific targets the client would like

tested. Which of the following accurately describes this work?

A. Internal Audit

B. External Audit

C. Whitebox Penetration Testing

D. Blackbox Penetration Testing

26. A token device is a handheld device that can be used to authenticate a user in a synchronous or asynchronous manner. What mechanism does an asynchronous token-generating method employ?

A. Counter based mechanism

B. Challenge/response mechanism

C. Accept/Reject mechanism

D. Start/Stop mechanism

27. In which security mode can users access all data once they have proper clearances and comply with certain other requirements?

A. Multilevel security mode.

? B. Compartmented security mode.

C. Dedicated security mode

D. System high security mode

28. Liz is a network engineer and is finding it difficult to troubleshoot a network cable fault. In which topology would it be difficult to detect cable faults?

A. Linear Bus Topology

B. Mesh Topology

C. Star topology

D. Ring Topology

29. A consultant is called in to advise on aspects of creating a business continuity and disaster recovery plan. She insists on establishing clear goals for the plans. What key information must a goal contain?

A. Responsibility, Priorities, References

B. Responsibility, Authority, Priorities

C. Responsibility, Email addresses, Organization Structure

D. Responsibility, Target Dates, Email Addresses

30. If the same key is being used to encrypt and decrypt a payload, what is the encryption method in use called?

A. Asymmetric

B. Public Key Exchange

C. Public Key Infrastructure

D. Symmetric

31. Which of the following will be curbed by implementation of the Least Privilege principle?

A. Information Breaches via fax

B. Network sniffing

C. Information Breaches via email

D. Browsing

32. Which of these access control models is the best system for a company that has high employee turnover?

A. LDAP

B. RBAC

C. MAC

D. DAC

33. In what mode should a door access system that relies on magnetic locks fail in the event of a complete power failure?

    A. Fail Secure

    B. Fail Local

    C. Fail Remote

    D. Fail Safe

34. The CEO of a drug-manufacturing company was aware of malpractices in the manufacture of certain drugs by the company. These drugs resulted in loss of life to some users of those drugs. The CEO is likely to be tried under:

    A. Civil and criminal laws

    B. Civil and administrative laws

    C. Administrative, criminal and civil laws

    D. Administrative and criminal laws

35. Which statement best describes a properly implemented incident handling program?

    A. Incident reporting should be decentralized

    B. Incident handling should be approached in a reactive manner

    C. Incident handling should be part of the business continuity plan

    D. Incident handling should be aligned with the disaster recovery plan

36. A publicly listed company was due to announce its quarterly results in a few days' time. How would the company classify information pertaining to its results, prior to the day of the results?

    A. It would be classified as private.

    B. It would be classified as public.

    C. It would be classified as sensitive.

    D. It would be classified as confidential.

37. Of the protection rings used by operating system security, in which of the following would I/O drivers and utilities reside?

    A. Ring 2

    B. Ring 1

    C. Ring 0

    D. Ring 3

38. Among the components inside the Central Processing Unit of a computer, which of the following performs the logic and calculations?

A. Output Unit

B. Arithmetic Logic Unit

C. Registers

D. L1 Cache

39. In an effort to create additional free space on a computer's hard disk, a user unwittingly deletes a folder that contains critical operating system files. What security principle is affected by this action?

A. Integrity

B. Confidentiality

C. Authentication

D. Capacity

40. A file is encrypted and placed on a secure FTP server. An MD5 hash is taken of the file and also placed on the FTP server. The authorized user logs in to the server and downloads both files, however, the hash fails to match the archive. In this case, which basic goal of a cryptosystem has failed?

A. Nonrepudiation

B. Authenticity

C. Confidentiality

D. Integrity

CISSP Mock Exam (LITE) - 3
Answer Key and Explanations

1. B - Diffie-Hellman is the only public key exchange asymmetric technology. All the other choices listed are pre-shared key or synchronous. [Cryptography]

2. B - DSA, based upon the Digital Signature Standards created by NIST, can not be used for encryption. The other options can be used for encryption. [Cryptography]

3. C - The first step in the backup process would be to run a full backup. This can then be followed by a differential or an incremental backup. However, differential and incremental backups should not be mixed up. [Business Continuity and Disaster Recovery Planning]

4. B - During the business impact analysis (BIA), the organization needs to identify its critical systems and determine the maximum outage time the organization can tolerate without these critical functions. This is referred to as the maximum tolerable downtime (MTD). General categories of MTDs are: Nonessential: 30 days, Normal: 7 days, Important: 72 hours, Urgent: 24 hours and Critical: Up to 4 hours Hence the server would be classified with an MTD of Urgent. [Business Continuity and Disaster Recovery Planning]

5. D - Dynamic separation of duties allows for flexibility in operations. Static separation of duties results in rigid policies. Job rotation will not help and conditional separation of duties is not a valid type of separation of duties. [Access Control]

6. B - Each of the three technologies - Password synchronization, SSO (single sign on) and Federation, help in using the information entered once by a user while signing on, for accessing other systems. Password network is not a valid response. [Access Control]

7. A - EAL 5 involves semiformal design and testing of systems. It ensures that a higher level of assurance is met through practices that have been thoroughly tested in rigorous commercial development. Therefore, it is supported by the use of specialist security engineering techniques. [Security Architecture and Design]

8. A - Eavesdropping is the act of intercepting and viewing unauthorized information that is being transmitted over the network. Use of routers will not prevent this activity. [Telecommunications and Network Security]

9. C - Electrically Erasable Programmable Read Only Memory is a non-volatile storage technology that can be "flashed" with reprogramming and updates. It is used to store the BIOS on most modern computer systems. [Security Architecture and Design]

10. D - Encrypting a message does not provide integrity. It is hashing which provides integrity. Digitally signing it provides authentication, nonrepudiation and integrity. [Cryptography]

11. A - When IPSec is used in transport mode, only the payload of the message is encrypted. [Cryptography]

12. C - Excessive privileges' is the most common security issue faced by companies. This occurs when a user possesses more rights, privileges, and permissions than required to fulfill their duties. Users can often cause the most damage to resources because of the privileged access they have been granted. [Legal, Regulations, Compliance and Investigations]

13. D - Fault tree analysis is useful in identifying failures that can take place in complex environments or systems. In this process, each failure situation is added to a tree as a series of logic expressions. This helps in determining where exactly a failure is

likely to occur. [Information Security and Risk Management]

14. C - Fiber-optic cable is the most secure cabling among the choices listed. Fiber-optic cable cannot be easily tapped into since it is made of glass. It is also very difficult to eavesdrop on since it does not radiate any signals that can be captured. [Telecommunications and Network Security]

15. C - Loki is a client/server program that is used by hackers to setup backdoors on systems. The server portion of the Loki software is installed on compromised systems and monitors a particular port which is the backdoor into the system. [Telecommunications and Network Security]

16. B - Identification ensures that a subject is the entity that it claims to be. This is achieved by use of a username, or account number. Authentication ensures that an additional credential such as a password or PIN number matches previously stored values for the subject. [Access Control]

17. A - Ping is a diagnostic program to determine if a host is on a network. A ping works by sending an ICMP echo packet to the target host. If this is greater than a legal packet size of 65,636 bytes, a large number of operating systems crash or become

unstable. The source of attack is sometimes difficult to find because a ping might seem like a harmless entry in a log. [Telecommunications and Network Security]

18. D - From a security perspective, it is better to restrict remote administrative access. This is especially true for critical applications or servers. By doing so, the possibility of an attacker gaining control of an administrative userid and password to attack the system is minimized or eliminated. [Software Development Security]

19. D - Hardware encryption is costlier than software encryption, but provides high speeds of operation in comparison to software encryption. [Cryptography]

20. D - HTTP is an application layer protocol. It is used to transfer information between a web browser and a web server. It is not a presentation layer standard. [Telecommunications and Network Security]

21. B - HTTPS, because of the asymmetric key exchange, is good for preventing man-in-the-middle attacks. Smurf, Teardrop, and Fraggle are all network based attacks that overwhelm a victim host with network traffic. [Cryptography]

22. D - Ideally, Ring 3 applications would never be able to directly access processes belonging to lower numbered security rings. In fact, in some cases an additional level of security is added in to applications like web browsers to even further abstract processes away from more critical ones. This is usually called sandboxing. Ring 3 is often called User mode or User land software. [Security Architecture and Design]

23. B - Lack of management support is the most likely reason the continuity planning project team is facing difficulties in getting the rest of the organization to participate and contribute to the plan. BCP/DRP needs to be a top-down initiative with support coming in from the highest level. [Business Continuity and Disaster Recovery Planning]

24. A - In a blackbox test, the penetration tester is only given enough information to ensure that the correct enterprise is tested. No specifics are given to the testers about the systems themselves. The advantage of blackbox testing is that it may yield unexpected results. A disadvantage is that extensive testing of particular controls may not take place simply because they are not uncovered in the test. [Security Operations]

25. C - In a whitebox test, an external tester is given information on

specific targets to be tested. This can included IP addresses, operating systems, and protection technologies. While these tests may not discover unexpected results, they can be very useful at drilling down on specific security controls. [Security Operations]

26. B - In an asynchronous token method, the device uses a challenge/response scheme whereby it authenticates a user. The authentication server sends the user a random value (a challenge). This value is entered by the user into the token device which returns an encrypted value. This value is entered by the user and sent to the authentication server for authentication. [Access Control]

27. C - In dedicated security mode, once a user has the necessary clearances, he/she can access all data. This is in contrast to the other modes where users can only access some of the data subject to approvals. [Security Architecture and Design]

28. B - In mesh topology, computers are connected to each other, providing a good amount of redundancy. This is however more expensive and cable faults can be quite effort-intensive to detect. [Telecommunications and Network Security]

29. B - In order for goals to be useful, it needs to contain key information

such as responsibility, priorities, authority and implementation / testing dates. [Business Continuity and Disaster Recovery Planning]

30. D - In symmetric encryption, a single key is used to both encrypt and decrypt the message. [Cryptography]

31. D - Implementation of the Least Privilege access principle ensures that personnel who have unnecessary access to systems do not end up "browsing" or looking through data that they should not have access to. Least Privilege access will not prevent any of the other choices. [Security Operations]

32. B - An RBAC model is well suited for a company with high employee turnover. This is because if an employee is mapped to a specific role, when he/she leaves, his/her replacement can easily be mapped to the same role. The administrator need not continually change ACLs on individual objects. [Access Control]

33. D - In this instance, failing safe means that the doors would be unlocked in case of a power failure. This will ensure that personnel are not trapped behind the door in case of emergencies. [Physical (Environmental) Security]

34. C - In this scenario, the CEO is likely to be tried under all the three types

of laws: 1. Civil law - because of the wrongs to certain individuals. 2. Criminal law - because the CEO willfully violated government laws. 3. Administrative law - because of the violation of regulatory standards. [Legal, Regulations, Compliance and Investigations]

35. D - Incident handling should align with the company's disaster recovery plan. Both plans are designed to quickly respond to incidents so that the company can return to normal operations as soon as possible. However, incident handling is a recovery plan that specifically addresses malicious technical threats. [Legal, Regulations, Compliance and Investigations]

36. C - Information within the company can be classified as public, sensitive, confidential or private. In the case of such financial information, it would typically be classified as sensitive, prior to the declaration of results. [Information Security and Risk Management]

37. A - Input/output system drivers and operating system utilities reside at the Ring 2 level. This ring is at an intermediate level between User mode (Ring 3) and Privileged Mode (Rings 0 and 1) rings. [Security Architecture and Design]

38. B - The Arithmetic Logic Unit (ALU) handles all of the logic and mathematical calculations. The control unit schedules the work to be done, and the local memory registers, or L1 cache, hold working data for quick reference. [Security Architecture and Design]

39. A - When a user deletes files that are required, the integrity of the system is affected. Unlike a virus attack which deliberately affects data integrity, a user deleting files usually happens in error. [Information Security and Risk Management]

40. D - Integrity means that the file or message was not modified in transmission, either by accident or on purpose. This is not a breach in confidentiality since the intended recipient also cannot read the file. [Cryptography]

Domain Area Test: Security Architecture and Design Practice Questions

Test Name: Domain Area Test: Security Architecture and Design
Total Questions: 15
Correct Answers Needed to Pass: 11 (73.33%)
Time Allowed: 25 Minutes

Test Description

This practice test specifically targets your knowledge of the Security Architecture and Design domain area.

Test Questions

1. A high security environment requires that every keystroke made by a user be recorded. What is this called?

   A. Trojan Horse

   B. Spyware

   C. Keystroke logging

   D. Biometrics

2. Which of the following does the Common Criteria use in its evaluation process?

   A. Protection profiles

   B. Application hosts

   C. Application profiles

   D. Protection hosts

3. A security perimeter is an imaginary boundary. Which of these statements correctly explains the concept of a security perimeter?

   A. Both trusted and untrusted components are outside the perimeter.

   B. Trusted components are outside the perimeter and untrusted components are within it.

   C. Trusted components are within the perimeter and untrusted components are outside it.

   D. Both trusted and untrusted components are within the perimeter

4. In many instances, firmware is preferred over software. Which of the following is a likely reason for this to be the case?

   A. Firmware is difficult to tamper with since it needs to be physically accessed.

FIRMWARE = EMBEDDED

B. Code written in firmware has lesser security needs.

C. Firmware runs faster than software.

D. Software is difficult to program in comparison with firmware.

5. A product vendor comes out with a new package called "Unified threat management system". The vendor claims that their product obviates the need for all other network security devices / software. If a company decides to use only this package, what major tenet of network security would this violate?

   A. Defense in Depth

   B. Network Segregation

   C. Separation of Duties

   D. Least Privilege

6. John works in accounting and Marsha in payroll. Both of them have always had the same privileges to the financial data files. In particular, both use one of Marsha's files named Payroll.xls. Marsha uses Payroll.xls to track and input weekly timesheet data, and John uses the data as an input for a different spreadsheet. A recent external audit firm has recommended that the company apply the concept of Least Privilege. How would this best be implemented?

   A. Set John's access for the file to read-only

   B. Remove John's access to the file completely

   C. Set both John's and Marsha's access for the file to read-only

   D. Remove Marsha's access to the file completely

7. A contractor assigned to work on a critical application introduced certain pieces of code that he planned to exploit at a later time. How can such activity be detected?

   A. By thoroughly testing the code.

   B. By implementing a structured code walkthrough process.

   C. By implementing an IDS

   D. By doing a thorough background check on the contractor prior to hire.

8. Secure systems are dependent on the use of effective security models. Which of these models protects integrity of information within a system?

A. The Biba model

B. The Clark-Denning Model

C. The Bell-LaPadula Model

D. The Brewer-Wilson Model

9. Full hard drive encryption on laptops mitigates some of the risk of loss or theft of the unit.   Under what security realm is this classified?

A. Host Security

B. Network Security

C. Data Security

D. Software Development Security

10. A covert channel is a way in which an entity can get information in an unauthorized manner. The number of covert channels that can be considered acceptable depends on the assurance rating that the system has. Which of these will have the least number of covert channels?

A. EAL0

B. EAL6

C. EAL3

D. EAL1

11. What ITSEC rating is concerned with a high level of integrity during communications?

A. F5

B. F6

C. F7

D. F8

12. The Information Technology Security Evaluation Criteria (ITSEC) is a single standard for evaluating security attributes of computer systems. Which of the following regions uses this?

A. United States only

B. Europe only

C. United States and Canada

D. United States and Europe

13. An operating system has many protection mechanisms to ensure that processes that are running do not negatively affect each other or other components.   One such mechanism is a protection ring.   The ring architecture is dictated by:

A. The security mode

B. The processor

C. The operating system

D. The processor and the operating system

14. Which rule is also classified as the "no read down" rule?

A. Star property rule

B. Simple integrity axiom

C. Simple security rule

D. Star integrity axiom

15. The sensitivity of the data being processed dictates the security modes in which systems operate. If users need to access some data subject to clearances and formal access approvals, what security mode would this likely be?

A. System high security mode.

B. Partitioned security mode.

C. Multi-level security mode.

D. Dedicated security mode

Domain Area Test:
Security Architecture and Design
Answer Key and Explanations

1. C - This is called keystroke logging. This is usually done in high risk situations, such as air traffic control or nuclear power operations to enforce accountability. [Security Architecture and Design]

2. A - The Common Criteria uses protection profiles as part of its evaluation process. The profile typically contains the set of security requirements, their meaning/reasoning and the EAL rating that the product will require. [Security Architecture and Design]

3. C - A security perimeter is an imaginary boundary with trusted components within it and untrusted components outside it. [Security Architecture and Design]

4. A - Firmware requires physical access and that makes it difficult to tamper with. Hence it provides excellent security. The other choices do not present valid reasons. [Security Architecture and Design]

5. A - Defense in depth is an information assurance strategy that relies on using multiple methods to defend a system. No single technology is ultimately secure; therefore strong security can only be had by adding layers of effective security rather than stripping them out. Although the vendor may claim that no other software is required if their product is used, it is preferable to use multiple layers for security. [Security Architecture and Design]

6. A - John only needs to read-access to the payroll xls. He may never have attempted to change any of the values in the payroll xls but the principle of least privilege states that he should only have as much access as needed. Hence the file needs to be read-only for John. The other answers are incorrect because both people need access to the file and Marsha needs to be able to write her changes since she needs to update timesheet data. [Security Architecture and Design]

7. B - Such types of activities are difficult to catch since they are at the programming level. A code review is the only way in which they can be caught. [Security Architecture and Design]

8. A - The Biba model is one in which the integrity of information within a system is protected, along with the activities that take place. [Security Architecture and Design]

9. C - The goal of hard drive encryption is to protect the data and this is classified as data security. This

does not protect the host itself. [Security Architecture and Design]

10. B - The higher the assurance level, the better the protection. Hence a system with a rating of EAL6 will have a lesser number of covert channels compared to the other values listed. EAL0 doesn't exist. [Security Architecture and Design]

11. D - The Information Technology Security Evaluation Criteria (ITSEC) is an evaluation standard developed and endorsed by the European Union (EU). EU countries wanted a broader standard that included integrity and availability, as well as confidentiality. The ITSEC ratings are broken down into two areas, which are Functionality "F" and Assurance "E". Functionality rating F8 requires a high level of data integrity during communications. [Security Architecture and Design]

12. B - The ITSEC is used in European countries. The United States uses the Orange book. However, most countries have started migrating towards Common Criteria. [Security Architecture and Design]

13. D - The ring architecture that a system uses, is dependent on the processor and the operating system. This is also the reason that an operating system designed for one platform (chip) do not work with

another. [Security Architecture and Design]

14. B - The simple integrity axiom rule is also classified as the "no read down" rule. This rule stipulates that a user at a specific integrity level cannot read information at an integrity level that is lower than their current level. [Security Architecture and Design]

15. C - This would be multi-level security mode. All users need to have formal approvals and an NDA. They access only some of the data on the system based on clearances, a formal approval and a need-to-know. [Security Architecture and Design]

CISSP Mock Exam (LITE) – 4
Practice Questions

Test Name:
CISSP Mock Exam (LITE) - 4
Total Questions: 40
Correct Answers Needed to Pass:
30 (75.00%)
Time Allowed: 60 Minutes

Test Description

This is a cumulative CISSP Mock Exam which can be used as a benchmark for your CISSP aptitude. This practice test includes questions from all ten domains of the CISSP CBK.

Test Questions

1. After a computer system is believed to have been used in a crime or incident, it is most important that which of the following be saved securely before electricity is removed?

   A. Internet cache

   B. Memory dump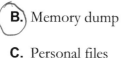

   C. Personal files

   D. Documents

2. Access to secure and / or critical areas should be always requested by _____, and only granted when a valid _____ is demonstrated.

   A. The Asset Owner / Signed Statement

   B. Division Director / Criminal Background Check

   C. An Employee's Supervisor / Business Need

   D. An Employee / Photo Identification

3. Joann has been given the task of maintaining the Backup Control Center box. A list of Master passwords, install media, and other essentials are contained inside. In the event of a disaster, she is to keep possession of the box at all times. Which of the four elements of a business continuity plan does this exemplify?

   A. Testing

   B. Authority

   C. Priorities

   D. Responsibility

4. Which of these is a key factor to keep in mind while selecting a directory service based product for Identity Management and Access Control?

   A. The X.501 standard is the best and preferred over the X.500 standard

   B. The directory service shows tangible benefits only when the number of entries in the directory exceeds 4000.

   C. The directory service shows tangible benefits only when the number of entries in the directory exceeds 400.

   ✓ **D.** Legacy applications may still need to be configured and managed individually by the system administrator.

5. Which of these is NOT an example of a detective physical control?

   A. Security guards

   B. Alarms and sensors

   C. Smoke and fire detectors

   D. Library control systems

6. Which of the following refers to the likelihood that an agent will exploit a weakness?

   A. Risk

   B. Exposure

   C. Threat

   D. Vulnerability

7. What statement is not true in regard to maintenance hooks?

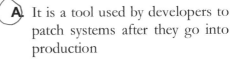

   A. It is a tool used by developers to patch systems after they go into production

   B. It is a security risk if not removed before the software goes into production

   C. It is a type of backdoor created by the developer

   D. It is a method used to bypass access controls to alter software code during the development process

8. Which statement best describes maintenance hooks?

   A. They are cycles of downtime for software access controls.

B. They are periods of time in which the software security is lax.

C. They are Trojan horses placed in the software by hackers.

D. They are backdoors into software that only the developer knows about.

9. Floyd is the chief compliance officer for a multi-million dollar concern that deals with medical records. It was reported to him that the firewalls currently in place are weak and have well-known exploits. However, in order to save money, he decides to ignore this. Which of the following has he violated?

A. Due diligence

B. Privacy rights

C. Prudent person rule

D. ISO-9000

10. Most companies outsource their security guard services requirements to external contractor companies. This results in a higher risk and is a vulnerability for information security requirements. Which of the following will be the least effective in reducing the risk?

A. Have a robust set of training procedures.

B. Monitor specific performance metrics.

C. Have strong contract management procedures.

D. Have a policy to mandatorily change the guards every week.

11. Employees in the accounting department in a company are required to mandatorily take off on vacation for two weeks every year. What is the purpose of such a requirement?

A. Mandatory vacations are a well known financial practice.

B. Mandatory vacations are a well-known HR practice.

C. Mandatory vacations are very useful for job rotation.

D. Mandatory vacations are well known as a security practice.

12. A biometric system weighs people entering a facility to ensure that only one person is being granted access. Where would such a system typically be used?

A. In a dual-surveillance system

B. In a fail-safe system

C. In a fail-secure system

D. In a mantrap

13. Which of the following would the first priority of a disaster recovery plan?

   A. Fast data recovery

   B. Transportation

   C. Human safety

   D. News media statements

14. Which of these is not a Crime Prevention Through Environmental Design (CPTED) guideline?

   A. Natural access control

   B. Natural response

   C. Territorial reinforcement

   D. Natural surveillance

15. A memory leak occurs when poorly written applications use up memory but do not free it back to the operating system. How would a hacker use such a flaw to disrupt systems?

   A. By a Buffer Overflow attack

   B. By a Teardrop attack

   C. By Denial of Service (DoS) attacks

   D. By introducing a Trojan horse

16. Doug is the manager of a large switched network. He notices that the network is very slow and with the use of a network sniffer, he diagnoses a broadcast storm. What causes a broadcast storm?

   A. Repeaters

   B. Pings

   C. Bridges

   D. Routers

17. The length of outage that can be survived by a company is called:

   A. Minimum Time Between Failure

   B. Maximum Backup Recovery Time

   C. Maximum Tolerable Downtime

   D. Minimum Tolerable Downtime

18. Certain information has an MTTR of close to zero. What action should an Information Security Professional advise for such a requirement?

   A. Such information should be accessed only by the system administrator

   B. It is not possible to have an MTTR of close to zero

   C. Such information need not have any backup planned.

   ✓ **D.** Such information should be mirrored / duplexed.

19. An object oriented programming (OOP) environment has certain key characteristics that need to be looked at carefully from a security point of view. Which of the following OOP features has an associated set of security issues?

   A. Objects

   B. Multiple Inheritances

   C. Encapsulation

   D. Classes

20. A company purchased anti-virus software from a leading vendor and installed it. However, the signatures were not kept up-to-date. This is a:

   A. Vulnerability

   B. Risk

   C. Countermeasure

   D. Threat

21. Threats to data integrity can be reduced through separation of duties and rotation of duties. What other security principle will help protect against threats to integrity?

   A. Social engineering

   B. Dumpster diving

   C. Need-to-know

   D. Collusion

22. Public key certificates provide a high level of trust. Certificates need to be issued, maintained, may expire, or may need to be revoked. Which authority keeps track of expired certificates?

   A. No authority keeps track of expired certificates

   B. Certificate Repository (CR)

   C. Certificate Authority (CA)

   D. Registration Authority (RA)

23. The Local Area Networking team at a company has commenced work on a Business Continuity Plan. They have followed all recommendations and procedures and have come up with an exhaustive plan. However, they have forgotten a very important step in the process. What could this be?

   A. Obtain a hardware Budget

   B. Get management support

   C. Test the plan

   D. Choose between hot site and cold site

24. Will an operating system that works with one microprocessor chip work with another?

   A. Yes, this is part of the portability built into operating systems.

   B. Yes. The ring architecture of operating systems is designed to be flexible across different chips.

   C. No. Even though the ring architecture used by chips is the same, the ring architecture system used by an operating system is different.

   D. No. Different microprocessors have different architectures and instruction sets.

25. A sender challenged a recipient that a message did not originate from him. If this message was sent using cryptography and used a trusted third party, what feature of cryptography allows this statement to be verified?

   A. Authentication

   B. Nonrepudiation

   C. Integrity

   D. Access Control.

26. If you are designing a cryptosystem and require a mathematically intensive algorithm, which one should you use?

   A. IDEA

   B. Blowfish

   C. RSA

   D. Data Encryption Standard (DES)

27. Two computers are communicating at the transport layer. Which of these is not a protocol used at the transport layer?

A. Remote Procedure Call (RPC)

B. Transmission Control Protocol (TCP)

C. User Datagram Protocol (UDP)

D. Sequenced Packet Exchange (SPX)

28. Which of these correctly depicts the structure of a business continuity plan?

A. Initiation phase, Activation phase, Reconstruction phase, Recovery phase

B. Activation phase, Initiation phase, Reconstruction phase, Recovery phase

C. Activation phase, Initiation phase, Recovery phase, Reconstruction phase

D. Initiation phase, Activation phase, Recovery phase, Reconstruction phase

29. Which of these is not a characteristic of a signature-based intrusion detection system?

A. Identifies new types of attacks

B. Needs constant updating

C. Uses pattern matching

D. Can be host-based

30. Which of the following types of evidence can stand on its own merit in court and needs no corroboration?

A. Opinion evidence

B. Direct evidence

C. Circumstantial evidence

D. Hearsay evidence

31. Which of the following is NOT a physical security control?

A. Padlocks

B. CCTV

C. A password

D. Guards

32. An audit of the password management process of an enterprise organization revealed that users were never required to reset their network passwords. This was flagged as a red item and the administrator was asked to enforce password changes. What is a good frequency for change of passwords?

A. 180 to 365 days

B. 30 to 60 days

C. 15 to 30 days

D. 90 to 120 days

33. Visitors to a high security prison are marked with an invisible hand stamp. This is then verified by a Corrections Officer behind a bullet proof glass enclosure, after which the visitor is allowed through a second door. What type of preventative control is this?

A. Technical Control

B. Administrative Control

C. Resident Control

D. Physical Control

34. What of these is the best way to prevent piggybacking from occurring at the access points into a facility?

A. Security guards

B. Programmable locks

C. Swipe cards

D. Proximity cards

35. Which of the following is Personally Identifiable Information (PII)?

A. First Name and Address

B. Last Name

C. First Name, Last Name, Account Number

D. Last Name and Address

36. A bank wishes to install wireless access within their main branch. Because of FFIEC guidelines to encrypt transmitted data, however, they must find a way to do so securely. Which of the following implementations would be most secure?

A. Connect the wireless access point to the internal network and allow DHCP to provide addresses to client machines.

B. Connect the wireless access point to the internal network and implement WPA.

C. Connect the wireless access point to the Internet and use WEP.

D. Place the wireless access point in a DMZ and allow only VPN connections to the internal network.

37. Why should plenum-rated cabling be used in data centers?

A. Prevents crosstalk

B. Improves signal strength

C. Reduces attenuation

D. Reduces fire hazards

38. Which of the following technologies is not used for Virtual Private Networking?

A. L2TP

B. IPSec

C. PPTP

D. PPP

39. Which of the following is primarily at a management level and states a high-level overview of an entity's stance towards a certain issue?

A. Policy

B. Procedure

C. Standard

D. Guideline

40. Which of the following firewall architectures is the fastest?

A. Stateful firewall

B. Application-level proxy firewall

C. Circuit-level proxy firewall

D. Kernel proxy firewall

CISSP Mock Exam (LITE) – 4
Answer Key and Explanations

1. B - Internet cache, personal files, and documents are all stored on the hard drive. However, evidence in RAM will disappear forever when the machine is turned off. Special software tools must be used to do this. [Legal, Regulations, Compliance and Investigations]

2. C - It is good practice to require requests for access to come from an employee's supervisor. This prevents an employee from gaining access levels about which his or her management does not know. This should be based on a business need. [Security Operations]

3. D - This refers to responsibility. Joann has accepted the responsibility of the backup control center box (BUCC). She does not necessarily have the Authority to declare a disaster, and she may have other priorities before and after the responsibility of the BUCC. [Business Continuity and Disaster Recovery Planning]

4. D - Legacy applications may still need to be configured and managed individually by the system administrator since they were not built to work with a directory service. These legacy entities need to be managed using their original management software. [Access Control]

5. D - Library control systems are classified as preventive technical controls, not detective physical controls. Library control systems avoid unauthorized data modification by ensuring that only library control personnel can implement changes to production programs. [Physical (Environmental) Security]

6. A - A risk is the likelihood that a threat agent will take advantage of a vulnerability. It ties the vulnerability, threat and the likelihood of being exploited, to the business impact that could result. [Information Security and Risk Management]

7. A - Maintenance hooks are backdoors into software that were created by the developer. Generally, developers use them to bypass access controls to easily make changes to software code or alter development. They become a serious security issue when they are not removed after the software is sent to production. Many developers still use maintenance hooks even though they are considered a security issue. [Security Architecture and Design]

8. D - Maintenance hooks are software backdoors created by the developer. Generally, developers use them to bypass access controls in order to

easily change software code or alter development. They become a serious security issue when they are not removed after the software is sent to production. Many developers still use maintenance hooks even though they are considered a security issue. [Security Architecture and Design]

9. C - Management must follow the prudent person rule in performing due care. In other words, they must do what a prudent and responsible person would do in the situation. Due diligence takes place in planning, and is done to ensure that all possible weaknesses and threats were considered. Due care is the set of actions to mitigate weaknesses in the current situation. [Legal, Regulations, Compliance and Investigations]

10. D - Mandatorily changing the guards every week will actually add to the risk. Security guards will need some time to be trained and be familiar with the system requirements and understand what the security expectations are. If guards are frequently changed, there is a loss of knowledge. This option does not reduce the risk of outsourcing the security guard services. [Physical (Environmental) Security]

11. D - Mandatory vacations are well known as a security practice. Frauds committed by employees can come to light during their absence. The company has a better chance of finding this out if the employee is away for a week or longer. Hence companies often mandate that employees in key departments be covered by such policies. [Security Operations]

12. D - Mantraps typically consist of a small room with two doors. An individual must first authenticate through the first door to enter the room. Then, the individual must authenticate through the second door to gain access into the facility. Sometimes, mantraps have biometric systems that weigh individuals to make sure that only one person enters the facility at a time. This is an effective way to prevent unauthorized individuals from piggybacking and gaining access to the facility. [Physical (Environmental) Security]

13. C - Human safety is the first priority of a disaster recovery plan. Many regulatory bodies also require that human concerns be considered ahead of all others in every emergency response plan. [Business Continuity and Disaster Recovery Planning]

14. B - Natural response is not a valid CPTED guideline. CPTED primarily outlines how a well-designed physical environment can reduce/minimize crime by affecting human behavior. [Physical (Environmental) Security]

15. C - Memory leaks can be exploited by hackers who can launch a Denial of Service (DoS) attack. Hackers can potentially cause systems to be disrupted by continually sending requests to the server. This results in more and more memory being used up, because the application does not release allocated memory. At some point, it will run out of memory. [Security Architecture and Design]

16. C - Bridges forward all traffic and as a result they broadcast all packets as well. This can congest the network and result in a broadcast storm. [Telecommunications and Network Security]

17. C - MTD, or Maximum Tolerable Downtime is the length of time a company can withstand an outage It is based on the best technical facts available, but is a purely business decision. [Business Continuity and Disaster Recovery Planning]

18. D - MTTR refers to Mean Time to Repair. If the MTTR is close to zero, it means that the information needs to be continuously available. This would call for mirroring / duplexing the information. [Security Operations]

19. B - Multiple Inheritances have the potential to be incorrectly used, resulting in a security breach for object access. Aspects such as name clashes need to be resolved by the programming language or else a situation may arise where a subclass has inherited excessive privileges from a superclass and can misuse its privileges. [Software Development Security]

20. A - This is a vulnerability since the company is now prone to virus attacks. The threat is that a virus will actually show up and disrupt systems. Risk is the likelihood of the virus showing up. [Information Security and Risk Management]

21. C - Need-to-know, or least privilege, is a security principle that will help protect against threats to data integrity. Employees should only be granted access to the resources required to perform their duties [Information Security and Risk Management]

22. A - No authority keeps track of expired certificates. The certificate authority (CA) keeps a list of all certificates that have been revoked but not of those that have expired. [Cryptography]

23. B - A continuity plan can never be successful without the involvement of other departments. Management support needs to be enlisted to make this happen. [Business Continuity and Disaster Recovery Planning]

24. D - No. Hardware chips are designed to have a certain number of rings. Operating systems also need to be designed to work within this ring structure. Different microprocessors have different architectures and instruction sets thus preventing operating systems from being portable. [Security Architecture and Design]

25. B - Nonrepudiation. Digital signatures and public key encryption provide tools for non-repudiation or origin. Use of a third party can allow verification of the origin of the message. [Cryptography]

26. C - Of the choices given, RSA is an asymmetric algorithm while the other choices Blowfish, DES and IDEA are symmetric algorithms. Asymmetric algorithms are mathematically intensive compared to symmetric algorithms. Hence RSA is the right choice. [Cryptography]

27. A - Of the protocols listed, remote procedure call (RPC) works at the session layer and not at the transport layer. [Telecommunications and Network Security]

28. D - A good business continuity plan will be structured as Initiation phase, Activation phase, Recovery phase, and Reconstruction phase. [Business Continuity and Disaster Recovery Planning]

29. A - A major drawback of signature-based intrusion detection systems is that they are weak against new types of attacks. For this type of intrusion detection system to perform optimally, it must be continually updated. If a new type of attack is discovered, a new signature must be created by the vendor. Intrusion detection systems must then be updated to be able to detect this type of attack in the future. [Access Control]

30. B - Only direct evidence, such as an eye-witness, does not need backup information. Conclusive evidence also needs no corroboration - it is irrefutable. [Legal, Regulations, Compliance and Investigations]

31. C - Passwords are not physical controls, they are cyber or electronic controls. [Physical (Environmental) Security]

32. B - Passwords may be easily compromised over a period of time. Enterprise organizations typically force users to change passwords in a timeframe of 30 to 60 days. More frequent changes are a hindrance to users while less frequent changes lower the security. [Access Control]

33. D - Physical controls attempt to prevent physical access by unauthorized persons to secure objects. Other examples are guard dogs, antenna badges, and swipe cards. [Information Security and Risk Management]

34. A - Piggybacking occurs when an individual obtains unauthorized access to a facility by simply following another individual who had valid credentials. One of the best ways to prevent piggybacking from occurring is to place security guards at each access point into the facility. [Physical (Environmental) Security]

35. C - PII does not include information that is readily available from a telephone directory. However, when it is combined with a third item of information, such as an account number, it becomes private. A social security number would always be considered private. [Legal, Regulations, Compliance and Investigations]

36. D - Placing the access point in a firewall DMZ and using a strong technology such as VPN is the safest way to implement wireless networking. Placing the device on the LAN with no protection is dangerous. The other options do not provide the security of VPN. [Telecommunications and Network Security]

37. D - Plenum is more expensive than non-plenum cable. This is due to the special cabling material that does not let off hazardous gases if it burns.

[Telecommunications and Network Security]

38. D - Point to Point Tunneling Protocol (PPTP), Layer 2 Tunneling Protocol (L2TP), and IPSec can all be used for VPN connections. PPP is a non secure connection protocol, as it does not tunnel. [Telecommunications and Network Security]

39. A - Policies present a high-level view of a company's attitude toward protecting a particular asset, or dealing with a single issue. For instance, a Server Security Policy may only state that the entity will use NIST guides as a gold standard. It should then refer to detailed server administration procedure documentation. [Information Security and Risk Management]

40. D - A kernel proxy firewall is a fifth-generation firewall. This firewall is faster than other firewalls because inspection and processing takes place in the kernel and does not need to take place in a higher layer in the OS. [Telecommunications and Network Security]

Domain Area Test: Telecommunications and Network Security Practice Questions

Test Name:
Domain Area Test: Telecommunications and Network Security
Total Questions: 15
Correct Answers Needed to Pass: 11 (73.33%)
Time Allowed: 25 Minutes

Test Description

This practice test specifically targets your knowledge of the Telecommunications and Network Security domain area.

Test Questions

1. A company needs to install a customer-facing sales web server so that their backend customer database is accessible over the internt. They install this server between two firewalls so that one stands between the internet and the server and the other between the server and the internal systems. This arrangement would be called a:

   A. WEP

   B. DMZ

C. WAN

D. LAN

2. A firewall is essentially a special-purpose type of device. Which of the following could be used to describe a firewall?

   A. Bridge

   B. Switch

   C. Repeater

   D. Router

3. On which layer of the OSI model does a hub or repeater operate?

   A. Layer 1 - Physical

   B. Layer 2 - Data Link

   C. Layer 3 - Network

   D. Layer 4 - Transport

4. On which layer of the OSI model does a network router operate?

   A. Layer 2 - Data Link

   B. Layer 3 - Network

   C. Layer 4 - Transport

D. Layer 1 - Physical

5. On which layer of the OSI model does a basic network switch operate?

A. Layer 4 - Transport

B. Layer 1 - Physical

C. Layer 2 - Data Link

D. Layer 3 - Network

6. What solution would you use if you needed to make a secure connection over an unsecure network?

A. None. It is not possible to make a secure connection over an unsecure network.

B. VPN

C. ADSL

D. PPP

7. At which layer of the OSI model are communications channels setup and released using protocols such as remote procedure calls (RPC)?

A. Data Link Layer

B. Session Layer

C. Network Layer

D. Transport Layer

8. At which layer of the OSI model do connection-oriented protocols operate?

A. Session Layer

B. Application Layer

C. Transport Layer

D. Physical Layer

9. Which of these is not a requirement for a computer to communicate across a router using TCP/IP?

A. Gateway Address

B. IP Address

C. Subnet Mask

D. DNS Server

10. Which of the following is a fringe benefit of using a Network Address Translation (NAT) gateway?

A. The shortage of IP addresses is resolved because companies can reuse private IP addresses within their networks as long as these don't access the internet.

B. When attackers attack a network, they are unable to find out the internal details about the company's network and topology.

C. Since the internal topology of a company is not known, it is completely immune to viruses.

D. Even though the acceptance of IPv6 is taking time, NATs have allowed companies to put the problem off for a while.

11. When a firewall proxies many computer systems using private IP addressing to the Internet over a single public IP address what is it called?

  A. NAT

  B. DNS

  C. WAN

  D. DNA

12. Which layer of the OSI model is responsible for interfacing between the network stack and the application?

  A. Network Layer

  B. Physical Layer

  C. Session Layer

  D. Application Layer

13. A connection-less protocol has no way of detecting transmission errors that may occur due to connectivity or network problems. What can a connection-less protocol use to test connectivity and troubleshoot problems on IP networks?

  A. ARP

  B. MAC

  C. RARP

  D. ICMP

14. At which layer of the OSI model are transformations made to prepare datagrams for use between disparate systems, such as an EBCDIC to ASCII conversion?

  A. Session Layer

  B. Physical Layer

  C. Application Layer

  D. Presentation Layer

15. A programmer wants to use a connection-oriented protocol that provides handshaking so that the application can identify whether

packets were dropped and which ones to resend. Which protocol would he use in the application?

A. UDP

B. Telnet

C. TCP

D. SSL

Domain Area Test:
Telecommunications and Network
Security
Answer Key and Explanations

1. B - A De-Militarized Zone is the traditional name for a secure segment that is still firewalled away from the internal network. They are used commonly for Internet-facing services. [Telecommunications and Network Security]

2. D - A firewall is a router with packet inspection and filtering capabilities. In fact, many routers have optional features that may be installed to transform them into firewalls. [Telecommunications and Network Security]

3. A - A repeater or hub (which is just a multiport repeater) simply amplifies electrical impulses it receives and broadcasts the same impulses out on all ports. It operates on the physical layer only. [Telecommunications and Network Security]

4. B - A router is a network layer device that only forwards directed traffic. Broadcasts are not forwarded. [Telecommunications and Network Security]

5. C - A basic network switch operates at the data-link layer (Layer 2) of the OSI model. [Telecommunications and Network Security]

6. B - A VPN permits a secure, private connection using an unsecure environment. This is achieved through the use of encryption and tunneling protocols. [Telecommunications and Network Security]

7. B - At the session layer, communications channels (called sessions) between applications are set up and released. Remote procedure calls (RPC), Structured Query Language (SQL) and Network File System (NFS) are some of the protocols used in this layer. [Telecommunications and Network Security]

8. C - Connection-oriented protocols such as TCP are found at the Transport layer. [Telecommunications and Network Security]

9. D - DNS Servers are not needed to just communicate to another network segment. A network node requires a unique IP address and a subnet mask to communicate on a network. To communicate to another network (across a router), a gateway address is required. [Telecommunications and Network Security]

10. B - NATs were originally intended to address the shortage of IP address problem. However, a fringe benefit

is that attackers are unable to obtain internal network topology details of companies since the NAT gateway stands in between attackers and the company's internal networks. Use of NATs does not make the company immune to viruses. [Telecommunications and Network Security]

11. A - Network Address Translation allows many hosts behind a firewall to access the Internet from only one public address. [Telecommunications and Network Security]

12. D - The application layer does not refer to the end application itself but refers to the interface between the OSI network stack and that application. It is the topmost layer and interfaces with the system and applications. [Telecommunications and Network Security]

13. D - The Internet Control Message Protocol (ICMP) reports routing information and errors and delivers status messages. It can be used as a means of sending back error messages to sending systems that use connectionless protocols. [Telecommunications and Network Security]

14. D - The presentation layer is responsible for making conversions between formats so that the data can be properly processed by the end system. Handling a conversion from EBCDIC to ASCII would be done at this layer. [Telecommunications and Network Security]

15. C - The programmer would use TCP, which is a connection-oriented protocol that uses handshaking. Packets which are dropped are identified and can be resent. In contrast, UDP is a connection-less protocol and UDP will not know which packets were dropped. Telnet and SSL do not fit in here. [Telecommunications and Network Security]

CISSP Mock Exam (LITE) – 5
Practice Questions

Test Name:
CISSP Mock Exam (LITE) - 5
Total Questions: 40
Correct Answers Needed to Pass:
30 (75.00%)
Time Allowed: 60 Minutes

Test Description

This is a cumulative CISSP Mock Exam which can be used as a benchmark for your CISSP aptitude. This practice test includes questions from all ten domains of the CISSP CBK.

Test Questions

1. Which of the following is a document that lists step-by-step tasks and is intended to be used by operations staff?

   A. Guideline

   B. Procedure

   C. Standard

   D. Policy

2. The temperature inside a data center started to go up due to a malfunction of the air-conditioning system. Which of the following will be most resistant to such a rise in temperature?

   A. Hard copy of a report

   B. A printer

   C. A data tape

   D. A keyboard

3. Which of the following is NOT an advantage of maintaining a Hot Site?

   A. Fast Recovery Time

   B. Highly Available

   C. Less Expensive

   D. Available for Annual Testing

4. There are two main types of Risk Analysis: _____ which uses the knowledge of the workers who know the processes best, but also includes some amount of guesswork. There is also _____, which requires more complex calculations, but can also be more easily automated and provides cost / benefit information.

   A. Auditory / Preemptive

   B. Qualitative / Quantitative

C. Quantitative / Qualitative

D. Preemptive / Auditory

5. What type of interference can be caused by fluorescent lights that are commonly found in office buildings?

    A. Electrostatic discharge

    B. Radio modulation

    C. Radio frequency interference

    D. Intermodulation

6. If cost is not an issue, which of the following storage systems provides the best combination of performance and availability?

    A. RAID 1

    B. RAID 10

    C. RAID 5

    D. RAID 0

7. Which algorithm is not a hashing algorithm?

    A. RC4

    B. SHA

    C. HAVAL

    D. MD5

8. Which of the following statements best describes the objectives of a Recovery Strategy?

    A. They are measures put into place to help detect when a disaster strikes.

    B. They are predefined activities that will be used to prevent a disaster from occurring.

    C. They are measures put into place to help reduce the likelihood of a disaster.

    D. They are predefined activities that will be used when a disaster strikes.

9. What is the process of transferring transaction logs or journals to an offsite facility known as?

    A. Disk duplexing

    B. Disk-shadowing

    C. Remote journaling

    D. Electronic vaulting

10. Which of the following choices is not a basic principle used to help protect against threats to data integrity?

A. Separation of duties

B. Repudiation

C. Rotation of duties

D. Need-to-know

11. When managing risks, which of the following statements is true?

A. Risk Management provides complete security.

B. Risk Management should be outsourced whenever possible to professionals in the Risk Management industry.

C. Risk Management cannot mitigate risk in any way, it is merely an exercise to become aware of existing or possible risks.

D. Risks are best managed with a layered approach, sometimes called defense-in-depth.

12. Java uses a security scheme to prevent an applet from having undue access to the rest of the system. What is this called?

A. Ivory Tower

B. Sandboxing

C. Browser-level

D. Safe-mode

13. A software application development project had already proceeded into the design phase when it was discovered that security aspects had not been taken into consideration. What should be done to address this?

A. Prepare the necessary security guidelines and checklists so that they can be used in the build/coding phase.

B. Prepare necessary test plans so that security aspects are properly taken care during Integration testing.

C. Restart the design phase and include security as part of this phase.

D. Revisit the requirements phase to incorporate security requirements and ensure that these are input to the design phase.

14. At what point should security requirements be addressed while developing a new system?

A. At the end of the design phase.

B. At the start of the project.

C. At the end of the testing phase

D. At the start of the integration testing phase.

15. In order for security plans to be effective, the time-period for which they must be designed is at least:

A. Three years.

B. Ten years.

C. One year.

D. Six months.

16. The security policy of a company had the following statement: "Employees of the company should not share their passwords with anyone." Is this statement worded correctly? If not, how would you reword it for it to be effective as a policy?

A. The statement is okay and can be left as-is.

B. No, it is not worded correctly. It should be rewritten as "Employees of the company

should avoid sharing their passwords with anyone."

C. No, it is not worded correctly. The statement should be rewritten as "Employees of the company shall not share their passwords with anyone."

D. No, it is not worded correctly. It should be rewritten as "Employees of the company shouldn't share their passwords with anyone."

17. A RAID consists of multiple drives but appears as a single drive to applications. A technique used is to divide and write data over several drives. This results in dramatically increased read performance since data is simultaneously read from several drives. Such a technique is called:

A. Multiple-mirroring

B. Strobing

C. Swapping

D. Striping

18. In a HTTPS connection, the web server generates a cookie which is sent to the browser. This may be stored on hard disk or in memory. Which of these is not a valid 'best practice' with regard to cookies in a HTTPS connection?

A. Cookies should not contain sensitive information such as account numbers and passwords.

B. Cookies should not have timestamps on them.

C. Cookies containing sensitive information should be only resident in memory and not stored on hard disk.

D. Cookies containing sensitive information should be encrypted by the server

19. Certain audit standards required that records be maintained for 3 years. In order to comply with these standards, what is the recommended duration for which data should be maintained?

A. 4 years

B. 6 years

C. 1 year

D. Exactly 3 years

20. Under what law would a person caught stealing a computer be prosecuted?

A. Civil Law

B. Copyright Law

C. Criminal Law

D. Regulatory Law

21. Which of the following protocols is easily susceptible to hacking?

A. VPN

B. HTTPS

C. 3DES

D. SMTP

22. A person enters a business claiming to be a printer service engineer. He talks his way into secure areas and manages to copy some confidential data. What is this usually called?

A. Black boxing

B. Dumpster diving

C. Phreaking

D. Social engineering

23. Jen would like to have more control over VPN connections made to her corporate network. Additionally, she would like to save effort and money

by eliminating costly VPN client licenses. Which technology would be the best solution?

A. SSL VPN

B. IPSec VPN

C. IPSec / L2TP VPN

D. S/MIME

24. Which of the following refers to a mandatory rule (either internally or externally mandated) implemented across an organization?

A. Policy

B. Guideline

C. Standard

D. Procedure

25. Which of these is not an example of a physical control?

A. Subnets

B. Building location

C. External lights

D. Data backups

26. The Computer Emergency Response Team (CERT) has an advisory that companies should use legal banners that pop up when employees log in. What would be the purpose of such banners?

A. Using such legal banners absolves the company from any legal action in case of security violations.

B. They permit personal information of the employee to be captured and used by the company.

C. They will prevent employees from violating security policies.

D. They can be used to strengthen a case against an employee in case of a security violation.

27. Kate is the director of risk management at a large financial institution. Once each year, she is required by the board of directors to convene a table-top exercise based upon a disaster scenario. After several milestones are discussed in the exercise, she makes sure that the lessons learned are folded back into the BCP for more efficiency. This exemplifies which of the four elements of a business continuity plan?

A. Responsibility

B. Maintenance

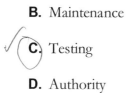 **C.** Testing

D. Authority

28. What network device can you implement between end systems on a network to reduce the possibility of sniffing and monitoring attacks by potential intruders?

A. Gateways

B. Routers

C. Switches

D. Firewalls

29. Dan has been tasked to employ an encryption methodology for his company's data network. Management has identified performance as the number one concern. Which of the following should Dan use for encryption?

A. MD5

B. RSA

C. DSA

D. DES

30. Greg is designing a cryptosystem to provide encryption and decryption. He weighs the pros and cons and finally decides to use a symmetric cryptosystem as opposed to an asymmetric cryptosystem. Which of the following could have been a key influencing factor in his decision?

A. Key management is very simple and straightforward in symmetric cryptosystems.

B. Symmetric cryptosystems are very scalable.

C. Symmetric cryptosystems are much faster than asymmetric systems.

D. Symmetric cryptosystems provide strong authenticity and nonrepudiation.

31. At John's company, there is a software policy in place that prevents the use of unencrypted flash storage devices, such as USB thumb drives. What type of control is such a preventative measure called?

A. Resident Control

B. Physical Control

C. Administrative Control

D. Technical Control

32. Which of the following is an example of a technical control?

    A. Policies and procedures

    B. Encryption

    C. Mantraps

    D. Background checks

33. Administrative, technical, and physical controls are used by security administrators to meet the organization's security requirements. Which of these is an example of a technical control?

    A. Closed-circuit TV (CCTV)

    B. Separation of duties

    C. Use of guard dogs

    D. Firewall

34. The remote administration security policy of a company states that no administration technology that utilizes clear-text transmission over a routable protocol should be employed on any network system. Which of the following protocols will not be allowed as per the policy?

    A. Serial Console Port

    B. USB Console Port

    C. SSH

    D. Telnet

35. Which of the following is NOT a step in contingency Planning?

    A. Testing and Implementation

    B. Identifying Critical Business Functions

    C. Estimating Potential Disasters

    D. Identifying Resources and Systems that Support Critical Business Functions

36. Which of these security models ensures that you cannot write to an object that resides at a security level lower than the one you possess?

    A. Clark-Wilson model

    B. Lattice model

    C. Biba model

    D. Bell-LaPadula model

37. Which of the following is a benefit of job rotation?

    A. All of the options

B. Cross Training enhances Efficiency of Employees

C. Fraud Prevention

D. Skill Redundancy in case of Emergency

38. You are currently meeting with management to have them formally approve the products, systems, and components within your organization. What is this process referred to as?

A. Certification

B. Accreditation

C. Affirmation

D. Verification

39. When databases are updated in a distributed environment, protecting the integrity of the data becomes very important. The ACID test is often used as a guideline to how the database software should be implemented. This stands for:

A. Atomicity, Consistency, Inter-operability and Dependability

B. Atomicity, Concurrency, Inter-operability and Dependability

C. Atomicity, Concurrency, Isolation and Durability

D. Atomicity, Consistency, Isolation and Durability

40. A bank's rating was lowered post an audit by the Federal Deposit Insurance Corporation (FDIC). Lack of proper administrative controls in the IS department was cited as a key non-conformance. Which of the following would NOT be the Board of Directors' primary response?

A. Hire an Internal IT Auditor into the Risk Management Department

B. Approve an Information Security Program

C. Hire an Internal Auditor into the IS Department

D. Approve a plan to create a procedural manual for the IS department.

CISSP Mock Exam (LITE) – 5
Answer Key and Explanations

1. B - Procedures are detailed in nature. They typically include step-by-step tasks that need to be done to achieve a specific goal such as configuring operating systems, setting up new user accounts etc. [Information Security and Risk Management]

2. A - Products made of paper can withstand temperatures up to 350 deg Fahrenheit. Magnetic products start to degrade first, as early as 100 deg Fahrenheit. [Physical (Environmental) Security]

3. C - Purchasing, implementing, and maintaining two sets of hardware and software is very expensive. However, once in place, a hot site offers the fastest recover time over cold and warm Sites. [Business Continuity and Disaster Recovery Planning]

4. B - Qualitative Risk Analysis uses personal and subjective opinions of people involved with the processes. Quantitative Risk Analysis seeks to apply mathematical values and formulae to the process and can best achieve hard numbers. [Information Security and Risk Management]

5. C - Radio frequency interference (RFI) can be caused by devices that produces radio waves and is commonly caused by fluorescent lights in buildings. Shielded cabling and proper placement of cables are ways to help prevent interference due to fluorescent lighting. [Physical (Environmental) Security]

6. B - RAID stands for Redundant Array of Independent Drives. RAID 0 stripes data across two drives, which is extremely fast but has no redundancy. Raid 1 is drive mirroring or duplexing, but can suffer from performance issues. Raid 5 offers a fairly good protection with striping plus parity data and is only moderately expensive. The most expensive is RAID 10 which is a combination of RAID 1 and RAID 0. RAID 10 offers the best performance and best protection. [Physical (Environmental) Security]

7. A - RC4 is a symmetric key algorithm that provides key distribution services. Hashing is used to verify the integrity of a message. If you want to ensure that a message has not been altered in transmission from source to destination, you can use a hashing function. A one-way hash will take the variable-length message that you want to send and produce a fixed-length value to send to the recipient. Once the recipient receives the message, they will perform the same hash function to determine if they get the same result. If the results are the same, the message has not been altered. [Cryptography]

8. D - Recovery strategies are predefined activities that will be used when a disaster strikes. They identify how the disaster and recovery should be handled. The recovery strategy should include documents about alternate sites and facilities, costs and alternatives, emergency response procedures, contact information, security procedures, and other systems that may need to be reviewed. [Business Continuity and Disaster Recovery Planning]

9. C - Remote journaling is the process of moving journals or transaction logs offsite to another storage facility. This type of solution does not include the actual files, but only the logs containing any changes that have been made to the files since the last transfer. If for some reason data becomes corrupted, the log files can be retrieved and used to quickly restore the data. This is a very efficient means of recovery as only the changes need to be retrieved and applied to the data. [Business Continuity and Disaster Recovery Planning]

10. B - Repudiation does not protect against threats to integrity. Repudiation refers to sending a message and then denying that you sent it. Digital signatures are used to provide a non-repudiation service,

which prevents the sender from denying that they sent the message. [Information Security and Risk Management]

11. D - Risk Management is just that - management of risk. Risks cannot be completely eliminated. Hence, risks are best managed by a layered approach. [Information Security and Risk Management]

12. B - Sandboxing constructs a walled, virtual environment to execute foreign code. In theory, an applet cannot pass commands directly to the underlying system, but it is instead abstracted away by the virtual layer. [Software Development Security]

13. D - Security needs to be built into a software application development project right from the requirements phase. If this has been missed out, the requirements phase needs to be revisited and reworked to address this gap. [Software Development Security]

14. B - Security requirements must be addressed right at the start of the project. [Software Development Security]

15. A - Security plans should be designed to be useful for at least three years. If not, it means that sufficient thought has not gone into its creation and it needs to be

revisited. [Security Architecture and Design]

16. C - Security policies should contain statements that are direct and commanding. They need to convey the effect and less forceful words like 'should' or 'may' should be replaced by use of the stronger words 'shall' or 'must'. [Information Security and Risk Management]

17. D - This technique is known as striping. Although a write operation might take longer time, a read is much faster since data is read simultaneously from multiple drives. [Business Continuity and Disaster Recovery Planning]

18. B - Since HTTP is a stateless protocol, cookies are very much essential for a secure connection using SSL. In order to prevent man-in-the-middle attacks, it is very important that the cookies contain timestamps. The web server periodically checks these. If the connection has been idle for a while, it is "timed out" by the web server. All the other choices are best practices. [Cryptography]

19. D - As a general principle, audit data should not be kept any longer than required since it can otherwise consume massive amounts of storage. Hence it is advised to maintain records for exactly 3 years in this case. [Security Operations]

20. C - Since this case involves a physical theft, at least the initial charges will be criminal. If it was later discovered that the perpetrator was sent by a competitor to steal trade secrets, then a civil case might also be brought on. [Legal, Regulations, Compliance and Investigations]

21. D - SMTP is the only protocol or technology listed that uses clear text for all of its transmissions. Hence it is particularly vulnerable to being hacked. The others are all encrypted in some way. [Security Operations]

22. D - Social engineering involves convincing or tricking a person into giving access to or parting with confidential information. It plays on the basic trusting and helpful nature of most people. [Legal, Regulations, Compliance and Investigations]

23. A - SSL VPNs make use of common web browsers and allow users to access applications in the organization's network. Back-end databases can also be accessed with the help of plug-ins. This approach is more cost-effective than the VPN using IPSec. [Cryptography]

24. C - Standards refer to mandatory activities or rules. They could be internally or externally mandated. For example, organizational security standards may specify in detail how hardware and software products are to be used by a company. [Information Security and Risk Management]

25. A - Subnets are an example of technical controls. Subnetting allows you to logically break up a network into segments. The other choices of external lighting, data backups, and physical location of the building are physical controls. [Access Control]

26. D - Such banners strengthen the legal case against an employee in case he/she is found to have violated security policies. This is because the company can show that the employee had acknowledged the security policy and given permission to be monitored. The other choices are not valid. [Legal, Regulations, Compliance and Investigations]

27. C - Kate is testing the plan. Testing is a key aspect of the BCP because environments continually change. When the plan is tested (or exercised), improvements and efficiencies can be uncovered. [Business Continuity and Disaster Recovery Planning]

28. C - Switches are used on networks to connect end systems to the network. Switches create a virtual private connection between two communicating end systems on a network. Therefore, data packets are not flooded throughout the network where they could be easily sniffed

and monitored. They are sent directly from end system to end system on the network. [Telecommunications and Network Security]

29. D - Symmetric algorithms are very fast when compared to asymmetric algorithms. Of the choices listed, only DES is a symmetric algorithm. [Cryptography]

30. C - Symmetric cryptosystems work much faster when compared to asymmetric cryptosystems. They use simple mathematical algorithms for encrypting and decrypting. The algorithm is applied multiple times during encryption / decryption. This also makes them much harder to break. The other choices listed are not valid. [Cryptography]

31. D - Technical controls are software or operating system based, and can include concepts such as encryption, passwords, smart cards, and biometrics. Sometimes the term technical controls and logical controls are used interchangeably. [Information Security and Risk Management]

32. B - Technical controls protect resources on a network by granting or denying access to them. They protect the integrity, availability, and confidentiality of resources through methods that include access control software, anti-virus software, passwords, smart cards, encryption, audit trails, and intrusion detection systems. [Access Control]

33. D - Technical or logical controls are mechanisms employed to enforce policy. They include elements such as firewalls, operating systems, filters or routing protocols. [Information Security and Risk Management]

34. D - Telnet is a routable protocol that operates in clear-text. SSH, or Secure Shell, is an encrypted technology. Serial cables and USB cables connected to console ports are not affected by this policy, as neither of them is a routable network protocol. [Cryptography]

35. A - Testing can only be done after a plan is implemented; it is not a part of designing one. The other choices listed are logical steps in contingency planning. [Business Continuity and Disaster Recovery Planning]

36. D - The *-property rule of the Bell-LaPadula model ensures that you cannot write to an object that resides at a security level lower then the one you possess. This is classified as the "No Write Down" rule. The "No Read Up" rule states that you cannot read information that is at a higher classification level then the one you possess. [Security Architecture and Design]

37. A - All of the choices listed are benefits of job rotation. Job rotation reduces the risk of fraud by reducing the risk of collusion between two individuals. Rotating individuals out of jobs helps build skill redundancy and cross training. [Business Continuity and Disaster Recovery Planning]

38. B - The accreditation process occurs after the certification process. It involves meeting with management and presenting the information derived from the certification process. This is done to have management formally approve the products, systems, or components within the organization. When management accredits the products, systems, and components within the organization they are stating that they know the potential threats, vulnerabilities, and weaknesses and are accepting the associated risks. [Security Architecture and Design]

39. D - The ACID test stands for Atomicity, Consistency, Isolation and Durability and should be implemented by all database software in distributed environments. [Software Development Security]

40. C - Auditing is a technical control, however, the question is specifically focused around administrative controls. Hiring an auditor in the IS department is not really a solution to the problem. [Access Control]

Domain Area Test:
Business Continuity and Disaster
Recovery Planning
Practice Questions

Test Name:
Domain Area Test: Business Continuity
and Disaster Recovery Planning
Total Questions: 15
Correct Answers Needed to Pass:
11 (73.33%)
Time Allowed: 25 Minutes

Test Description

This practice test specifically targets your knowledge of the Business Continuity and Disaster Recovery Planning domain area.

Test Questions

1. Which of the following is least likely to be considered a disaster for BCP/DRP purposes?

   A. A severe power outage

   B. A tornado

   C. A security guard falling ill

   D. A distributed denial-of-service attack

2. Nancy is auditing the business continuity / disaster recovery readiness in her organization. She finds that the continuity plan was last tested about 3 years ago. She raises this point as a non-conformance and presents it in her audit findings. How often should such a plan be tested?

   A. At least once every six months.

   B. At least once a year.

   C. At least once in two years

   D. At the discretion of the Information Security Officer.

3. Which of the following teams is responsible for getting the alternate identified site into operation in the aftermath of a disaster?

   A. Salvage team

   B. Mitigation team

   C. Restoration team

   D. Assessment team

4. A company takes daily overnight differential backups and a full backup each weekend. At 7:50 AM on Wednesday the server fails and needs to be restored. Which backup sets will be required to restore the server to the pre-failure state?

A. Weekend, Monday, and Tuesday

B. Weekend Only

C. Weekend and Tuesday

D. Tuesday Only

5. A Business Continuity Planning team is in the planning stage for a recovery site. A consultant advises them to use the most widely used model. Which of the following choices is he advising them to use?

   A. A warm site

   B. A cold site

   C. A frozen site

   D. A hot site

6. As a senior executive, you are in the process of setting up a robust business continuity and disaster recovery plan. Which of the following tests is the recommended way to assess that the processes are in place and actually work?

   A. Perform a full-interruption test

   B. Perform a walkthrough test.

   C. Perform a simulation test

D. Perform a checklist test.

7. Which fundamental security principle is addressed by use of geographically dispersed server clusters?

   A. Confidentiality

   B. Availability

   C. Integrity

   D. Durability

8. Marco is a plant manager for a large facility. In the event of a disaster, he is to serve as the Incident Commander. This role requires him to declare the disaster and activate the emergency response plan. This exemplifies which of the four elements of a business continuity plan?

   A. Priorities

   B. Responsibility

   C. Authority

   D. Testing

9. A company performs a risk assessment and determines that they are exposed to risk via an older, non-critical system that utilizes a bank of

modems. They decide to decommission the system completely. What is this an example of?

A. Mitigating Risk

B. Tolerating Risk

C. Treating Risk

D. Transferring Risk

10. A company performs a risk assessment and determines that the likelihood of a disaster caused by an earthquake is very remote, yet possible. To deal with this risk they decide to purchase more insurance. What is this an example of?

A. Tolerating Risk

B. Treating Risk

C. Terminating Risk

D. Transferring Risk

11. Cost is an important deciding factor in your planning for disaster recovery. Which of these would be a cheap option to use?

A. Redundant Site

B. Tertiary site

C. Offsite location

D. Reciprocal Agreements.

12. As the Information Security Officer in an organization, you are part of a team involved in business continuity and disaster recovery planning activities. The project is currently in the current state assessment phase. Which of these is not an output of this phase?

A. Business Impact Assessment (BIA)

B. Benchmark/Peer Review

C. Threat Analysis

D. Recovery Strategies

13. While designing a backup procedure for database recovery, an efficient procedure that can transmit data offsite and which can be used to rebuild the database data is:

A. Disk shadowing

B. Disk duplexing

C. Electronic vaulting

D. Remote Journaling

14. What data recovery solution would you recommend if systems need to be continuously available?

    A. A tape restore solution

    B. Synchronous replication

    C. Partial synchronous replication

    D. Asynchronous replication

15. An archive bit is used by the operating system to indicate whether data in a file has changed. This bit may be changed during the backup process. Which of these backup methods does not change the archive bit of files?

    A. Differential backup.

    B. Incremental backup

    C. Full backup and Incremental backup

    D. Full backup

Domain Area Test:
Business Continuity and Disaster
Recovery Planning
Answer Key and Explanations

1. C - A security guard falling ill is not likely to be considered a disaster for BCP/DRP purposes. All the other three choices may be considered as disasters. Note however that if executive management disruption takes place, that could also be viewed as a disaster. [Business Continuity and Disaster Recovery Planning]

2. B - A business continuity plan should be tested at least once every year. If there are other changes in the business or operating environment in the organization, the plan may need to be retested earlier. [Business Continuity and Disaster Recovery Planning]

3. C - The restoration team is responsible for getting the alternate identified site into operation so that it functions as a working environment. This team (like a salvage team) needs to know how to do many tasks such as installing operating systems, handling wiring requirements, setting up workstations, servers etc. [Business Continuity and Disaster Recovery Planning]

4. C - A full backup resets all of the archive flags on each file to be seen as "unchanged." Every time a file is modified, that file flips the flag to "changed." An Incremental backup backs up all of the files that have changed and resets their flags back to "unchanged." However, a Differential backup copies all of the modified files but leaves their status as "changed." Hence, only the most recent differential and the weekend's full backup is needed to restore the system. [Business Continuity and Disaster Recovery Planning]

5. A - A warm site is the most commonly used model for a recovery site. It is less expensive than a hot site since it is not completely configured, and can be set up to be operational in a reasonable timeframe. In contrast, a hot site is more expensive while a cold site may take a long time to be up and ready to use. [Business Continuity and Disaster Recovery Planning]

6. C - Although at first glance it might appear that the full-interruption test is the best one to do, it is not a recommended testing approach. This involves interrupting an actual production facility and could result in problems cropping up due to any issues with the BC/DR plan. It is best to use the simulation test to detect issues. [Business Continuity and Disaster Recovery Planning]

7. B - Availability is the fundamental security principle that information

should be accessible by users when needed. A geographically dispersed cluster ensures that information can be made available even if one of the locations goes down and is unable to provide services. [Business Continuity and Disaster Recovery Planning]

8. C - In a disaster, someone needs to be in charge or chaos ensues. It is Marco's responsibility to take charge, and perform a certain sets of activities in line with the Business Continuity and Disaster Recovery Plan. [Business Continuity and Disaster Recovery Planning]

9. A - In this case, the company has mitigated the risk by turning a system off forever. This is a little drastic, however it works in the current context. It may not always be possible to mitigate risk in so simple a manner. [Business Continuity and Disaster Recovery Planning]

10. D - This is a case of transferring risk. Insurance is a classic example of transferring risk from one party to another. [Business Continuity and Disaster Recovery Planning]

11. D - Reciprocal agreements are alternatives to offsite facilities. In this agreement, two companies agree to allow each other to use the other's facilities in the event of a disaster. Although this is a cheap option it is not very effective due to associated

problems. [Business Continuity and Disaster Recovery Planning]

12. D - Recovery strategies are not part of the current state assessment phase. They are prepared as part of subsequent phases in business continuity planning / disaster recovery planning (BCP/DRP). [Business Continuity and Disaster Recovery Planning]

13. D - Remote journaling is a method to transmit data offsite. This typically moves the transaction log and journal to an offsite facility rather than moving the actual files. In case of a disaster, the logs can be used to recreate the lost data. This is quite efficient in case of recovering a database where a sequence of changes to its records allows its recreation. [Business Continuity and Disaster Recovery Planning]

14. B - Synchronous replication is used if a system needs to be continuously available. In synchronous replication, the primary and secondary copies are always identical whereas in asynchronous replication, the two are a few milliseconds out of sync. Tape solutions will not serve the purpose. [Business Continuity and Disaster Recovery Planning]

15. A - A differential backup process only does a backup of all the files that have undergone a change since the last full backup was done. The

archive bit value is not changed. In case of full and incremental backups, the archive bit value is changed. [Business Continuity and Disaster Recovery Planning]

CISSP Mock Exam (LITE) – 6
Practice Questions

Test Name:
CISSP Mock Exam (LITE) - 6
Total Questions: 40
Correct Answers Needed to Pass:
30 (75.00%)
Time Allowed: 60 Minutes

Test Description

This is a cumulative CISSP Mock Exam which can be used as a benchmark for your CISSP aptitude. This practice test includes questions from all ten domains of the CISSP CBK.

Test Questions

1. What is the product of Single Loss Expectancy (SLE) and Annualized Rate of occurrence (ARO) i.e. SLE x ARO known as?

   A. Residual Risk

   B. Single Loss Expectancy per risk

   C. Exposure Factor

   D. Annualized Loss Expectancy

2. A data recovery solution is chosen based on business criticality of operations. The cost to recover needs to be balanced against the cost of disruption. What is this balancing point called?

   A. Point of Inflexion

   B. Recovery time objective

   C. Critical point

   D. Minimum damage point

3. Which statement best describes the Bell-LaPadula simple security rule?

   A. A user at any given security level cannot write data at a level that is higher than their current level.

   B. A user at any given security level cannot read data at a level that is lower than their current level.

   C. A user at any given security level cannot read data at a level that is higher than their current level.

   D. A user at any given security level can only read data

4. Dawn is designing a server room for her manufacturing company. She would like to reduce air-borne dust contamination as much as possible. Which of the following would best serve this requirement?

   A. Positive pressurization

B. Sealed server racks

C. Raised floor

D. Negative pressurization

5. Which of these is a good countermeasure to asynchronous attacks involving time-of-check/time-of-use (TOC/TOU)?

A. Use of software locks.

B. Good quality assurance testing

C. Use of bounds checking.

D. Use of hardware locks.

6. One of the best ways to keep a Business Continuity Plan (BCP) up to date is:

A. Include maintenance responsibilities in job descriptions

B. Integrate the BCP plan into the change management process

C. Maintain a record of any revisions made to the BCP plan

D. Review the BCP plan at least once a year

7. This early security model was constructed mainly for the purpose of preserving data integrity. It is typified by the concepts of "cannot read down" and "cannot write up". Which of the following security models best fits this description?

A. Bell-LaPadula

B. Clark-Wilson Model

C. Brewer and Nash Model

D. Biba Model

8. As an information security professional, what would be your biggest concern with open database connectivity (ODBC)?

A. The username and the password for the database are stored in plaintext, thus making them susceptible to inappropriate access.

B. In data exchanges over the network, the actual call is encrypted, but the returned data is in cleartext.

C. In data exchanges over the network, the actual call is in cleartext, but the returned data is encrypted.

D. The username is in plaintext but the password is encrypted and stored, thus making the username susceptible to inappropriate access.

9. Which model allows changes to occur dynamically for access controls based on previous actions that a user performed?

   A. Graham-Denning Model

   B. Chinese Firewall Model

   C. Brewer and Nash Model

   D. Lattice Model

10. A brokerage services company makes recommendations to clients to buy equity stocks and also issues analyst reports on equity stocks. In order to ensure that there is no conflict of interest between its two divisions, what information flow policy should it implement?

   A. Implement the Brewer-Nash model for information flow.

   B. Implement the Graham-Denning model for information flow.

   C. Implement the Bell-LaPadula model for information flow.

   D. Implement the Clark-Wilson model for information flow.

11. This security model was developed with a great deal of focus on information integrity and fraud prevention. It requires the use of an abstraction layer that prevents subjects from directly accessing the object. The abstraction layer enforces the integrity of the object. Which of the following models best corresponds to this description?

   A. Clark-Wilson Model

   B. Brewer and Nash Model

   C. Biba Model

   D. Bell-LaPadula Model

12. The Chief Information Security Officer of an organization wants to implement an effective model for IT governance procedures. Which of these would guide him in this endeavor?

   A. CoBit

   B. COSO

   C. BS7799

   D. ISO 17799

13. A company performs a risk assessment and determines that they are exposed to a very small amount

of risk from a possible robbery at the convenience store next door. They choose to do nothing. This is an example of what?

A. Terminating Risk

B. Transferring Risk

C. Tolerating Risk

D. Treating Risk

14. A company performs a risk assessment and determines that because of an older Windows NT 4.0 server that is directly attached to the Internet, they are exposed to risk. The system cannot be changed but an upgrade is available that places the server behind a strong firewall. The company decides to upgrade the system. What is this an example of?

A. Terminating Risk

B. Tolerating Risk

C. Transferring Risk

D. Mitigating Risk

15. A company lost some confidential data from a critical server due to an attack by hackers into its network systems and decided to implement an Intrusion Detection System (IDS). To provide the best

protection, which of the following options should the company pursue?

A. Install a NIDS and a HIDS on the critical server.

B. Install a HIDS on the critical server

C. Install a NIDS on the critical server

D. Install a HIDS on the network.

16. A company has hired a software developer who has a very good prior track record. Which of the following steps will help best ensure that the company's data is protected.

A. The company should have the employee undergo a security awareness training program.

B. The employee should be asked for two references prior to his joining and these references would be contacted for their feedback on the employee.

C. The company should have the employee sign a non-disclosure agreement.

D. The company should have a background check performed on the individual.

17. What is the concept of only granting a user the exact minimum access required to complete ordinary daily job functions called?

    A. Least Access

    B. Least Privilege

    C. Mandatory Access Control

    D. Role Based Access Control

18. Which security principle ensures that information is not disclosed to unauthorized individuals?

    A. Confidentiality

    B. Availability

    C. Integrity

    D. Authorization

19. An organization has outsourced a part of its software development and maintenance activities to an outside vendor organization. The outside organization requires test data. What would be the best way to go about this?

    A. Sanitize data obtained from production and ensure that no confidential data is supplied as part of the test data.

    B. Ask the vendor organization to connect to the company's network to access production data through a secure VPN connection.

    C. Avoid outsourcing work to a vendor organization. The associated risk is usually not manageable.

    D. Ask the vendor organization to create its own test data since this is their responsibility.

20. Which of the following types of encryption may allow an attacker to find out details (such as headers, addresses and routing) about an intercepted packet without needing to decrypt it?

    A. Link encryption.

    B. Inline encryption.

    C. End-to-end encryption.

    D. Online encryption.

21. If the requirement is that a user have flexibility in choosing what gets encrypted, which of these encryption methods should be used?

    A. Link encryption

    B. End-to-end encryption

C. PPTP encryption.

D. Online encryption

22. As part of the company's security activities, it wishes to monitor employees' email. Which of the following would be the first step in undertaking such an activity?

A. Put up a notification on the common notice board in the company indicating that all employees' email is going to be monitored.

B. Prepare a document informing employees that if they do not accept the policy, they will be terminated.

C. Introduce an email filter which permits employees' email to be monitored.

D. Outline the security policy around email monitoring.

23. Which of the following access control functionalities has controls that provide for an alternative measure of control?

A. Corrective

B. Directive

C. Deterrent

D. Compensating

24. An organization is performing quantitative risk assessment. In order to mitigate a particular risk, the company decides to apply a countermeasure. The cost of the countermeasure over a 5 year period is equal to 5 times the annualized loss expectancy. What would be the likely course of action for the company?

A. The countermeasure cost per year should always be greater than annualized expectancy. Hence the company may proceed with the countermeasure.

B. The value of the annualized loss is required to make a decision. Hence the data provided is insufficient to determine the course of action.

C. The countermeasure cost per year should always be less than the annual loss expectancy. Hence the company should look at an alternative way of handling the risk.

D. The company should proceed with the countermeasure since the countermeasure cost per year is less than the annualized loss expectancy.

C. Sally's manager

D. The Board of Directors

25. Crime Prevention Through Environmental Design (CPTED) provides guidance on the design of a physical environment and outlines how it can affect the crime rate. Which of the following choices would be a guideline from CPTED?

A. Avoid use of glass and have metal doors in garages and stair towers within the parking lots.

B. A side door at the facility, with restricted access, should not have a sidewalk leading up to it from the front of the building.

C. Provide for barriers and trees near secluded doors. This will prevent it from being visible to intruders.

D. Provide for a driveway right up to the entrance door of the facility to prevent incidents of crime against the employees.

26. Sally creates a digital file for her company. If the company uses a discretionary access control scheme, who owns the file according to the control methodology?

A. Sally

B. The network administrator

27. You connect to an external website on the internet, download, and play an MPEG file on your computer. In the OSI model, at what layer does the decompression of the MPEG file happen?

A. Application layer

B. Session Layer

C. Presentation layer

D. Transport Layer

28. Company security policy dictates that access to the company's networks from the internet must be highly restricted, and through a DMZ. How is a firewall setup to implement the DMZ?

A. Setup a firewall between the DMZ and external network only.

B. Setup a firewall between the internal network and DMZ and another firewall between the DMZ and external network.

C. Setup a firewall between the DMZ and the internal network only.

D. Setup a firewall between the internal network and DMZ and another between the internal network and the external network.

29. Which of the following is NOT useful for secure key distribution?

    A. DSA

    B. RSA

    C. El Gamal

    D. Diffie-Hellman

30. The commonly used form of IP is IP version 4 (IPv4) which uses 32 bits for its addresses. However, these have started to run out due to the high demand, and there is a move towards IP version 6 (IPv6). How many bits does IPv6 use?

    A. 64

    B. 32

    C. 96

    D. 128

31. What is the first level in the Orange Book that requires labeled security?

    A. B1

    B. B2

    C. C1

    D. C2

32. What is the first level in the Orange Book that requires users to be individually identified and accountable for their actions?

    A. B1

    B. C1

    C. C2

    D. B2

33. Disaster has struck at the facility of a company. Which of the following would be the first priority to the company when such an incident occurs?

    A. Restoration of customer service at the earliest.

    B. Start of operations from a backup site

    C. Assessment of the financial loss

    D. Safety of its employees.

34. What feature/tool can be used in cryptography to prevent messages from getting altered?

A. A message authentication code (MAC) can be used to prevent a message from getting altered.

B. A hash function can be used to prevent the message from getting altered.

C. None. Cryptographic tools cannot prevent a message from getting altered.

D. A digital signature can be used to prevent a message from getting altered.

35. A company uses a 10-key pad for door entry. However, concerns have been raised that the four-digit PIN numbers might be breached or guessed. Which of the following strategies will be least effective in preventing unauthorized individuals from entering through the door?

A. Use a thumbprint scan in addition to the PIN

B. Use an antenna card combination in addition to the PIN

C. Use a key token combination in addition to the PIN

D. Use video surveillance logging in addition to the PIN

36. Which of the following regulations requires financial institutions to develop privacy notices and allow customers an option to prevent their information from being shared with nonaffiliated third parties?

A. Glass-Steagall Act

B. SOX

C. GLBA

D. HIPAA

37. Katie is the director of Information Systems at her company. She is in the process of identifying a suitable facility to house a new data center. Which of the following four sites would be best suited for this purpose?

A. Top floor, center of building, carpeted, and site generator

B. Top floor, carpeted, site generator, and pre-existing network cabling

C. Ground floor, center of a building, no carpet, and site generator

D. Ground floor, no carpet, edge of a building, and pre-existing network cabling

38. In the realm of one-way hashing, which of the following can be configured to be the best choice against a birthday attack?

   A. MD0

   B. MD2

   C. MD5

   D. SHA1

39. Which of the following is a document that describes management's view on how databases are to be used and protected?

   A. Policy

   B. Practice

   C. Program

   D. Procedure

40. Within a Software Development Life Cycle, a process may be assigned a maturity level that describes its effectiveness and durability. According to the Capability Maturity Model, the final stage and highest level of maturity is which?

   A. Initial, Repeatable, Defined, Managed, Custom

   B. Initial, Repeatable, Defined, Managed, Auditable

   C. Initial, Repeatable, Defined, Managed, Optimized

   D. Initial, Repeatable, Defined, Managed, Quantized

CISSP Mock Exam (LITE) – 6
Answer Key and Explanations

1. D - The Annualized Loss Expectancy is derived by multiplying the SLE by the Annualized Rate of Occurrence (ARO). [Information Security and Risk Management]

2. B - The balancing point is called the recovery time objective. As part of the business continuity planning / disaster recovery planning, the team needs to strike a balance between the cost of disruption and cost to recover. [Business Continuity and Disaster Recovery Planning]

3. C - The Bell-LaPadula simple security rule states that a user at any given security level cannot read data at a level that is higher than their current level. Users can only read the information at their security level or lower. This protects the confidentiality of information at higher security levels by ensuring that unauthorized users cannot read the information. [Security Architecture and Design]

4. A - The best choice is a positive pressurization system that forces air out of the server room whenever a door is opened. The other choices listed do not help in preventing dust-contamination. [Physical (Environmental) Security]

5. A - The best way to avoid TOC/TOU attacks (asynchronous attacks) is by having the operating system apply software locks on the files being requested. [Security Architecture and Design]

6. B - The best way to keep a Business Continuity Plan (BCP) up to date is to integrate the plan into the change management process. The change management process could be updated to alert the individuals in charge of the BCP plan when any changes are about to occur. This ensures that when any change occurs in the organization, the BCP team is aware of it and can update the BCP plan accordingly [Business Continuity and Disaster Recovery Planning]

7. D - The Biba model was developed from the Bell-LaPadula model. It is primarily concerned with the protection of data integrity--making it ideal for the corporate world where the integrity of proprietary secrets is key. In the Biba system, a subject cannot read information from a lower integrity level that might be suspect or corrupt, in other words, it cannot read "down." At the same time it prevents the inappropriate assignation of integrity levels by preventing subjects from writing suspect or corrupt data to higher levels, in other words, it cannot write "up." [Security Architecture and Design]

8. A - The biggest concern with ODBC connectivity is that both the username and password are stored as plaintext. Hence if an HTML document is calling an ODBC source of data, it must be protected to ensure that the userid and password in the source is protected. [Software Development Security]

9. C - The Brewer and Nash model, also known as the Chinese Wall model was designed to allow access controls to dynamically change based on previous actions that a user performed. This model's main goal is to protect an organization's assets from a user's conflict of interests by automatically denying access to resources that would cause a conflict of interest. [Security Architecture and Design]

10. A - The Brewer-Nash model is also known as a Chinese Wall and is used in situations of conflict of interest. In the current scenario, the company should ensure that the activities of the two departments are clearly separated to avoid conflicts of interest. [Security Architecture and Design]

11. A - The Clark-Wilson model was developed as an extension to the Biba model. Concepts in the model revolve around the inability to directly access and/or manipulate

objects to prevent data corruption. [Security Architecture and Design]

12. A - The CoBIT stands for Control Objectives for Information and related Technology. This is published by the IT Governance Institute and is an effective IT Governance framework. COSO is a model for corporate governance, while ISO 17799 and ISO 27001 are enterprise security standards. [Information Security and Risk Management]

13. C - The company has accepted the risk by choosing to ignore it. This is based upon the fact that the risk of its occurrence is a remote possibility. Such a decision should also be documented well. [Business Continuity and Disaster Recovery Planning]

14. D - The company has decided to mitigate the risk. They have added protection to ensure that the risk has a smaller opportunity of occurring. Residual risk is the term for the amount of risk left after a mitigating control is put into place. [Business Continuity and Disaster Recovery Planning]

15. A - The company will need to install both a NIDS as well as a HIDS. The NIDS monitors network traffic whereas the HIDS detects anomalous activity on the critical server. [Access Control]

16. C - The company should have the employee sign a nondisclosure agreement. While the other choices go towards reducing the risk of hiring the employee or ensuring that he/she is aware of the security policies, it is the nondisclosure agreement which will protect the company's information and can be legally enforced. [Information Security and Risk Management]

17. B - The concept of least privilege is to start each account at zero privileges and add only the access needed to perform required job functions and no more. [Access Control]

18. A - The confidentiality security principle ensures that information is protected from unauthorized individuals, other programs, or processes. The actual level of confidentiality is usually determined by the overall level of secrecy required for the information. Therefore, information that requires a high level of security will usually also require a very high level of confidentiality. [Access Control]

19. A - The correct procedure would be to sanitize the production data and provide this to the supplier. The other options do not serve the purpose. Connecting through a secure VPN link to the organization ensures that the data is secure, however, it does not prevent the vendor organization from getting access to raw production data, which could then be misused. [Information Security and Risk Management]

20. C - The correct response is end-to-end encryption. In this form of encryption, details such as the addresses, routing information, header and trailer information are not encrypted, thereby enabling an attacker to gain details without the need for decryption. In contrast, link encryption (also known as online encryption) provides better security against packet-sniffers. [Cryptography]

21. B - The correct response is end-to-end encryption. This provides the user more flexibility in choosing how and what is encrypted. [Cryptography]

22. D - The correct response is that the security policy around email monitoring must first be outlined. The next step would be to prepare a document that employees can read and sign. [Legal, Regulations, Compliance and Investigations]

23. D - Compensating controls provide for an alternative measure of control. [Access Control]

24. C - The countermeasure cost per year should not exceed the annualized loss expectancy. Hence in the current case where both are equal, it may not be viable for the company to use this countermeasure. [Information Security and Risk Management]

25. B - A CPTED guideline is that a side door at the facility, with restricted access, should not have a sidewalk leading up to it from the front of the building. This will ensure that unwanted people are not aware of its existence and do not use it. The other choices are contrary to CPTED guidelines. [Physical (Environmental) Security]

26. A - The creator of a file is the owner in a discretionary access control model (DAC). An administrator may possess privileges to override this and take ownership, but that is only in case of emergencies. [Access Control]

27. C - The data decompression of the MPEG file would happen at the presentation layer. There are only services and no protocols that work at this layer. [Telecommunications and Network Security]

28. B - The DMZ is the demilitarized zone and is a network segmented between a protected and unprotected network. To implement this, setup a firewall between the internal network and DMZ and another between the DMZ and external network. [Telecommunications and Network Security]

29. A - DSA was primarily created for the purpose of digital signatures. It cannot encrypt data and cannot be used for key exchange. [Cryptography]

30. D - IPv6 is the next generation of IP addressing and uses 128 bits. It also provides many other capabilities that IPv4 does not. [Telecommunications and Network Security]

31. A - The first level in the Orange Book that requires labels is B1 (Labeled Security). At the B1 level each subject and object will have its own security label. To be granted access, the subject and object labels will have to be compared and match accordingly. This level has the ability to support classified data. [Security Architecture and Design]

32. C - The first level in the Orange Book that requires users to be individually identified and accountable for their actions is C2. C2 users are required to authenticate to the system which proves the individual's identity within the system. The system is then able to track the user's activities and associate this information with the user's account credentials in the system log files. [Security Architecture and Design]

33. D - The first priority in the aftermath of a disaster would be to ensure that

the employees are safe and there is no loss to life. [Business Continuity and Disaster Recovery Planning]

34. C - The fundamental application of cryptography is to detect whether a message has been altered (intentionally or otherwise). Cryptographic tools cannot prevent a message from getting altered. [Cryptography]

35. D - The goal is prevention, rather than detection. Use of video surveillance is the least effective of the options listed since an individual who has cracked the PIN code can still access the door. [Physical (Environmental) Security]

36. C - The Gramm-Leach-Bliley Act (GLBA) covers financial institutions. A bank may fall under Health Insurance Portability and Accountability Act (HIPAA) regulations as they apply to Human Resources and Benefits. Sarbanes-Oxley Act (SOX) would only apply if the bank is a publicly traded company. The Glass-Steagall Act of 1933 created the FDIC and does not apply. [Legal, Regulations, Compliance and Investigations]

37. C - The ground floor is more accessible to emergency crew in case of fires. The center of a building is better than the edges for protection against bombs, weather events, and intruders. Site generation for intermediate-term backup power is important for a data center. Finally, a carpet is to be avoided when dealing with equipment sensitive to static electricity. [Physical (Environmental) Security]

38. D - The SHA1 algorithm uses 160 bits. This makes it more resistant to the birthday attack which is a type of brute-force attack. [Cryptography]

39. A - Policies are overall general statements produced by senior management (or a policy board / committee). For example, system-specific policies could detail out management's view on how databases are to be used and protected. [Information Security and Risk Management]

40. C - The highest level of maturity in the Capability Maturity Model is a process that is optimized, or one that essentially cannot be made more efficient. [Software Development Security]

Domain Area Test: Cryptography Practice Questions

Test Name:
Domain Area Test: Cryptography
Total Questions: 15
Correct Answers Needed to Pass:
11 (73.33.00%)
Time Allowed: 25 Minutes

Test Description

This practice test specifically targets your knowledge of the Cryptography domain area.

Test Questions

1. Which type of attack is considered a passive attack?

   A. Sniffing attack

   B. Ciphertext-only attack

   C. Replay attack

   D. Chosen-plaintext attack

2. Which method does not provide integrity for a message?

   A. Encrypting a message

   B. Digitally signing a message

   C. Hashing a message

   D. Encrypting and digitally signing a message

3. Which term best describes the method used to transform plaintext information into ciphertext?

   A. Incipher

   B. Decryption

   C. Encryption

   D. Decipher

4. At what level of the OSI model does IPSec operate?

   A. Application

   B. Network

   C. Physical

   D. Session

5. Which of the following is a Hashing Algorithm?

   A. El Gamal

   B. 3DES

   C. MD4

D. DES

6. A securities clearinghouse receives several sales orders from a customer and executes them accordingly. The customer later claims that the sales orders did not come from him. However, due to the use of a digital signature, the clearinghouse can prove that the sales orders did in fact originate with the customer. In this case, what basic goal of a cryptographic system is being met?

   A. Nonrepudiation

   B. Integrity

   C. Authenticity

   D. Confidentiality

7. Which of the following is a Symmetric Key Algorithm?

   A. El Gamal

   B. Diffie-Hellman

   C. Digital Signature Algorithm

   D. IDEA

8. What is Pretty Good Privacy (PGP) known as?

   A. A web of trust

   B. Hierarchical certificate authority

   C. One time pad

   D. Multipurpose Internet mail extension

9. Which protocol relies on a "web of trust" for its key management approach instead of a hierarchy of certificate authorities?

   A. RSA

   B. SSL

   C. PGP

   D. Deffie-Hellman

10. In an asynchronous encryption system, Alan can only send an encrypted message to Bob if which of the following are true?

   A. Bob provides his private key to Alan

   B. Bob provides his public key to Alan

   C. Alan provides his private key to Bob

   D. Alan provides his public key to Bob

11. Which of the following is an asymmetric key algorithm?

A. RC4

B. Blowfish

C. RSA

D. DES

12. Which method involves the hiding of data within another form of media so that the existence of the original data is concealed?

A. Steganography

B. Stenography

C. Tasseography

D. Cryptography

13. Which type of cipher replaces bits, characters, or blocks with different bits, characters, or blocks?

A. Permutation cipher

B. Substitution cipher

C. Transposition cipher

D. Replacement cipher

14. What type of cipher moves bits, characters, and blocks around to hide the original plaintext message?

A. Scramble cipher

B. Replacement cipher

C. Substitution cipher

D. Transposition cipher

15. Which of the standards listed identifies the format for public key certificates?

A. X.21

B. X.400

C. X.500

D. X.509

Domain Area Test: Cryptography Answer Key and Explanations

1. A - A passive attack is an attack that does not alter or destroy information as it passes over the network. Passive attacks simply capture or monitor traffic as it crosses the network. Since no changes occur to the actual data, they are rather hard to detect. As such, methods are employed to try to prevent them from occurring rather then detecting and stopping them [Cryptography]

2. A - Encrypting a message only provides confidentiality. When you want to ensure that a message has not been altered in transmissions from source to destination, you can use a hashing function. This verifies the message's integrity. A one-way hash will take the variable-length message that you want to send and produce a fixed-length value to send to the recipient. Once the recipient receives the message, they will perform the same hash function to determine if they get the same result. If the results are the same, the message has not been altered. [Cryptography]

3. C - Encryption is the method that is used to transform plaintext information into ciphertext. A complex mathematical formula, also known as an algorithm, is used to

complete the transformation. [Cryptography]

4. B - IPSec runs at the Network layer of the OSI model. No encryption is possible at the physical layer. [Cryptography]

5. C - MD4 is a one-way hashing algorithm. It is one of a set of algorithms. MD2, MD4 and MD5 which were developed by Ron Rivest. [Cryptography]

6. A - Nonrepudiation means that the sender cannot deny, or repudiate, that the message was sent. The clearinghouse was simply doing what they were contracted to do. [Cryptography]

7. D - Of the choices, only IDEA is a symmetric algorithm. The rest of the choices are asymmetric algorithms. [Cryptography]

8. A - PGP is a web of trust rather than a hierarchical authority. There is no central certificate server in the PGP structure, and each endpoint manages their own public key and signs the public keys of other users. [Cryptography]

9. C - PGP is used as an e-mail security program and relies on a "web of trust" for its key management approach instead of certificate authorities. Users generate and distribute their own public keys and they will sign each others public keys to determine who will trust each other. With a certificate authority hierarchy, no one trusts each other. They only trust the CA. [Cryptography]

10. B - Private keys are never shared. Alan needs Bob's public key to encrypt a message that only Bob can decrypt using his (Bob's) private key. If Alan encrypts a message with his own public key, then only Alan's private key can decrypt it - which does not serve the purpose. [Cryptography]

11. C - RSA is the only asymmetric algorithm listed among the choices. The others are all symmetric algorithms. [Cryptography]

12. A - Steganography is a method that involves the hiding of data within another form of media so that the existence of the data is concealed. An excellent example of this is hiding a text message within a picture. You can accomplish this by changing some of the pixels to letters so that they can be read under a microscope but to the naked eye it appears as just a pixel that completes the entire picture. [Cryptography]

13. B - The substitution cipher replaces bits, characters, or blocks with different bits, characters, or blocks to create the ciphertext. For example, if you wanted to encrypt the plaintext

term "James" and you were using the English alphabet and moving three positions to the right, the new ciphertext would be "Mdphv". [Cryptography]

14. D - The transposition cipher rearranges and scrambles bits, characters, and blocks to hide the original plaintext message. A key is used to keep track of where the original bits, characters, and blocks would normally be. A transposition cipher can be very simple or very complex. It can use mathematical calculations to create a very strong cipher that is difficult to break. [Cryptography]

15. D - A digital certificate is a very important piece of a Public Key Infrastructure (PKI). The X.509 standard defines the different types of fields that are used within the certificates as well as the possible values that could be used within those fields. The most current X.509 version is 4. A certificate would usually include a serial number, a version number, identity information, algorithm information, lifetime dates, and the signature of the issuing authority. [Cryptography]

CISSP Mock Exam (LITE) - 7
Practice Questions

Test Name:
CISSP Mock Exam (LITE) - 7
Total Questions: 40
Correct Answers Needed to Pass:
30 (75.00%)
Time Allowed: 60 Minutes

Test Description

This is a cumulative CISSP Mock Exam which can be used as a benchmark for your CISSP aptitude. This practice test includes questions from all ten domains of the CISSP CBK.

Test Questions

1. A reporting structure is being prepared for the Information Security Officer of a high security organization. Which of the following would best serve the purpose?

    A. Information Security Officer reporting to the CEO.

    B. Information Security Officer reporting to the Internal Audit department.

    C. Information Security Officer reporting to the Corporate Security department.

    D. Information Security Officer reporting to the Information Technology department.

2. Which layer of the TCP/IP model maps to the Network layer of the OSI model?

    A. Host-to-Host

    B. Application

    C. Internet

    D. Network Access

3. If you are looking for a less expensive but secure encryption method, you would prefer to use:

    A. Internet Security Protocol (IPSec)

    B. End-to-end encryption method

    C. Secure Electronic Transaction (SET)

    D. Link Encryption method

4. Of the protection rings used by operating system security, which of the following would host privileged mode (or supervisor mode) processes that specifically deal with the kernel of the system?

A. Ring 2

B. Ring 3

C. Ring 1

D. Ring 0

5. Which of the following is the most important component of a Kerberos system?

A. Key Distribution Center (KDC)

B. Privileged Attribute Certificate (PAC)

C. Ticket Authentication Service (TAS)

D. Authentication Grant Service (AGS)

6. Bert is a security officer in his organization. He is asked by HR to provide some DOs and DON'Ts that can be incorporated into an employees manual. Which of the following may have been a suggestion from Bert?

A. Employees may not reveal their network login IDs and passwords, except if asked by their supervisors.

B. Employees need to disclose all removable media that they are

carrying with them, except in the case of music CDs or DVDs.

C. Employees shall confront individuals inside the organization premises who do not have a clear identification badge prominently displayed, and politely ask them who they are. Also ask them why they are not displaying an ID and escort them to the nearest security officer.

D. Employees need to prominently display their Identification badge while at work, except on weekends.

7. Change management, separation of duties, and logging are implementations of the concept of:

A. Execution

B. Accountability

C. Cooperation

D. Prosecution

8. Communications utilizing an asymmetric encryption method are most susceptible to which of the following attacks?

A. Birthday

B. Man-in-the-middle

C. Smurf

D. Teardrop

9. Which of these is not a protocol at the transport layer?

A. User Datagram Protocol (UDP)

B. Secure Sockets Layer (SSL)

C. NetBios

D. Transmission Control Protocol (TCP)

10. Which access control model is also referred to as non-discretionary access control?

A. Rule-based access control

B. Role-based access control

C. Discretionary access control

D. Mandatory access control

11. Which security model has the ability to address the inference attack?

A. Lattice model

B. Noninterference model

C. Biba model

D. Graham-Denning model

12. What is the first priority of an individual during a disaster?

A. Protect Systems

B. Protect Data and Assets

C. Evacuate

D. Render Humanitarian Aid

13. Which of the following would be true if you were using Kerberos security technology?

A. Redundancy is necessary for the Key Distribution Center (KDC)

B. Kerberos is insulated from password guessing

C. Kerberos protects the network traffic even when encryption is not enabled

D. Secret keys are never stored on users' workstations

14. Of the protection rings used by operating system security, in which of the following would the operating system kernel reside?

A. Ring 4

B. Ring 6

C. Ring 2

D. Ring 0

15. What is the correct order of sensitivity levels for data classification in commercial business (from lowest to highest)?

    A. Private, Confidential, Sensitive and Public

    B. Sensitive, Confidential, Private and Public

    C. Public, Private, Sensitive and Confidential

    D. Public, Sensitive, Private and Confidential

16. A company needs to selectively encrypt e-mail messages. What choice would you recommend?

    A. Pretty Good Privacy (PGP)

    B. Private Signed Mail (PSM)

    C. Kerberos

    D. Link encryption

17. Radio frequency interference (RFI) frequently occurs in buildings. Which of the following is the primary cause of RFI?

    A. Backup generators

    B. UPS equipment

    C. Telephone lines

    D. Fluorescent lighting

18. How are rows uniquely identified in a relational database model?

    A. By a column key

    B. By a primary key

    C. By a tuple key

    D. By a row key

19. Which of the following is not a recommended procedure to handle a system crash or failure?

    A. It is best to have an administrator validate configuration and system files after a crash.

    B. It is best to have an administrator physically present at a console to recover files.

C. It is best to boot to a Recovery console to recover files.

D. It is best to enter into multi-user mode to recover files.

20. Which of these books mainly addresses government and military expectations for their computer systems?

   A. Aqua Book

   B. Red Book

   C. Orange Book

   D. Blue Book

21. Which term best describes an abstract machine that ensures all subjects have the access rights necessary before accessing objects.

   A. Security perimeter

   B. Security kernel

   C. Reference monitor

   D. Secure state

22. What technique utilizes anonymous opinions by members of the risk analysis team?

   A. Classification

   B. Quantitative

   C. Delphi

   D. Safeguard

23. In which phase are threats and vulnerabilities determined?

   A. Risk Assessment

   B. Vulnerability Assessment

   C. Threat Assessment

   D. Agent Assessment

24. Ben works for an auditing firm on a team that specializes in social engineering. At a client site, he carries an armload of boxes to a secure entrance and waits for a helpful employee to open the door for him. Once inside, he poses as a printer repair person and accesses data from the stations of several administrative assistants. Which of the following would be options would be successful in preventing such breaches in the future?

   A. Security awareness training for all employees

   B. Use of additional video surveillance cameras

C. Use of sensitive alarms

D. Use of ID cards by all employees

25. Which of these accurately depicts the relationship between total risk, countermeasures and residual risk?

A. Total risk + Residual Risk = Countermeasures

B. Total risk - Countermeasures = Residual risk

C. Total risk + Countermeasures = Residual risk

D. Countermeasures - Total Risk = Residual risk

26. What does the Asset Value multiplied by the Exposure Factor yield?

A. Single Loss Expectancy

B. Exposure Factor

C. Residual Risk

D. Annualized Loss Expectancy

27. From a security perspective, if you wish to ensure that internal and external resolution requests to the DNS server are handled separately, how can this be achieved?

A. Implement a split DNS

B. Use a proxy server to handle requests separately

C. Implement a parallel DNS

D. Place internal resources within the DMZ

28. Which of the following passwords is the strongest of the choices listed?

A. PasswordBob123

B. P999000

C. kathy!

D. KaJM22!4

29. A company is concerned that the system administrator might abuse his elevated privileges. They implement a plan that removes all of the administrator's privileges to the server logs and charge a security auditor with the task of viewing them. What would this be known as?

A. Separation of duties

B. Change Management

C. Least Privilege

D. Regulatory Compliance

30. Which of the following refers to the level of trust a system provides rather than the level of security it provides.

    A. ISO-9000

    B. Trusted Computer System

    C. Trusted Systems Specification

    D. Trusted Computer Base

31. Which of these is the correct order in which the Zachman framework for enterprise architecture should be approached?

    A. Scope context boundary, Business model concepts, System model logic, Technology model physics.

    B. Scope context boundary, System model logic, Business model concepts, Technology model physics.

    C. Business model concepts, Scope context boundary, System model logic, Technology model physics.

    D. Technology model physics, Scope context boundary, Business model concepts, System model logic.

32. When working with United States military classifications, which answer best ranks the level of classification in order from low to high?

    A. Top Secret, Secret, Classified, Sensitive, Public

    B. Unclassified, Sensitive but Unclassified, Confidential, Secret, Top Secret

    C. Top Secret, Confidential, Classified, Unclassified but Confidential, Sensitive

    D. Confidential, Secret, Top Secret, Public, Proprietary

33. Fire code regulations dictate that data centers and server areas should have two doors. What is the usual best practice followed to minimize security issues?

    A. Have separate doors for entry and exit purposes respectively. Ensure that a security guard is posted at each of the doors.

    B. Have one door for daily entry and exit into the secure area. The other door should be used only in emergencies and should have a panic bar.

C. Have only one door for entry and exit into a data center. In the interests of security, the fire code regulations can be overruled in case of data centers.

D. Have two doors into the facility, but only one door should be conspicuous. The other door should be known to only a handful of people and should not be publicized.

34. Which of the following is a solution to DNS poisoning?

A. Increase penalties for attackers indulging in DNS poisoning

B. Implement an NIS

C. Enable DNSSEC on all DNS servers on the internet

D. Use better firewalls

35. Which of the following is a robust security architecture framework?

A. The Starkey framework

B. The Zachman framework.

C. The Zimmerman framework

D. The Zarkov framework

36. Several measures can be taken to help protect against electric power issues. Which of these is NOT a recommended method of protecting devices?

A. Plug all devices into surge protectors.

B. Use shielded cables.

C. Plug power bars into other power bars to help provide additional protection

D. Do not run cables close to fluorescent lights.

37. Which is NOT an integrity goal that is addressed by the Clark-Wilson model?

A. Separation of duties is enforced

B. Constrained data items can be manipulated only by transformation procedures

C. Auditing is required

D. Subjects can access objects through any program

38. The primary feature of an application design that uses a web-based data warehousing thin client, as compared to a thick client application is:

A. It will run much faster but requires specialized software to be installed on the client machine.

B. It provides redundancy if the connection to the internet is dropped, but runs relatively slowly.

C. It runs faster and by choosing an application that provides redundancy, data access is possible even if the connection to the internet is disrupted.

D. It will run much faster but cannot provide redundancy in case the connection to the internet is dropped

39. A cybercriminal wants to redirect traffic from a competitor's website. When a prospective customer tries to visit the competitor's website, the cybercriminal redirects him to another website. What form of attack does he use to achieve this?

A. Trojan horse

B. DNS poisoning

C. A worm

D. DNS reconfiguring

40. A biometrics system rejects access to an authorized subject. What is this called?

A. Type II Error

B. Type III Error

C. Type IV Error

D. Type I Error

CISSP Mock Exam (LITE) - 7
Answer Key and Explanations

1. A - Such a reporting structure reduces any message filtering that may happen due to any hierarchy structure that exists and improves communication. This is ideally suited for firms that have high security needs. [Information Security and Risk Management]

2. C - The Internet layer of the TCP/IP model maps to the Network layer of the OSI model. [Telecommunications and Network Security]

3. A - The Internet Protocol Security (IPSec) allows a secure channel to be set up between two devices that wish to exchange data in a protected manner. It is flexible and the least expensive of the options listed. [Cryptography]

4. D - The kernel is the most protected area of the operating system. The Protection Ring security mechanism prevents higher ring levels from directly accessing lower rings. For example, Ring 0 can directly access Ring 1, however, the reverse is not true. Rings 0 and 1 are considered System, Supervisor, or Privileged Modes [Security Architecture and Design]

5. A - The Key Distribution Center is a single point of failure and is the most important component of a Kerberos system. TAS and AGS are not valid choices while PAC is used by SESAME. [Access Control]

6. C - The likely input given by Bert is that employees should confront any individuals inside the organization premises who do not have a clear identification badge prominently displayed, and politely ask them who they are. Employees should also ask them why they are not displaying an ID and escort them to the nearest security officer. This will go a long way in preventing any adverse incidents. [Security Operations]

7. B - Change management, separation of duties, and logging are implementations of the concept of accountability since they help establish who carried out a particular activity. The other choices are not valid. [Security Operations]

8. B - A common problem with a communications channel using asymmetric encryption (besides a full denial of service attack) is the man-in-the-middle attack. [Cryptography]

9. C - NetBIOS is a protocol that operates at the session layer. UDP, TCP and SSL operate at the transport layers. [Telecommunications and Network Security]

10. B - A role-based access control (RBAC) model is also called a non-discretionary access control model. Access to objects is granted or denied based on the role a user has within the organization. [Access Control]

11. B - The Noninterference model has the ability to address the inference attack. An inference attack occurs when someone has just enough information to infer (guess) about other information that they are not allowed to access or view. The Noninterference model addresses this attack by ensuring that any actions that occur at a particular security level do not affect or hinder the actions that occur at a lower security level. This prevents information from leaking from higher security levels down to lower security levels. [Security Architecture and Design]

12. D - The first priority of an individual is to render immediate medical care and aid. This should also be clearly stated in the Business Continuity and Disaster Recover Plan. [Business Continuity and Disaster Recovery Planning]

13. A - Redundancy is necessary for the KDC in a Kerberos system. The KDC can turn out to be a single point of failure and if it goes down, no one will have access to the required resources. [Access Control]

14. D - The operating system kernel is in ring 0. Subjects in other rings cannot access this ring directly but need to make requests to access this ring. [Security Architecture and Design]

15. D - The order of sensitivity from lowest to highest in commercial business is Public, Sensitive, Private and Confidential. Information classified as Public is available to the general public to access. Sensitive information should not be disclosed to or modified by unauthorized users. Private information, which must be kept internal, is considered personal and should be viewed by the intended users only. Confidential information is the most sensitive, and if disclosed, could have a severe, negative effect on the company. [Information Security and Risk Management]

16. A - The preferred choice is Pretty Good Privacy (PGP). This is a public key encryption program and is a complete cryptosystem to protect email and files. The other choices are not valid responses. Link encryption may be used if all data on the company's network needs to be encrypted. Kerberos may be implemented when single sign-on is required. Private Signed Mail does not exist. [Cryptography]

17. D - The primary cause of radio frequency interference in office buildings is fluorescent lights. The solution is to use shielded cables and to ensure that power and data lines are separate and don't run over fluorescent lights. [Physical (Environmental) Security]

18. B - A primary key uniquely identifies a row within a relational database. The other choices are not valid. [Software Development Security]

19. D - An administrator must be involved in the aftermath of a system crash and it is best to use 'single user' mode so that unauthorized connections are kept out. [Security Operations]

20. C - The Orange Book mainly addresses government and military expectations for their systems. However, there are a number of deficiencies in the Orange book and the focus is now to move towards Common Criteria. [Security Architecture and Design]

21. C - The reference monitor is an access control concept. It is responsible for mediating subject access to objects. This ensures that subjects are provided with access rights that are necessary for them to access objects, and to ensure that the objects are protected from modification and unauthorized access. It is important to note that the reference monitor is not an actual physical component; it is an abstract machine. [Security Architecture and Design]

22. C - A risk analysis team may use the Delphi technique when conducting qualitative risk analysis. Each member of the team anonymously submits their opinions with regard to asset values, security threats, and their probabilities of occurring in the organization. The comments are collected and shared among the team, after which another series of anonymous contributions are made to gather feedback. This process continues within the group until a consensus is reached. [Information Security and Risk Management]

23. A - Threats and vulnerabilities are determined in the risk assessment phase. At this time the total risk is obtained by multiplying the value of the assets being assessed and the possibility of a vulnerability being exploited. [Security Architecture and Design]

24. A - Social engineering involves playing on the emotions of employee such that they unwittingly help in a crime. This can be addressed by better and more regular security awareness training. In the current scenario, a helpful employee allowed an unknown person to enter the facility. More cameras, better alarms

etc will not stop social engineering. [Physical (Environmental) Security]

25. B - Residual risk is the risk that remains after a company implements countermeasures to handle risks. Hence at a conceptual level, Total risk - Countermeasures = Residual risk.

Note that this is not a mathematical formula, but depicts the relationship between the three entities. [Information Security and Risk Management]

26. A - The single loss expectancy is the dollar amount an organization might assign to a single event representing the potential loss if a specific threat took place. It is determined by multiplying the asset value and the exposure factor (exposure factor is the percentage of loss a realized threat could have on an asset). [Information Security and Risk Management]

27. A - The solution is to implement a split DNS. In this, a DNS server is installed in the DMZ to handle external resolution requests. This ensures that the internal DNS is not directly accessible through the internet and has additional layers of protection since both external and internal requests are handled separately. [Telecommunications and Network Security]

28. D - The strongest passwords are those with a mix of upper and lower case letters, numerical digits, and special characters. The best passwords are constructed via a phrase that can be easily remembered rather than made up of dictionary words. The other passwords are not as strong since they are susceptible to being guessed. [Security Operations]

29. A - The system administrator in this example is prevented from covering his tracks by editing the log files. The auditor views the logs to make sure nothing is inappropriately used. This separates the administration and the auditing duties. [Security Operations]

30. D - The Trusted Computing Base, or TCB, was developed after the Orange Book, but is more concerned with trust levels rather that system security. Communications between trusted components and untrusted components must be regulated. [Security Architecture and Design]

31. A - The correct order in which the layers of the Zachman framework are approached are: Scope context boundary, Business model concepts, System model logic, Technology model physics, Component configuration and Functioning enterprise instances. [Security Architecture and Design]

32. B - The US Military classifies information in the following way from highest to lowest: Top secret, Secret, Confidential, Sensitive but unclassified, Unclassified. Note that the question asked for the reverse order. [Access Control]

33. B - The usual best practice is to have two doors to the facility. However, only of these should be used for daily entry and exit from the facility. The other should be equipped with a panic bar so that the door can open only from the inside. The other option of using multiple doors and posting security guards may also work but is not a preferred solution since it will increase costs. [Physical (Environmental) Security]

34. C - Installation of DNSSEC on all DNS servers will prevent this type of attack because two DNS servers communicating with each other will authenticate each other. However, in practice if DNSSEC has to work properly, all DNS servers on the internet would need to participate in a PKI to validate digital signatures and this is quite impractical. [Telecommunications and Network Security]

35. B - The Zachman framework serves as a model that can be used to create robust security architectures that deal with multiple components across the organization. [Security Architecture and Design]

36. C - There are a number of things that can be done to help protect against electric power issues. Power bars and extension cords should always be plugged into their own wall sockets to prevent possible fire hazards. Plugging power bars into other power bars, or extension cords results in safety issues. [Physical (Environmental) Security]

37. D - One of the ways in which the Clark-Wilson model addresses a goal of integrity is that subjects can access objects only through authorized programs and not just any program. [Security Architecture and Design]

38. C - Thin client applications normally use an Internet browser to connect to a central server. The web-based data warehousing thin client runs very fast and also provides redundancy in case the connection to the internet is dropped. [Security Architecture and Design]

39. B - This can be done using a DNS poisoning attack. In this attack the cybercriminal will listen for requests from a particular DNS server when it is trying to resolve a particular hostname. When this happens, he quickly sends a request to the server with the incorrect mapping and causes a false redirection. [Telecommunications and Network Security]

40. D - This is a called a Type I error, or a False Negative (Reject). In this case an authorized subject is prevented access and this is usually more of an inconvenience rather than a breach. [Access Control]

Domain Area Test: Software Development Security Practice Questions

Test Name:
Domain Area Test: Software Development Security
Total Questions: 15
Correct Answers Needed to Pass: 11 (73.33%)
Time Allowed: 25 Minutes

Test Description

This practice test specifically targets your knowledge of the Software Development Security domain area.

Test Questions

1. Which attack involves sending malformed packets to a system in order to cause it to crash or end processing?

   A. Denial of Service (DoS) attack

   B. Smurf attack

   C. Fraggle attack

   D. SYN flood attack

2. What type of mobile code control serves as a protected area for a program to execute?

   A. Sandbox

   B. Access matrix

   C. Kernel

   D. Covert channel

3. Which form of malware has the ability to reproduce itself and is classified as self-contained?

   A. Trojan horse

   B. Logic bomb

   C. Virus

   D. Worm

4. Aggregation is a database security issue. Which of the following statements about aggregation is true?

   A. A user has the permissions to access information, and does not have the required permissions to access subsets of the same information.

   B. A user lacks the permissions to access information, but has the required permissions to access subsets of the same information.

C. A user has the permissions to access information, and also has the required permissions to access subsets of the same information

D. A user lacks the permissions to access information, and does not have the required permissions to access subsets of the same information.

5. Which of these is NOT a type of programming language?

A. High-Level

B. Assembly

C. Machine

D. Interpreter

6. Pre-compiled code runs faster than interpreted code but can be considered less secure. Is this statement correct?

A. Yes. Pre-compiled code runs so quickly that it can tie up CPU resources and cause availability issues.

B. No. This is a common fallacy. Pre-compiled code is actually significantly more secure than interpreted code.

C. Yes. Interpreted code relies on the integrity of the host system for security. Therefore it has no security holes. This is not the case with Pre-compiled code.

D. Yes. Pre-compiled code is transformed into a binary file that is unreadable by humans. Unauthorized changes are extremely hard to detect.

7. The senior loan officer of a large financial institution is preparing to travel to a conference. To make more effective use of travel time, he copies a large number of customer files to his laptop to work on during flight. While at the airport, he uses free WiFi to check email. During this time, another WiFi user compromises the security of the Loan Officer's laptop and copies the customer data. The malicious user then overwrites the customer information with similar files containing random edits as a prank. This is an example of what kind of breach(es)?

A. Integrity and Availability

B. Confidentiality Only

C. Integrity Only

D. Confidentiality and Integrity

8. What is the strategy of providing security at many points, including at the application level, known as?

    A. Security Bifurcation

    B. Monolithic Security

    C. Defense-in-depth

    D. Layer Cake Security

9. What type of database interface language is used for structuring data so that it can be shared between applications and web technologies?

    A. ADO

    B. OLE DB

    C. ODBC

    D. XML

10. Every foreign key in a relational database refers to an existing primary key. This type of integrity is known as:

    A. Database Integrity

    B. Referential Integrity

    C. Entity Integrity

    D. Key Integrity

11. Which of the following provides a simple and effective mechanism to protect against buffer overflow vulnerabilities?

    A. Input Validation

    B. Policies

    C. Firewalls

    D. High Availability

12. A database server in a hospital data center is an active-node member of a geographically dispersed active/passive cluster that is synchronized across three locations. Due to a software defect an improperly calculated value is written back into the database tables. What type of breach is this?

    A. Availability Only

    B. Integrity and Availability

    C. Integrity Only

    D. Confidentiality

13. Which of these is a system that employs Artificial Intelligence to solve problems, recognize patterns, and mine data.

A. Software Escrow

B. Expert System

C. Dynamic Data Exchange

D. Database Cluster

14. What type of attack occurs when an attacker sends packets that are too small?

    A. Fraggle

    B. Teardrop

    C. SYN flood

    D. Smurf

15. A set of procedures that are used to carry out changes that affect software, individual systems or the network is called:

    A. Application management

    B. Configuration management

    C. Baseline management

    D. Migration management

Domain Area Test:
Software Development Security
Answer Key and Explanations

1. A - A Denial of Service (DoS) attack is performed by sending malformed packets to a system in order to cause it to crash or end processing. The attacked system is unable to recognize the format of the packets that it receives. This causes it to crash or stop processing other valid packets. [Software Development Security]

2. A - A sandbox is a type of mobile code control that serves as a protected area for a program to execute. The sandbox limits the amount of memory, processor, and hard drive resources that a process can utilize. If the process exceeds the limits of the sandbox, process is terminated. [Software Development Security]

3. D - A worm has the ability to self reproduce, and is classified as self-contained. It does not require any type of host application. It is commonly transferred through email messages over the Internet. [Software Development Security]

4. B - Aggregation occurs when a user has the permissions to access subsets of information but does not have the required permissions to access the information as a whole. The user will collect (aggregate) the subsets of information and attempt to create the information as a whole from it. When the user succeeds, this is known as inference. Using this method a user could access information that he/she is not supposed to. [Software Development Security]

5. D - An interpreter is a program (translator) that is used to convert a high-level language into a lower level language such as assembly or machine. It is not a type of programming language. [Software Development Security]

6. D - Changes made to the code base of an interpreted program can be easily found by human eyes. Most interpreted programs include in-line documentation (comments) that describe the function of each section of code. A change, either mistakenly or maliciously, is easy to track down. Since pre-compiled code is in machine language, it is extremely difficult to detect changes. [Software Development Security]

7. D - Confidentiality was breached because a copy of the private data was made. Integrity was breached because bad data was merged into the files. Availability is not an issue in this scenario. [Software Development Security]

8. C - Defense-in-depth seeks to employ the best security possible at each level of a system. The overarching idea is to slow down an attacker to such a degree that they are either detected or give up the attack entirely. [Software Development Security]

9. D - Extensible Markup Language (XML) is a database interface language standard used for structuring data so that it can be shared between applications and web technologies. XML is flexible and provides a lot of options for how data can be presented in the database. [Software Development Security]

10. B - In a relational database model, referential integrity implies that a foreign key actually exists. Entity integrity means that each table must have a unique and non-null primary key. Key integrity requires that a key must be maintained if referenced by another. Database integrity refers to the overall validity of the data contained in a database. [Software Development Security]

11. A - Input validation prevents unexpected data from being entered into database fields and provides a simple form of protection against buffer overflow errors. [Software Development Security]

12. C - Integrity was breached due to the fact that bad data was written to the database. Because of the role of a node in the Active/Passive configuration, the bad data was propagated to the other sites. Availability is not an issue, as the bad data was available. Confidentiality too is not an issue. [Software Development Security]

13. B - An expert system is also called a knowledge-based system and uses Artificial Intelligence (AI) to solve problems. It uses nonnumeric algorithms to solve complex problems. [Software Development Security]

14. B - Teardrop attacks occur when an attacker sends packets that are too small and result in a system locking up or rebooting. This type of attack takes advantage of the fact that systems do not check to see if a received packet is too small. The attacker creates these small packets in such a way that when the receiving system attempts to recombine the fragments, they can not be reassembled properly. [Software Development Security]

15. B - Configuration management is the set of procedures that are used to carry out changes that affect software, individual systems or the network. [Software Development Security]

CISSP Mock Exam (LITE) – 8
Practice Questions

Test Name:
CISSP Mock Exam (LITE) - 8
Total Questions: 40
Correct Answers Needed to Pass:
30 (75.00%)
Time Allowed: 60 Minutes

Test Description

This is a cumulative CISSP Mock Exam which can be used as a benchmark for your CISSP aptitude. This practice test includes questions from all ten domains of the CISSP CBK.

Test Questions

1. A database administrator wishes to restrict certain tables of a database from being accessed or used by certain users. This is accomplished by using:

    A. Access controls at the program level.

    B. Database restrictors which restrict a set of users from seeing certain information.

    C. Database controls which can be configured to let some users see only certain information.

    D. Database views which restrict a set of users from seeing certain information.

2. A hacker is trying to exploit the vulnerability of a software program. He inserts a large amount of data and hopes to execute malicious code in system memory. This pattern is called:

    A. Buffer overflow

    B. Covert channel

    C. Memory reuse

    D. Trapdoor attack

3. A database administrator of a database containing very sensitive information is trying to misdirect attackers. He does this by inserting fake information into the database. This would be termed as:

    A. Noise and falsification

    B. Cell suppression

    C. Noise and polymorphism

    D. Noise and perturbation

4. A film distribution company creates a website that advertises "Click Here

for Free Movies." They record all individuals who download these files and attempt to prosecute for copyright infringement. What would such an activity be termed as?

A. Entrapment

B. Scandal

C. Enticement

D. Libel

5. During a code walkthrough, a systems analyst uncovered unauthorized code installed in a production system program. This could have potentially been used to gain access to the program. The most likely explanation is:

A. A programmer inadvertently inserted the code into the program during the development stage.

B. This is normal programming practice. The code is known only to the group of people who programmed it, so it is unlikely to be exploited by a hacker.

C. A hacker gained access to the production system and inserted code which could be used to exploit the system later.

D. A programmer inserted the code into the program during development to access the system if the access control mechanism failed during development.

6. A malicious programmer inserted code which would cause serious problems if activated. This did not cause problems during normal operation and he intended to activate this if he was laid-off from the company. This is referred to as:

A. Spyware

B. Remote Access Trojan (RAT)

C. A prank

D. Logic bomb

7. An algorithm has been chosen such that a minor change in the key results in a completely different ciphertext being produced. This is referred to as:

A. Weak Hashing

B. Avalanche effect

C. Diffusion

D. Confusion

8. Andy receives a mail which informs him that if he forwards the email to ten other people he will have 'good luck' for the rest of the day. Andy promptly complies with this request. This would be termed as a:

   A. Meme virus

   B. Multi-part virus

   C. Human virus

   D. Social Engineering virus

9. Which of the following techniques is used in detecting spam?

   A. Gaussian filtering

   B. Curtis filtering

   C. Polynesian filtering

   D. Bayesian filtering

10. Servers are placed on one network segment and all of the workstations on a second segment. The router in between these two networks is configured to only pass traffic a handful of required ports. What is this termed as?

   A. Network Address Translation

   B. Domain Services

   C. Dynamic Host Control Protocol

   D. Network Segregation

11. Rick performs certain critical operations at work. Due to a serious illness, Rick is unable to report to work. The company is ill-prepared for this and work suffers for many days before normalcy is restored. This could have been avoided by implementing:

   A. Job Rotation

   B. Mandatory Reporting

   C. Separation of Duties

   D. Periodic company sponsored health checks.

12. An employee became aware of a computer crime in which a colleague was involved. However, he did not bring it to the notice of the company. This was most likely because:

   A. The crime did not have serious ramifications.

   B. It is the responsibility of the security team in the company to detect such crimes.

   C. The employee was also involved.

    D. Incident handling procedures were poorly defined in the company.

13. A policy that outlines what is acceptable behavior within an organization and also outlines the repercussions of not complying with such a policy would be considered as what category of policy?

    A. An advisory policy

    B. A regulatory policy

    C. An Informative policy

    D. A standard policy

14. A protester hacked a government website and put up protest banner images on it. This type of cyber-crime would be classified as:

    A. A computer-targeted crime.

    B. A computer-assisted crime

    C. A computer-violation

    D. A 'computer is incidental crime'.

15. The entity that takes advantage of a vulnerability to endanger systems is called:

    A. Threat

    B. Threat-agent

    C. Risk

    D. Exposure

16. An audit board found that a bank was poorly prepared to handle disasters and that the bank's current choice of backup site would not be operational in a timely manner following a disaster. If cost is not an issue and the bank needs to be fully operational within TWO hours of a disaster, what kind of site should the bank use?

    A. Cold Site

    B. Warm Site

    C. Dead Site

    D. Hot Site

17. While preparing a BCP/DRP, goals are established so that everyone involved is aware of the ultimate objective. Which of these is not key information that is part of a goal?

    A. Responsibility

    B. Strategies

    C. Authority

D. Priorities

18. A _____ law protects a resource that a company uses as a competitive advantage, while _____ law protects certain resources that a company produces.

    A. Trademark , Trade Secret

    B. Copyright , Trade Secret

    C. Trade Secret , Copyright

    D. Trade Secret , Trademark

19. Which of these is a very important consideration for accurate event correlation and forensics?

    A. Chain of Custody

    B. Separation of Duties

    C. Chain of responsibility

    D. Accurate Time Stamping

20. A man-in-the-middle attack can happen when an attacker intercepts a communication and spoofs the identities of either of the two parties involved. How can such a type of attack be countered?

    A. Such attacks can be countered by having an authentication done through the use of a digital signature, before accepting someone's public key.

    B. Such an attack can be countered by a cyclic redundancy check (CRC)

    C. Such an attack can be countered by use of a parity bit.

    D. Such attacks can be countered by using two-way hashing algorithms.

21. A programmer is developing an application which would reside on a server and send out status information to the network where it would be received by listening nodes. Which transport protocol would she prefer to use?

    A. OSP

    B. CP

    C. TCP

    D. UDP

22. In order to minimize the expenses involved in acquiring alternative resources like computer workstations, network circuits and backup hardware, the CFO of a company downplayed the potential

revenue loss. What will be the most likely impact of this?

A. The continuity planning project team (CPPT) will need to find cheaper alternatives to cope with a disaster.

B. The savings in the cost of the backup equipment will make up for the potential revenue loss when a disaster strikes.

C. The continuity planning project team (CPPT) will be held responsible for drop in customer service levels when a disaster strikes.

D. The customer service level will likely drop when a disaster strikes and the company may be unable to service customers properly.

23. Jim is caught spending a great amount of time and resources sending non-work related emails on subjects the leadership of the company would not approve. He is summarily fired. Jim sues for wrongful termination on the basis that he never gave permission for his email to be monitored. If his case succeeds, which of the following options is most likely to be the reason?

A. Chain of custody

B. Freedom of speech

C. Legal council

D. Reasonable expectation of privacy

24. A junior network technician has approached you and wishes to know what type of cable is the least resistant to electromagnetic interference (EMI). Which of these would you select?

A. Unshielded Twisted Pair

B. Coaxial

C. Fiber-optic

D. Shielded Twisted Pair

25. You wish to implement a control mechanism for mobile code. A good option is:

A. Introduction of an efficient error logging system.

B. Use of a sandbox that provides a protective area for program execution.

C. Introduction of proper audit control procedures.

D. Use of a blackbox that provides a protective area for program execution

26. A certain organization has multiple teams that take turns with off-hours support duty. Their work requires that they have elevated privileges on the firewalls, servers, and infrastructure devices. What type of access control scheme would best be used in this situation?

A. MAC

B. RBAC

C. LDAP

D. DAC

27. What is the most common method used to locate unsecured wireless networks?

A. War dialing

B. War driving

C. Piggybacking

D. Salami

28. What is a Type II error in a biometric system?

A. Crossover error rate

B. False rejection rate

C. Equal error rate

D. False acceptance rate

29. As part of the business impact analysis, individual threats are identified and loss criteria are applied. Which of the following is an incorrect criterion while considering business impact due to a potential disaster?

A. Decrease in operational expenses.

B. Loss in revenue

C. Violations of contractual agreements

D. Loss of reputation

30. On a device-by-device basis, which of the following should be included in documentation demonstrating the application of standards?

A. All deviations from the written standard, serial number, date, and technician name

B. Deviations that lower security level from that of the standard, serial number, date, and technician name

C. The date and name of the technician

D. The machine type and serial number

31. In which of the following situations could you say that the integrity of data has not been lost?

A. A New Year's greeting sent by the CEO of a company to all its employees is intercepted and altered.

B. The equity stock balance in an individual's account shows 50000 instead of 5000.

C. A consumer receives a telephone bill of $75 instead of $ 750.

D. The credit card number of a cardholder finds its way into public domain.

32. When a data center facility has been flooded, what is the best way to handle the situation?

A. Scrap all equipment and invest in new equipment.

B. Allow the moisture to evaporate on its own.

C. Increase the room temperature to 150 deg Fahrenheit (about 65 deg Centigrade) so that the moisture evaporates.

D. Use dehumidifiers that are of industry-strength to dry up the moisture.

33. Your company is implementing wireless technologies to provide users with the mobility they require to perform their day to day activities. Management has approached you and is questioning the security of the wireless technologies in relation to war driving. You need to assure them that the network will be secured against war driving. Which of the following measures will not provide protection against war driving?

A. Enable 'broadcasting SSID' on the access points.

B. Physically place the access points within the middle of the buildings.

C. Use 128-bit WEP as the encryption standard on the wireless network.

D. Change the default SSID of each access point

34. Which of the following is not a type of response to operating system failure?

A. System jumpstart

B. Emergency system restart

C. System reboot

D. System cold start

35. A large bank and a hospital decide that in the event of a disaster at either of their facilities, the other will provide facilities for short term business continuity. Under this agreement, the Information Technology staff of the affected entity will be provided with workstations, necessary connectivity, electricity, and office space. What is this known as?

A. Joint BCP

B. Reciprocal Agreement

C. Warm Site

D. Active/Active Agreement

36. Which of the following cabling strategies is cost-effective and resistant to electromagnetic interference (EMI)?

A. STP

B. Fiber-optic

C. XTP

D. UTP

37. A hard drive containing evidence of a possible breach is given to several local computer stores for general advice before finally handing it over to a professional data forensics expert. What principle has been violated by not maintaining a signed history document?

A. Chain of custody

B. GLBA

C. SOX

D. Protocol

38. Which of these roles is responsible for data protection and will be held liable in case of any negligence that resulted in the breach of the data?

A. Chief Legal Counsel

B. Security Officer

C. Systems Administrator

D. Network Administrator

39. The main difference between compartmented security mode and the other security modes is:

   A. Formal access approval is not required.

   B. All users must have proper clearance for the highest level of data classification in the system.

   C. All users need to sign an NDA for the information they will access.

   D. All users must have proper clearance for the lowest level of data classification in the system.

40. If employees find a USB drive labeled "Beach Vacation Pics" plugged into a computer system at work, what should they be trained to do?

   A. Follow procedures for a security incident

   B. Attempt to find the owner

   C. Access the drive to determine who lost it

   D. Throw it away

CISSP Mock Exam (LITE) – 8
Answer Key and Explanations

1. D - This is accomplished by using database views which can place restrictions on the information that users can access. [Software Development Security]

2. A - This is called 'Buffer Overflow' and is a common problem in poorly written software programs. An attacker enters a larger amount of data than the program can handle and attempts to execute malicious code when the excess data overflows into system memory. This can be avoided by doing proper bounds checking. [Software Development Security]

3. D - This is called noise and perturbation and is a technique to confuse and mislead attackers so that their attacks do not succeed or yield poor results. [Software Development Security]

4. A - This is called entrapment because the company was advertising "free" movies to trick the victims into clicking. [Legal, Regulations, Compliance and Investigations]

5. D - This is known as a trapdoor / backdoor. Software developers often use this route to provide access to a program in case they are locked out of the program during development

due to a failure of the access control mechanism. So, it is most likely that a programmer inserted this code as a backdoor route. This poses a risk to the system and could be dangerous. [Software Development Security]

6. D - This is referred to as a logic bomb and should be caught by proper code review procedures. If this is not caught and slips through, an employee may activate this code with malicious intent at a later time. [Software Development Security]

7. B - This is referred to as 'Avalanche Effect' and forms a key consideration while selecting an algorithm. A strong hashing algorithm will also have this feature. This makes the algorithm difficult to crack. [Cryptography]

8. A - This is termed as a meme virus and is not actually a virus. Such email messages, hoax virus alerts, religious messages that are continually forwarded on the Internet by people waste valuable resources. [Software Development Security]

9. D - Bayesian filtering is used to detect spam. This is a mathematical method and it reviews prior events to predict future events and quantifies uncertainty to detect spam. [Software Development Security]

10. D - This is network segregation and helps segregate networks and

subnets from each other. [Telecommunications and Network Security]

11. A - This type of situation is best handled by job rotation. Job rotation would have allowed an individual other than Rick to do the job and the company would not have struggled to handle this situation. The other choices listed would not help in this matter. [Information Security and Risk Management]

12. D - This was most likely due to poor incident-handling procedures in the company. Employees need to be aware how such incidents are handled and should not feel threatened by reporting such incidents. [Legal, Regulations, Compliance and Investigations]

13. A - This would be classified as an Advisory policy. Such policies typically advise employees on acceptable behavior within an organization and the result of not conforming to such behavior. For example, such an advisory policy could be put into effect while handling confidential data. [Information Security and Risk Management]

14. B - This would be termed as a computer-assisted crime since the protester uses the computer as a tool to carry out an attack such as a protest against the government. In

contrast a 'computer-targeted' crime targets a computer to gain some information while a 'computer is incidental' crime is a situation where the computer is just incidental to the attack and not the primary purpose of the attack. [Legal, Regulations, Compliance and Investigations]

15. B - The entity that takes advantage of a vulnerability is referred to as a threat-agent. This could be an intruder accessing the network or even an employee making an unintentional error and deleting confidential information. [Information Security and Risk Management]

16. D - A hot site is recommended as a recovery site since the requirement is to begin operations within two hours of the disaster. Warm sites and cold sites do not provide this level of turnaround and require much longer to become operational. [Business Continuity and Disaster Recovery Planning]

17. B - Strategies are not part of the goals established while preparing a BCP/DR plan. The goals usually contain key information such as: Responsibility, Authority, Priorities, Implementation and testing [Business Continuity and Disaster Recovery Planning]

18. C - Trade secrets are usually proprietary to the company. They are

used to create products, but they are not the products themselves. Copyrights protect the products (such as software) from being sold as original works by some other company. [Legal, Regulations, Compliance and Investigations]

19. D - Two events from two different systems can be very meaningful when correlated together. This requires an accurate and precise time stamp on each of them. [Security Operations]

20. A - Two parties communicating with each other can use digital signatures for authentication purposes before accepting each other's public key. This will allow them to securely authenticate each other and communicate safely. [Cryptography]

21. D - For the given application, even if there is a node on the network which does not receive the status information due to a dropped packet, it is acceptable since it will receive it on the next update. Hence UDP is preferred in such cases. Using TCP for this requirement may not be efficient since TCP requires a higher overhead. [Telecommunications and Network Security]

22. D - Understating the loss of revenue results in poor and inadequate readiness to cope with disaster. The most obvious impact will be that the company will be unable to restore customer service levels adequately in a manner required by the business. [Business Continuity and Disaster Recovery Planning]

23. D - Unless employees sign or in some other way acknowledge that they have no expectation of privacy, in most states they do have a legitimate (and legal) expectation of privacy. To mitigate this risk, all employees should be required to sign an acceptable use agreement as a condition of employment. [Legal, Regulations, Compliance and Investigations]

24. A - Unshielded Twisted Pair (UTP) cable provides very little protection against EMI. It contains insulated copper wires that are surrounded by an outer jacket. The wires are twisted into pairs to provide protection against EMI. However, UTP is more susceptible to EMI as compared to the other choices. [Telecommunications and Network Security]

25. B - Use of a sandbox is a good control mechanism for mobile code. The sandbox places a limit on the memory and resources available to a program. If this is exceeded, an error is logged and the program is terminated. [Software Development Security]

26. B - Using RBAC, roles are created for various job functions. Permissions to perform certain operations are then assigned to specific roles. Anyone in the role has the ability to access the resources needed. DAC and MAC do not provide this flexibility. LDAP is a directory system, not an access methodology. [Access Control]

27. B - War driving is a technique that is used on wireless networks. It involves driving or walking around with a laptop and searching for unsecured wireless networks. [Telecommunications and Network Security]

28. D - When a biometric system accepts an individual who should have been rejected, it is referred to as a Type II error or false acceptance rate. Type II errors are dangerous, as an unauthorized individual obtains access to resources that they should not have access to. [Access Control]

29. A - When a disaster strikes, the operational expenses will most likely increase rather than decrease. All the other choices are correct and need to be included as part of loss criteria. [Business Continuity and Disaster Recovery Planning]

30. A - When applying standards, all deviations should be recorded on a device-by-device basis. This paper trail should be reviewed at least annually to ensure that the device still matches the documented settings. One advantage of using a standard is that all settings do not have to be recorded, only those that deviate need to be recorded. [Security Operations]

31. D - When the credit card number of a cardholder is released into public domain, the confidentiality of data or information is lost since the information is now available to unauthorized people. In the other three instances, the integrity of data is lost since the original value or content has been altered. [Access Control]

32. D - When there is water-related damage in a data center, it is advisable to use dehumidifiers of industry-strength to remove moisture. This will prevent the formation of mold which could cause problems and render equipment unusable. [Physical (Environmental) Security]

33. A - War driving is a common attack on wireless networks and involves people who try to identify Access Points (APs) and break into them. Best practices for wireless LANs include disabling and not enabling 'broadcast SSID" on the network. [Telecommunications and Network Security]

34. A - System jumpstart is not a valid response. The other choices are valid responses. System reboot happens when the system shuts itself down in a controlled manner. Emergency restart happens after a system failure in an uncontrolled manner. System cold start takes place if an unexpected kernel or media failure takes place. [Security Operations]

35. B - Reciprocal agreements are alternatives to offsite facilities. Two companies mutually agree to aid the other in the event of a disaster. This is a cheap option but it may not always work out when an actual disaster strikes. [Business Continuity and Disaster Recovery Planning]

36. A - While fiber-optic is impervious to EMI, it is an expensive option. Shielded Twisted Pair (STP) provides protection against EMI and is comparatively economical to implement. [Telecommunications and Network Security]

37. A - Evidence that has been handled without proper controls would not be admissible in court. [Legal, Regulations, Compliance and Investigations]

38. B - A security officer is responsible for data protection and is held liable in case of any breach of data. [Information Security and Risk Management]

39. B - The main difference between compartmented security mode and the other modes is that all users must have proper clearance for the highest level of data classification in the system. In the other modes proper clearance is required for all information in the system. [Security Architecture and Design]

40. A - This incident may be part of an organized attack and hence appropriate security procedures need to be followed to handle this. This method of attack is often used to run background scripts to steal passwords, copy the entire email history, etc. and email it to the hacker's address. [Physical (Environmental) Security]

Domain Area Test:
Physical (Environmental) Security
Practice Questions

Test Name: Domain Area Test: Physical (Environmental) Security
Total Questions: 15
Correct Answers Needed to Pass: 11 (73.33%)
Time Allowed: 25 Minutes

Test Description

This practice test specifically targets your knowledge of the Physical (Environmental) Security domain area.

Test Questions

1. Some personnel are trained in CPR and other procedures and stationed throughout an organization to aid their colleagues when the need arises. What is this group normally called?

   A. Backup and recovery team

   B. Disaster recovery team

   C. Emergency response team

   D. Business continuity team

2. Of the following, which is the most appropriate to include as part of an Emergency Response Plan?

   A. Detailed HVAC Diagrams

   B. Server Passwords

   C. Door Access Logs

   D. Evacuation Routes

3. Susan is driving by her office late one night and sees intruders attempting to gain entrance through a darkened front window. She follows a procedure and calls the control room, which is staffed on a 24 x 7 basis to report what she has seen. What type of procedure would this be?

   A. Control Reporting Plan

   B. Incident Handling Procedures

   C. Emergency Response Plan

   D. Governance Procedures

4. Which of the following groups provides classifications and guidelines to ensure the necessary level of protection in physical security?

   A. Underwriters Laboratory (UL)

B. National Institute of Standards (NIS)

C. Sherwood Applied Business Security Architecture (SABSA)

D. Laboratory Standards (LS)

5. Which of the following physical security controls are detective rather than preventative?

A. Moat

B. Fence

C. CCTV

D. Six Wall Enclosure

6. Which of the following physical security schemes is comparatively expensive to maintain?

A. Flood Lighting

B. Guard Dogs

C. Perimeter Fencing

D. CCTV

7. For what class of fires would you use carbon dioxide (CO2)?

A. Class C and D

B. Class B and C

C. Class A and B

D. Class A and D

8. Which of the following power fluctuations results in a loss of power?

A. Spike

B. Brownout

C. Sag

D. Fault

9. While away on business you are forced to leave a company laptop unattended in your hotel room for several hours. What would be the best method of securing the sensitive data stored on this laptop from theft?

A. Maintain backups of the sensitive data in a secure location

B. Place the laptop in an unmarked bag

C. Have the laptop engraved with an ID number

D. Use encryption software to encrypt the sensitive data

10. Which type of lock allows for a certain amount of individual accountability?

   A. Combination lock

   B. Smart lock

   C. Cipher lock

   D. Electronic combination lock

11. A company has two feeder supplies for electrical power. In addition, it has a provision for backup generators. Which of the following choices would offer the best benefits while planning for backup in case of a power failure?

   A. The generator room should be located close to the data center so that there is minimum loss of power during transmission.

   B. The two feeders should be connected to the same electrical station, but via different paths.

   C. The two feeders should be connected to two separate electrical stations.

   D. The capacity of each generator should be equal to one quarter the maximum load of the data center.

12. Locks act as delaying devices and hold up intruders if they are properly installed. Which of these locks provides the highest level of security?

   A. A tumbler lock

   B. A warded lock

   C. A grade III lock

   D. A cipher lock

13. Lighting is an important aspect of security planning. In which of the following situations is the lighting requirement incorrectly mentioned?

   A. Lights used for protection in the exterior of buildings require less illumination intensity than those in the interior.

   B. Lighting should be directed away from the gates and inwards to deter intruders.

   C. Locations where security guards physically verify identification credentials should be brightly lit.

   D. Guard locations should have lower amounts of illumination and should be in the shadows.

14. Procedural security involves procedural controls within the

company. Which of the following procedural controls may require special consents from employees?

A. Use of smartcards to access a data center

B. Use of CCTV to monitor personnel.

C. Use of security guards at the entrance of a facility

D. Use of guard dogs on the campus

D. Institute a security awareness program so that employees are aware of the procedures.

15. An audit of physical security measure revealed vulnerabilities. It appeared that the procedures were relaxed because the employees had a different understanding than what was documented. What is the first step that should be taken to overcome this?

A. Penalize employees who violate documented policies by linking violations to the employees' salaries.

B. Have a policy of job-rotation so that the same employees do not handle the same responsibility all the time.

C. Publicize security procedures so that all employees in the company are aware of them.

Domain Area Test:
Physical (Environmental) Security
Answer Key and Explanations

1. C - An emergency response team is made up of volunteers who have been trained in evacuation routes and life-saving techniques. Unlike a disaster recovery team, they are not usually senior decision-makers. [Physical (Environmental) Security]

2. D - An Emergency response plan (ERP) should be simple and easy to follow. Evacuation routes need to be part of such a plan. Server passwords may not really be part of an emergency response plan although they may be part of a recovery plan. [Physical (Environmental) Security]

3. B - Any suspicious behavior is an incident. Incident handling procedures typically detail out the set of activities to handle such incidents. In this scenario, Susan has kicked off the procedures by informing the control center. [Physical (Environmental) Security]

4. A - Underwriters Laboratory (UL) is a non-profit organization that provides the necessary classifications and guidelines for physical security. This organization inspects, tests and classifies various devices and equipment used in physical security. [Physical (Environmental) Security]

5. C - Closed Circuit Television (CCTV) is a simple surveillance camera that is usually monitored in real-time by a human (as opposed to a DVR type recording device). It can only detect an attack, it does not specifically deter attacks. [Physical (Environmental) Security]

6. B - Among the options listed, guard dogs are the most expensive to maintain. [Physical (Environmental) Security]

7. B - Carbon dioxide (CO_2) is used to put out class B and class C fires. It is bad for most types of life forms since it works by removing oxygen from the air. Hence a delay mechanism is often used so that CO_2 is applied after people have had time to evacuate. [Physical (Environmental) Security]

8. D - A fault is a type of power fluctuation that occurs when there is a momentary loss of power. In contrast, a blackout is a type of power fluctuation that occurs when there is a prolonged, total loss of power. The other options listed are situations where the voltage is above or below normal. [Physical (Environmental) Security]

9. D - In most cases it is best to never leave your laptop unattended. If you must leave your laptop unattended for any extended period of time, the

best way to secure the sensitive data on the laptop hard drive would be to encrypt it. This would ensure that the data is not accessible even if it is stolen. [Physical (Environmental) Security]

10. B - A smart lock is a type of cipher lock that can allow for individual accountability by assigning specific codes to each individual. Smart locks can also be configured to allow certain codes access to the facility only at certain times. [Physical (Environmental) Security]

11. C - The two electrical feeders should ideally be connected to different electrical power stations else the whole purpose of having two feeders is lost. The other choices don't help as much. Having two separate paths to the same station for the feeders will not help in case of an outage at the power station. The generator room should not be located near the data center and the total generator capacity should be planned such that it can handle the load of the data center. [Physical (Environmental) Security]

12. D - Cipher locks provide the best level of security. They are expensive compared to traditional locks but they have a number of additional features which makes them very desirable for office environments. [Physical (Environmental) Security]

13. B - Lights should be directed towards an area from which an intruder is likely to come, rather than away from it. Hence it should be directed at gates. The other choices mentioned are correct uses of lighting. [Physical (Environmental) Security]

14. B - Use of CCTV to monitor personnel has the potential to violate the privacy of individuals. Hence it needs specific consents from employees. [Physical (Environmental) Security]

15. D - The first step would be to institute a security awareness program which trains employees and increases their awareness of security policies. A key point to note here is that some of the security policies will be on a need-to-know basis so ALL security procedures cannot be publicized. Penalizing employees is too drastic a step and may come in at a later stage. [Physical (Environmental) Security]

CISSP Mock Exam (LITE) – 9
Practice Questions

Test Name:
CISSP Mock Exam (LITE) - 9
Total Questions: 40
Correct Answers Needed to Pass:
30 (75.00%)
Time Allowed: 60 Minutes

Test Description

This is a cumulative CISSP Mock Exam which can be used as a benchmark for your CISSP aptitude. This practice test includes questions from all ten domains of the CISSP CBK.

Test Questions

1. Joe wants to exchange data with 100 other users using symmetric key encryption. How many separate keys does Joe need to have?

   A. 101 keys

   B. 100 keys

   C. 1 key

   D. 99 keys

2. A computer data center hosts 10 servers. At any given time, it is expected that only 1 server may fail. The cost of each of the servers is $ 10,000. The frequency at which a server may fail in a year is 0.1. What would be the annualized loss expectancy (ALE) for the data center due to a file server failure?

   A. $10,000

   B. $1,000

   C. $100

   D. $100,000

3. A company has a trade secret that is proprietary to the company. The company's business depends on this trade secret. What is the typical expiry period for trade secrets?

   A. 75 years

   B. They never expire in most cases.

   C. 10 years

   D. 100 years

4. A high-speed LAN network needs to operate at 1000 Mbps (1 Gbps). Which of the following technologies will support this?

   A. Ethernet

   B. 100VG-AnyLAN

C. FDDI

D. Token Ring

5. Which of the following correctly brings out the difference between a copyright and a patent?

A. A copyright deals with the representation of an invention whereas a patent deals with the actual subject matter of an invention.

B. A copyright deals with the actual subject matter of an invention whereas a patent deals with the representation of an invention.

C. A copyright protects a specific resource whereas a patent protects a name, shape, color or symbol.

D. A copyright deals with the actual subject matter of an invention whereas a patent deals with something that is proprietary to the company.

6. For disaster and backup planning purposes, which of the following would not be called a disaster impacting a company?

A. Introduction of a worm into a computer system

B. A financial emergency

C. A distributed denial of service attack (DDOS).

D. A hurricane that hits the facilities

7. The Recovery Time Objective (RTO) is identified as 4 days for a business operation. In such a case, which of the following recovery alternatives cannot be used?

A. A warm site

B. A hot site

C. A cold site

D. A mobile site

8. A trigger event that most incident response and handling models consider as the first step that starts off the process is called:

A. A flash

B. A rubric

C. A precursor

D. A triage

9. The operations team would like to use a backup method that allows

quick restores. They also have an additional criterion that the method should be cost-effective. Which of these will fit the requirement?

A. A differential backup process

B. An incremental backup process.

C. A full backup process

D. A pseudo-incremental backup process.

10. A company has facilities in the midwest region in the US. This region is prone to tornadoes. Since the processing done in the facilities is very critical, the company decides to shift its facilities to a different region where tornadoes are not active. This would be called:

A. A preventive measure.

B. A recovery objective

C. A crisis-management strategy

D. A recovery strategy.

11. An employee of a bank made changes to the software such that small sums of money were diverted to his account from inactive accounts. Such an attack would be labeled as:

A. Data diddling

B. Data manipulation

C. A rosalin attack

D. A salami attack

12. An inexperienced network engineer used a nearly obsolete identification service which allowed a hacker to exploit certain security loopholes associated with it. What is this likely to be?

A. Finger service

B. StopID service

C. NTP

D. HAND service

13. Which of the following events is least likely to be the cause of a fire inside a computer room?

A. A component on the motherboard of a computer catches fire due to the DC current flowing through it.

B. A transformer coil in a UPS short-circuits and starts a fire.

C. The plastic surrounding an overheated component catches fire and this starts a fire.

D. The wire insulation in an electrical line gets heated up and starts a fire.

14. An attack occurred on a computer network system and some data was compromised. If the company proceeds to court and initiates action against the attacker, which of the following people can testify and present their opinion of the case?

A. A user of the application who first noticed the issue.

B. An expert witness

C. The security officer

D. The chief executive officer (CEO)

15. Company Z's systems are infected due to a virus attack through the network systems of company Q. If company Z sues company Q, this would be termed as:

A. Downstream liability

B. System liability

C. A virus chain

D. Upstream liability

16. An auditor observed that the data center of a company was poorly secured and lacked necessary security controls to prevent unauthorized access. What activity should be performed to correct this situation?

A. Access to the data center should be controlled.

B. The data center should be physically secured.

C. The data center security controls should be hardened.

D. The data center security controls should be softened.

17. Your company wishes to purchase some safes to store backup tapes and valuable documents such as contracts. You would like to have added protection against possible tampering of the safes. Which of these features should you include?

A. Duplex relocking and anti-thermal functions

B. Passive relocking and thermal relocking functions.

C. Active relocking and Fire-safe functions

D. Realtime relocking and Fire protection functions

18. You are currently meeting with management to have them formally approve the products, systems, and components within your organization. What is this process usually called?

A. Affirmation

B. Certification

C. Verification

D. Accreditation

19. A security administrator is creating a procedure for setting up a new account and giving out the password of the new account to employees. Which of the following will best serve the purpose?

A. After a new account is set up, a temporary password should be revealed to the employee over telephone and the system should force the user to change the password on first logon.

B. After a new account is set up, a standard temporary password should be used. The system should then force the user to change the password on first logon.

C. New accounts should be set up such that they do not require any password. Once an employee is intimated about the account creation, she can change the password on first logon.

D. After a new account is set up, the ID and the password should be emailed to the supervisor or reporting manager of the employee. The manager can than reveal the password to the employee.

20. Which of the following is a good operational practice?

A. Service accounts should not be allowed multiple log-on session capabilities, but individual accounts should be allowed multiple-logon session facilities.

B. All service and individual accounts should not be allowed multiple log-on session capabilities.

C. All service and individual accounts should be allowed multiple log-on session capabilities.

D. Some service accounts may be allowed multiple log-on session capabilities, but individual accounts should not be allowed multiple-logon session facilities.

21. Which of the following best expresses the objective of having an access control policy?

   A. An access control policy should specify how users of resources are identified, processes used to authenticate them, and the level of access they must be granted to access resources.

   B. An access control policy should specify authentication processes and the level of access they must be granted to access resources.

   C. An access control policy should specify the level of access users must be granted to access resources.

   D. An access control policy should specify the tools used for authenticating resources and the level of access users must be granted to access resources.

22. During an external audit of a company's information security, you find that employees do not need to periodically change their passwords, and have access to all servers in the company. This is very likely due to:

   A. An error on the part of the security administrator.

   B. Poor access control policies.

   C. Employees needing to access all the data.

   D. An open communication policy.

23. A company laid out a policy on how financial transactions and other confidential information should be handled. This type of policy would be classified as:

   A. An advisory policy.

   B. A mandatory policy.

   C. An informative policy.

   D. A regulatory policy.

24. You would like to ensure that in the event of a fire, the smoke is pushed outwards rather inwards, if a door in your workplace is opened. Which of these air-ventilation combinations would you select?

   A. A closed-loop, recirculating air-conditioning system and using positive pressurization.

   B. A closed-loop, recirculating air-conditioning system and using negative pressurization.

   C. An open-loop, recirculating air-conditioning system and using positive pressurization.

D. An open-loop, recirculating air-conditioning system and using negative pressurization.

25. If two systems need to transfer large amounts of data, which form of communication is preferred?

    A. Analog communication

    B. Mixed-mode communication

    C. Asynchronous communication

    D. Synchronous communication

26. Two applications need to communicate with each other using full-duplex mode. Which layer of the Open Systems Interconnection (OSI) network model is responsible for establishing the connection and controlling the release of the connection?

    A. Session layer.

    B. Network layer.

    C. Interface layer.

    D. Transport layer.

27. A company has just completed a series of security training programs and has covered about 95% of its employees. A good measure of the effectiveness of this program would be to:

    A. Obtain feedback from the employees on a clearly articulated scale of 1 to 5.

    B. Check the retention of the course participants by sending out a questionnaire 1 year after the training.

    C. Compare the number of security incidents reported before and after the training.

    D. Artificially create some test situations and monitor the response of the employees.

28. Which of the following types of languages provides better security and enforces coding standards?

    A. Low-level languages

    B. Binary-level languages

    C. High-level languages

    D. Assembly-level languages

29. A risk analysis technique that obtains opinions from a group of experts, requires no calculations and does not provide a cost/benefit analysis is:

    A. Delphi technique

B. Quantitative risk analysis

C. Annualized loss expectancy

D. Automated risk analysis

30. Power failures could have disastrous consequences if not properly planned for. Which of these backup options provides the best protection from power failures?

   A. Inverters

   B. Battery packs

   C. Online UPS systems

   D. Standby UPS systems

31. A certain system required frequent granting and revoking of permissions. Why is a biometric means of authentication a poor choice for this system?

   A. Revoking credentials is a key issue in biometrics.

   B. Biometric devices are very expensive

   C. Biometrics are unreliable in verifying credentials.

   D. The danger that a hacker may misuse the system is very high.

32. A large organization decided to perform a penetration test of its network systems. Which of these choices would be the most appropriate to test for internal penetrations?

   A. Black box penetration testing

   B. Zero knowledge penetration testing

   C. Full knowledge penetration testing

   D. Partial knowledge penetration testing

33. While classifying the data in your company, how would you select a data custodian and a data owner?

   A. The data custodian is an IT role whereas the data owner is a business role

   B. Both, the data custodian and the data owners are IT roles.

   C. Both, the data custodian and the data owners are business roles.

   D. The data custodian is an business role whereas the data owner is an IT role

34. You are responsible for a project which has just gone through the software development life cycle (SDLC). For which of the following activities would you need to get management sign-off?

    A. Testing

    B. Accreditation

    C. Certification

    D. Build

35. As the security officer of a company, you are preparing a security program for physical safety. Which of these will not be a major metric as part of your security performance measurements?

    A. Business impact of disruptions.

    B. Number of unsuccessful crimes in the company.

    C. Number of successful crimes in the company.

    D. Number of employees who left the company the previous year.

36. A company deals with very sensitive and confidential information that needs to be available with zero downtime. Which of these steps can it take to ensure that it is completely able to provide this service even during a disaster?

    A. By using a backup site.

    B. By using a tertiary site.

    C. By having a reciprocal agreement.

    D. By having a warm site available.

37. Piggybacking is a common issue faced while using mantraps. Which of the following is the best option to counter this?

    A. By using a closed circuit camera

    B. By using a weight-based biometric system.

    C. By having a clear warning sign at the entrance that piggybacking is prohibited.

    D. By having a timing-based alarm circuit on the closure of the door.

38. In the financial sector, many software applications used by companies are critical. Vendors do not provide the source code for these applications. How can companies protect themselves from a scenario where the application

vendor goes bankrupt or out of business?

A. By having alternate software applications identified and ready to implement.

B. By signing non-disclosure agreements and insisting that the vendors supply the source code.

C. By using a software escrow.

D. Through a trust mechanism.

39. An administrator failed to verify the authenticity / integrity of a patch and downloaded a patch file for an application from a disreputable site. This caused a host of issues by introducing a Trojan horse into the system. This could have been avoided by:

A. Using a setting of auto-update mode to enable auto-installation of patches.

B. Researching the patch, verifying the authenticity of the download and performing an integrity check.

C. Avoiding the use of patches unless they are obtained in CD/DVD format directly from the vendor

D. Installing only the essential patches and omitting the non-essential ones.

40. An employee used a bootable USB flash drive to boot a workstation and copy confidential information. How could this situation have been prevented?

A. By installing a BIOS password and setting up only specific drives as boot drives.

B. By implementing a policy that employees should not be allowed to bring USB flash drives onto the company campus.

C. By implementing CCTV to monitor all workstations.

D. By removing USB ports from all workstations.

CISSP Mock Exam (LITE) – 9
Answer Key and Explanations

1. B - In symmetric cryptography, the sender and receiver will use two instances of the same key to encrypt and decrypt. So if Joe needs to exchange data with 100 other people, he would need to have as many separate keys, so the correct answer is 100. [Cryptography]

2. B - Since each server has a cost of 10,000, the total asset value of the servers in the data center is 10 x 10,000 = $ 100,000. It is expected that only 1 out of 10 servers may fail at a time. Hence the exposure factor is 1/10 = 0.1 Hence, the single loss expectancy (SLE) is given by asset value x exposure factor = 100,000 x 0.1 = $ 10,000. The frequency at which a server may fail in a year is given as 0.1, hence the annualized rate of occurrence (ARO) is 0.1. The annualized loss expectancy (ALE) is given by SLE x ARO = 10,000 x 0.1 = $ 1,000 [Information Security and Risk Management]

3. B - Trade secrets are proprietary to companies and vital for their survival. In most cases, trade secrets do not expire. [Legal, Regulations, Compliance and Investigations]

4. A - Ethernet technology has developed over the years. Modern Ethernet technology supports upto 1Gbps using UTP and is called 1000base-T Gigabit Ethernet. [Telecommunications and Network Security]

5. A - A copyright deals with the representation of an invention and protects the rights of an author so that the original work may not be copied or reproduced. In contrast, a patent deals with the actual subject matter of an invention and grants individuals or companies legal ownership of the invention. [Legal, Regulations, Compliance and Investigations]

6. B - A disaster would include anything that causes physical damage to the assets of an organization. A financial emergency may not be classified as a disaster for business continuity / disaster recover purposes. [Business Continuity and Disaster Recovery Planning]

7. C - Cold sites cannot be used when the RTOs are less than a week. Cold sites only consist of a shell location that does not have any supporting equipment. While they are cost-effective, they do not serve the purpose for RTOs of less than a week. [Business Continuity and Disaster Recovery Planning]

8. D - The trigger event that kicks off the incident handling process is called a triage. This would be the first in the entire incident handling

process with other activities following it. [Legal, Regulations, Compliance and Investigations]

9. A - A differential backup process backs up files that have been modified since the last time a full backup was done. The back up process takes longer than an incremental backup, but is faster during a restore. [Business Continuity and Disaster Recovery Planning]

10. A - This would be called a preventive measure. A company would do a thorough investigation and analysis to arrive at such a decision. Since this will ensure that the company is no longer in a tornado hit area, it is called a preventive measure. This is usually taken up proactively. [Business Continuity and Disaster Recovery Planning]

11. D - An attack in which the attacker commits a large crime, but does it in smaller phases is called a salami attack. In such an attack, the attacker hopes to avoid being discovered because insignificant amounts are involved in the individual smaller crimes. [Legal, Regulations, Compliance and Investigations]

12. A - The finger service is an almost obsolete identification service. It can be easily exploited and has raised many privacy and security concerns. It is no longer used unless there is no

alternative available. [Telecommunications and Network Security]

13. A - The DC voltage at the motherboard level is normally in the range of 3 to 5 volts. This is usually unlikely to cause fires. All the other options listed are more likely to occur and cause fires. [Physical (Environmental) Security]

14. B - In a court of law, the opinion rule applies. As a result, witnesses may only state facts pertaining to an issue and not their opinion. Only expert witnesses, who are considered subject matter experts, may testify and present an opinion of the issue. [Legal, Regulations, Compliance and Investigations]

15. A - This is termed as downstream liability. It is an important reason for companies to take proper precautions and protect their networks and systems. [Legal, Regulations, Compliance and Investigations]

16. C - System hardening should be performed on the data center. Hardening is a process of securing the data center and would involve implementation of various security controls to prevent unauthorized access. Hardening is also applied as a term when the security controls are increased. [Security Operations]

17. B - A passive relocking function can detect if someone attempts to tamper with the lock. When this happens, the mechanism causes extra bolts to fall in place. A thermal relocking function can detect when a certain temperature is met. For example if the lock is being drilled, its temperature will potentially rise. In such a case, the lock automatically causes extra bolts to fall into place. [Physical (Environmental) Security]

18. D - The accreditation process occurs after the certification process. It involves meeting with management and presenting the information derived from the certification process. This is done to have management formally approve the products, systems, or components within the organization. When management accredits the products, systems, and components within the organization they are stating that they know the potential threats, vulnerabilities, and weaknesses and are accepting the associated risks. [Security Architecture and Design]

19. A - Once a new account is set up, it is preferable to use an out-of-channel distribution method such as telephone to reveal the password to the employee. The second level of security can be provided by forcing the employee to change the password on first logon. Emailing passwords should be avoided since they will then travel as plain text and may be potentially intercepted. [Security Operations]

20. D - Some service accounts may be allowed multiple log-on session capabilities, but individual accounts should not be allowed multiple-logon session facilities. Preventing this facility will allow unauthorized sharing of accounts to be detected. Further, if an account has been stolen, this will prevent access by the attacker. [Security Operations]

21. A - An access control policy should specify how users of resources are identified, authentication processes, and the level of access they must be granted to access resources. It does not need to specify what tools are to be used for authentication, and only provides a guideline on standards and best practices. [Access Control]

22. B - This is most likely due to poor access control policies. Administering access to users and controlling what they can access are key aspects of access control. [Access Control]

23. A - Policies which strongly advise employees on what behaviors and activities are acceptable and what are not, along with the repercussions of violations, would be classified as advisory policies. Handling of financial data and confidential information comes under this umbrella of policies. [Information Security and Risk Management]

24. A - A closed-loop recirculating system ensures that the air inside the building is reused after proper filtration, instead of bringing in outside air. Positive pressurization means that if a door opens, the air goes out and outside does not come in. This is important in case of a fire when smoke should go out rather than be pushed back in. [Physical (Environmental) Security]

25. D - When large amounts of data are involved, systems are usually setup to transmit data synchronously. This involves the use of a clocking mechanism. In contrast, asynchronous communication is preferred for small amounts of data. [Telecommunications and Network Security]

26. A - Application-to-application communication happens at the session layer. This layer is responsible for setting up the connection between the applications and controlling the release of the connection. [Telecommunications and Network Security]

27. C - A good indication of whether a security training program was effective or not can be obtained by looking at details such as number of security incidents before and after training. A decrease in number can

point to effective training whereas an increase likely means that the training has not done much to help. [Information Security and Risk Management]

28. C - High-level languages provide better security and enforce coding standards. They are also easier to use and can be used to produce code very fast. [Software Development Security]

29. A - A risk analysis technique that obtains opinions from a group of experts, requires no calculations and does not provide a cost/benefit analysis is the Delphi technique. This is a type of qualitative risk analysis. [Information Security and Risk Management]

30. C - Online UPS systems provide the best protection in case of power failures. In these systems, primary power passes through the UPS even for normal operation. Hence they are ideally suited to detect power failures and supply backup power from the battery pack when required. [Physical (Environmental) Security]

31. A - The key challenge in using biometrics is that the credential is tied down to a user attribute as a result of which the process of granting / revoking accesses is very cumbersome. Hence this is a poor choice for systems that require frequent granting and revoking of accesses. [Access Control]

32. C - In full knowledge penetration testing, all information about the environment is typically provided to the tester. Here the intent is to explore what can be done rather than what can be discovered. Hence, this is appropriate in testing for internal penetration and a greater level of information can be shared with the testers. [Access Control]

33. A - The data custodian is an IT or security role and the personnel are responsible for maintaining and protecting the data. In contrast, the data owner is a business role and is typically the in-charge of a business unit. [Information Security and Risk Management]

34. B - Accreditation is an activity that requires management authorization. This is typically done after reviewing the certification. Intermediate phases of the software development life cycle may not necessarily require management sign-off. [Software Development Security]

35. D - Key metrics for a security program include the number of successful and unsuccessful crimes and the business impact of disruptions. The attrition in the company may not be a major metric in the company's security program. [Physical (Environmental) Security]

36. B - A requirement that demands zero downtime needs to be available even in case of a disaster. So, a backup site is a minimum requirement. In this case, it would be logical to have a tertiary site which serves as a secondary backup site. This will ensure that even if the backup site is down, the company can provide its services. [Business Continuity and Disaster Recovery Planning]

37. B - A weight based system will be the most effective in countering piggy-backing. The other options may not be as effective. A closed circuit camera may also offer some protection, but it will require constant monitoring. [Physical (Environmental) Security]

38. C - Such a situation is usually handled by using a third party escrow service called software escrow. Agreements are drawn up such that a third party holds the source code and the company gets access to the code only if the vendor goes out of business. [Business Continuity and Disaster Recovery Planning]

39. B - Administrators need to make sure the source of a file is authentic by researching a patch thoroughly. An integrity check needs to be performed to ensure the file is not corrupted. This is particularly relevant since almost all software vendors release patches to application software. [Software Development Security]

40. A - Among the options listed, the option that will work best is the use of a BIOS password. A "soft" policy may not deter a malicious employee from getting a flash drive into the facility. Use of CCTV to monitor all workstations or removing USB ports from all workstations is impractical. [Security Architecture and Design]

Domain Area Test: Security Operations Practice Questions

Test Name:
Domain Area Test: Security Operations
Total Questions: 15
Correct Answers Needed to Pass:
11 (0.00%)
Time Allowed: 25 Minutes

Test Description

This practice test specifically targets your knowledge of the Security Operations domain area.

Test Questions

1. Operational planning involves identifying where a back-up of data should be stored. Typically, multiple backups are created. One of these is held locally for day-to-day restores. Which of the following locations is the best choice for storing the other back-up copy?

   A. A backup location within the same city.

   B. Another building within the same facility

   C. A backup location 100 miles away

   D. A backup location 1000 miles away

2. Which of the following is the best option to handle data security for portable devices such as a laptops?

   A. Restrict remote connectivity of laptops to company networks.

   B. Encrypt all data stored on a laptop.

   C. Stay alert in airports and public places to prevent loss of the laptop.

   D. Always carry a laptop in a nondescript carry bag or case.

3. A and B are communicating with each other over a TCP session when an attacker hijacks the session using Juggernaut. What action should the administrator take to avoid recurrence of such attacks?

   A. The administrator should look at implementing a protocol such as Kerberos/ IPSec.

   B. The administrator should discourage such communication between the two users.

C. The administrator should look at implementing a protocol such as IMAP/ ICMP.

D. The administrator should ask the users to discuss and introduce a formal set of protocols known only to them.

4. A computer application that accessed a very critical file server was developed such that it required two administrator-level users to simultaneously log in for either of them to gain access to the system. Such a precaution would be termed as:

   A. Separation of duties.

   B. Good authentication.

   C. Excessive authentication.

   D. Joint duties

5. A security administrator reports to the network administrator and provides weekly security reports on the security functions. You are asked to audit operations and report your findings to management. One of your key comments would be:

   A. The reporting structure looks flawed. The network administrator should report to the security administrator.

B. Weekly reports are too far apart and reporting needs to happen daily.

C. It is unnecessary to have weekly reports since they are just an overhead of time. A monthly report will suffice.

D. The reporting structure looks flawed. A security administrator should not report to the network administrator.

6. Which of these is not a control method used in Security Operations?

   A. Supervision

   B. Highest privilege

   C. Need-to-know

   D. Separation of duties

7. As part of object reuse assurance, software tools are used that overwrite sectors of magnetic media so that the average attacker or hacker is unable to retrieve information that was stored on it. What is the typical recommendation for such overwriting?

   A. A single overwrite for noncritical information and two rounds of overwriting for sensitive data.

B. At least two rounds of overwrite for noncritical information and seven rounds of overwriting for sensitive data.

C. A single overwrite for noncritical information and multiple rounds of overwriting for sensitive data (ideally 7 times).

D. Multiple rounds of overwriting for all kinds of data. (Ideally this should be done 7 times).

8. An optical disk was not properly purged, with the result that some of the company data was leaked out to a competitor. What is the best way to purge an optical disk?

   A. Grinding of the media surface

   B. Electroplating the disk surface

   C. Zeroization of the media

   D. Degaussing the media

9. An IT services company plans to upgrade its computer systems and donate the older systems for a social cause. What would your primary suggestion be?

   A. All hard disks and digital media should be destroyed and the systems should be dispatched without the media.

   B. The computers should be dispatched only after all data on hard disks has been deleted by using the basic format functionality of the operating systems.

   C. It is extremely risky to permit computer systems owned by the company to be used elsewhere, hence it is better to destroy them.

   D. All hard disks and digital media should be sanitized before the systems leave the company premises.

10. What configuration will ensure that received fax documents are kept confidential and secure?

   A. Configure the fax device to only accept faxes when a user is present to receive it.

   B. Configure a fax server to route the received faxes to the appropriate user's electronic mailbox.

   C. Configure the fax device to only accept faxes from known senders.

   D. Configure a fax server to print the faxes to the nearest printer and include a cover page that separates the printed faxes by user name.

11. What type of backup will contain any files that have changed since the last full backup?

A. Partial

B. Full

C. Differential

D. Complete

12. The HR director of a company had certain valuable data on her desktop computer. A hard disk crash wiped out important data that was hard to recreate. Which could have been done to avoid this?

A. Hard disk crashes are an operational risk. There is not much that can be done in case of a hard disk crash on a desktop.

B. The user should have avoided working on her desktop computer.

C. It is the user's responsibility to backup data. Nothing much can be done about such a failure.

D. The operations department should have included critical,

identified directories on the HR director's desktop as part of its backup procedures.

13. During the quarterly audit of software licenses being used in a company, it was discovered that there were two extra software installations for which no valid license was available. What should the next step be?

A. An investigation should be launched to ascertain who used those applications and how they came to be installed.

B. There appears to be a valid requirement for having two additional licenses. The company should take steps to procure the same.

C. This is an ethical issue. The applications must be immediately deleted from the computer systems.

D. This is a legal issue. The applications must immediately be deleted from the computer systems.

14. Ed works for a manufacturing company as a drafting engineer. He narrowly escapes being terminated for inappropriate Internet browsing. It was discovered that the inappropriate acts took place only at 2:00 AM when Ed was not at work. Which of the following would have prevented this confusion?

A. Night Watchmen

B. Biometrics

C. Personal Firewalls

D. Mandatory Screen Timeouts

15. Which of the following is not true about RAID 10?

A. It does not provide sufficient redundancy.

B. It combines the characteristics of RAID 0 and RAID 1.

C. It is considered as a multi-RAID level.

D. It requires a large amount of storage space.

Domain Area Test:
Security Operations
Answer Key and Explanations

1. C - A key consideration while deciding the off-site backup location is that the location should be sufficiently far enough so that it is not affected by the same natural calamity; at the same time, it should not be so far away that recovering the backup becomes difficult. The choice of a location 100 miles away is a good choice. The choices of a backup within the same facility and city are poor choices. A backup location 1000 miles away is too far away for quick retrieval. [Security Operations]

2. B - Although all of the choices listed contribute to better security while handling a laptop device, the choice of encryption of data on the laptop is the best and can help prevent loss of information even if the laptop is stolen. [Security Operations]

3. A - An administrator should look at implementing a protocol such as Kerberos/ ITSec. This will require the two users who are communicating to have mutual authentication. An attacker will be unable to authenticate to the users and launch an attack. [Security Operations]

4. A - At first glance, this might seem like a situation where security requirements have been exaggerated. However, if there is a mission-critical server, it might be necessary to have two individuals manage the system, thus ensuring that no one person can misuse it. Hence, this is separation of duties enforced to a very high degree. [Security Operations]

5. D - Each of the roles of security administrator and network administrator has a different function and focus. A network administrator focuses on ensuring that networks and resources are available. This could result in a lower security. In contrast the security administrator introduces security mechanisms that decrease the performance and reduce the availability. It is best to have a different reporting structure to handle this conflict of interest. [Security Operations]

6. B - Highest privilege is not a valid control method used in Security Operations. The other three choices are valid control methods. [Security Operations]

7. C - For non-critical data, a single round of overwriting is considered sufficient. For more critical and sensitive data, it recommended that the overwriting happen several times (the recommendation is seven). [Security Operations]

8. A - Grinding the data side of the optical disk such that the media is rendered unreadable is a very effective way of destroying it. At a minimum, the grinding can be used to scratch the surface to such an extent that the media is rendered unreadable. [Security Operations]

9. D - Not permitting company owned systems to be donated, or destroying hard disks before giving the systems away is an extreme measure. On the other hand, using a simple format command to delete files is ineffective and does not fully delete the contents of files. The best option is to completely sanitize the digital media, thus ensuring that no old data is retrievable. [Security Operations]

10. B - The best way to ensure that faxed documents are kept confidential is to implement a fax server. When a fax is received by the fax server, it determines who the fax is intended for and sends it to the electronic mailbox of that user so that they can view it with their email client. This ensures that only the user that is intended to see the fax will actually see it. This overcomes the issue with traditional fax machines where faxes could be easily compromised. [Security Operations]

11. C - The differential backup will contain any files that have changed since the last full backup, regardless of the fact that they have been backed up before. This is because the archive bit is left on to identify that these files have not yet been saved to a full backup. [Security Operations]

12. D - The operations department should have included critical, identified directories on the HR director's desktop as part of its backup procedures. It is better the operations department implements backup procedures. [Security Operations]

13. A - Unauthorized installations could range from being a simple oversight to a serious violation involving deliberate misuse and access to data. When such unauthorized installations are noticed, a detailed enquiry should be launched. This would be the first step in the process. [Security Operations]

14. D - When personnel do not lock their console or log out, they may be held liable for what is done on their equipment in their absence. Biometrics and firewalls do not help when someone leaves a session unattended. Mandatory screen timeouts will help in such cases. [Security Operations]

15. A - RAID 10 is considered a multi-RAID level since it combines the characteristics of RAID 0 and RAID 1. It provides excellent redundancy and has a superior performance. On the flip side, it requires a large amount of storage space. [Security Operations]

CISSP Mock Exam (LITE) - 10
Practice Questions

Test Name:
CISSP Mock Exam (LITE) - 10
Total Questions: 40
Correct Answers Needed to Pass:
30 (75.00%)
Time Allowed: 60 Minutes

Test Description

This is a cumulative CISSP Mock Exam which can be used as a benchmark for your CISSP aptitude. This practice test includes questions from all ten domains of the CISSP CBK.

Test Questions

1. An application programmer wrote a web program that used session cookies to keep track of unsuccessful login attempts. If a user tried multiple times, the session cookie value was decremented and the user would be locked out after 3 attempts. An attacker used web proxy software to change the number of allowable attempts to 10000 and the application did not detect this. How could this situation have been handled?

   A. By using cleartext

   B. By using hidden fields

   C. By using post-validation control

   D. By using adequate parameter validation

2. Which of the following access controls becomes unmanageable for large applications / large environments?

   A. Centralized access control

   B. Access control matrix

   C. Role-based access control

   D. Rule-based access control

3. The network administrator of a company is extremely busy and does not change cryptographic keys used for encryption. The result is that all the keys have remained unchanged for a year now. If the company deals with credit-card data, what should be the preferred frequency of changing the keys?

   A. Change the keys thrice a day

   B. Change the key once a week

   C. Change the keys once a quarter.

   D. Change the keys once in a month

4. If you are looking for a software development model that is simple, offers a fairly structured approach, works best for small teams, and allows for small, fully integrated releases, the best choice is:

    A. Waterfall model

    B. Spiral Method

    C. Cleanroom

    D. Extreme programming

5. A company publishes a policy that an employee who uses a sniffer in an unauthorized manner is liable to be fired, if detected. This type of policy is called:

    A. Corrective access control

    B. Directive access control

    C. Preventive access control

    D. Deterrent access control

6. What is the benefit of using clustering in your enterprise data management scheme?

    A. Creates a single point of failure

    B. Amount of data storage is increased

    C. Scalability and redundancy

    D. Requires less memory to operate

7. A hacker broke into a computer network and stole sensitive information. He subsequently sold this to the company's competitor. Such acts would be tried under:

    A. Criminal law

    B. Civil law.

    C. Cyber-law

    D. Regulatory law.

8. A database was designed to contain very critical and sensitive information. An effective way to ensure that a hacker cannot obtain access to all the critical data in one go is by dividing the database into different parts. This technique is called:

    A. Database duplication

    B. Database partitioning

    C. Database redundancy

    D. Database mirroring

9. A company uses off-site storage as part of its business continuity strategy. Regular backups are made on tapes and these are shipped off to off-site locations where they are held securely. Which of the following will help in improving its Recovery Time Objective (RTO) considering that the company does not require real-time response?

A. Storage Area Networks

B. Remote journaling

C. Electronic vaulting

D. Database mirroring

10. Which of the following is not an assessment used in vulnerability testing?

A. Physical testing

B. Personnel testing

C. System testing

D. Management testing

11. In a well-established security system, developers should have to access to which of the following environments?

A. Development, quality assurance and production environments

B. Development and quality assurance environments

C. Development environment only

D. Development and production environments

12. The owner of certain data required specific users to access certain data and granted them read permissions. However, the system determined that these users should not have access to the data. This will happen in:

A. Mandatory Access Control (MAC)

B. Rule Based Access Control

C. Directionary Access Control

D. Discretionary Access Control (DAC)

13. Which of the following is a best practice to follow in designing the door to a computer room, to prevent it from being broken down easily?

A. Doors should open inwards and there should be at least seven hinges per door.

B. Doors should open outwards and there should be at least three hinges per door.

C. Doors should open inwards and there should be at least three hinges per door.

D. Doors should open outwards and there should be at least seven hinges per door.

14. Which of the following is not a good practice in assigning userids or identification values to users?

A. Each userid or value should be unique to provide accountability.

B. The userid or value should not be shared across users.

C. A standard nomenclature should be used for each userid or value.

D. The userid or value should be descriptive of the user's position.

15. Which of the following algorithms can only detect unintentional modifications to messages?

A. Hash function

B. CBC-MAC function

C. JMAC function

D. HMAC function

16. Devices such as wireless equipment, cellular telephones may have limited processing capacity, power supply and bandwidth. If efficiency of use of resources is a key factor, what type of encryption functionality may be used?

A. Knapsack

B. Elliptic Curve Cryptosystem (ECC)

C. El Gamal

D. RSA

17. An application requires a PIN to be encrypted in the fastest and easiest mode using Digital Encryption Standard (DES) or another block cipher. The best choice would be to use:

A. Electronic Block Chaining (EBC)

B. Electronic Code Book mode (ECB)

C. Cipher Feedback (CFB)

D. Cipher Block Chaining (CBC)

18. An optical disk was not properly purged, with the result that some of the company data was leaked out to a competitor. What is the best way to purge an optical disk?

A. Electroplating the disk surface

B. Grinding of the media surface

C. Degaussing the media

D. Zeroization of the media

19. Collisions occur when too many computers on the network transmit data at the same time. This slows down the network performance. Which of the following technologies does not suffer from this problem?

A. Fast Ethernet

B. Token ring

C. Ethernet using star topology

D. Ethernet using bus topology

20. What are the two major disadvantages that processes using multi-threading run into?

A. Deadlocks and Blocking

B. Failed RPCs and Buffer overflow.

C. Deadlocks and Failed RPCs

D. Deadlocks and Thread-drop

21. Fences act as an effective first line of defense and deter intruders. Which of the following may be a poor practice while designing a fence?

A. The posts to which the fencing is connected should be deeply buried in the ground.

B. Fences should be at least 8 feet high with razor wire at the top.

C. Fencing should extend into the ground in terrain that is soft.

D. Bushes should always be planted in front of fences so that the buildings within are unnoticeable.

22. Which of the following security models does not address the issue of integrity?

A. Biba model

B. Clark-Wilson model

C. Bell-LaPadula model

D. Graham-Denning model

23. A hacker created an email attachment with a name that was greater than 64K in length. The longer name overwrote program instruction code and caused issues because the email application was only designed to handle 64K long filenames. This could be avoided by:

A. Security control

B. Granular control

C. Cryptography

D. Implementing parameter checking

24. An employee was hired for a specific role and a regular background check was performed. A year later, the employee is now being considered for a more sensitive role. What would be the course of action required?

A. Perform a more detailed background check since the initial back-ground check was just a regular one.

B. Nothing specific needs to be done. One year in the company is sufficient to prove the employee's trustworthiness.

C. Consider alternatives for the role. Ideally look for an employee who has at least 5 years of service in the company.

D. Have the employee sign a confidentiality agreement prior to starting his new role.

25. If a system of a higher trust level needs to work with a very high level of protection, what would be the best memory implementation to use?

A. Hardware segmentation of memory

B. Erasable Programmable Read-Only Memory (EPROM)

C. Under privilege level

D. Cache memory

26. A security professional would like to ensure that the anti-virus system implemented is proactive and detects new malware. Which of these techniques should the anti-virus system incorporate?

A. Non-heuristic techniques

B. Signature based techniques

C. Behavior blocking techniques

D. Immunizer techniques

27. An administrator was subject to criminal and civil liability because he authorized a certain type of activity. Which of these is it most likely to be?

A. Implementation of an IDS without informing the employees of the company.

B. Implementation of a mandatory vacation policy.

C. Use of keystroke monitoring as an audit trail.

D. Non-enforcement of a requirement to change the password every 30 days

28. Debbie communicates with 9 other people using symmetric cryptography. If each one of them has to communicate securely with every other person, what is the total number of keys involved?

A. 11 keys

B. 45 keys

C. 9 keys

D. 20 keys

29. Which of the following is typically the responsibility of a network administrator and not that of a security administrator?

A. Creation and maintenance of user profiles

B. Implementation of security devices.

C. Ensuring the availability of a system

D. Setting initial passwords for users

30. Which of the following choices correctly represents an action dictated by the chain of custody evidence?

A. After a backup of a compromised server is made, it can be restored to normal application immediately.

B. In a computer crime, the hard disks and media are the most important pieces of evidence.

C. All evidence in a cyber-crime should be properly backed-up.

D. All evidence in a cyber-crime should be properly labeled with information indicating the person who secured and validated it.

31. The Golay code is a 24-bit error-correcting and detecting code. Where might this be used to ensure that data processed is accurate?

A. In a secondary control

B. In an input control

C. In an auxiliary control

D. In an output control

32. Which of the following models enforces separation of user duties?

   A. Information flow model

   B. Bell-LaPadula model

   C. Biba model

   D. Clark-Wilson model

33. Certain information that was once sensitive and confidential is no longer confidential. What should be the next course of action?

   A. The information should be de-classified to ensure that excess protection is not applied to non-sensitive documents.

   B. The information should be de-rated to ensure that excess protection is not applied to non-sensitive documents.

   C. Information which was once confidential should continue to be held confidential. Hence no action should be taken.

D. The information should be destroyed so that it is no longer accessible.

34. Network Address Translation (NAT) was developed because IP addresses were running out and the address space needed to be extended. Which of the following implementations will help resolve the address issue?

   A. IPv6

   B. IPv8

   C. IPv5

   D. IPv4

35. Two users have exchanged communication using a symmetric algorithm. If the sender challenges the communication and says that he/she did not send the message, how can this be proved or verified?

   A. This cannot be verified. A symmetric algorithm does not provide nonrepudiation.

   B. It can be easily verified that a message was sent by a particular sender, since the sender's key and the receiver's keys are different

   C. This can be verified by a third party who has access to the keys held by both users.

D. The keys are known only to the sender and the recipient. So, neither the sender nor the recipient can repudiate the fact that he/she sent the message.

36. A network administrator needed to connect two machines that were located at a distance of 250 meters. She used an unshielded twisted pair (UTP) in a single cable segment to make the connection, however she found that the machines were unable to communicate. What is the likely issue?

A. It is likely that the cable was frayed and lost continuity. The administrator should look at replacing the cable.

B. When UTP cable is used in segments greater than 185 meters, the signal gets attenuated and the communication breaks down.

C. This is most likely a network settings issue and the administrator needs to check the settings.

D. When UTP cable is used in segments greater than 105 meters, the signal gets attenuated and the communication breaks down.

37. Virtual memory uses hard drive space and 'extends' memory through a process of page swapping. It also has its own set of security issues. Which of the following is not an issue associated with virtual memory?

A. It is possible that even when a process is terminated, pointers to the data are present in the hard disk space. These could potentially be retrieved and misused.

B. It is possible that in the process of using virtual memory space on the hard disk, critical data on the non-virtual memory areas of the hard-disk could get overwritten.

C. It is possible that an attacker may gain access to the hard disk space and copy the data even as the process is executing.

D. It is possible that a controlling program has written unencrypted data to disk while using it as virtual memory, and this could be potentially compromised.

38. Which of the following is not correct about Secure European System for Applications in a Multi-Vendor Environment (SESAME)?

A. It offers access control based on roles.

B. It offers SSO with additional distributed access controls.

C. Components are not accessible through Kerberos v5 protocol.

D. It uses public key cryptography to distribute private keys.

39. A publicly listed company was due to announce its quarterly results in a few days' time. How would the company classify information pertaining to its results, prior to the day of the results?

A. It would be classified as private.

B. It would be classified as sensitive.

C. It would be classified as confidential.

D. It would be classified as public.

40. How would responsibilities be divided in a good application programming setup?

A. Software developers should focus on functionality and the security team should focus on the functionality and security of the program.

B. Software developers should focus on functionality and the security team should focus on the security of a program.

C. Software developers should focus both on functionality as well as security of a program.

D. Modern application development environments automatically take care of security requirements, so software developers only need to focus on functionality.

CISSP Mock Exam (LITE) - 10
Answer Key and Explanations

1. D - This situation could have been avoided by proper input parameter validation. If the session cookies are the only means of validation, it opens up the application to brute-force attacks. [Software Development Security]

2. B - An access control matrix (ACM) is a table structure of an access control list. Users, data and permissions are identified and incorporated into the matrix. This becomes unmanageable for very large systems. [Access Control]

3. B - A general rule of cryptography is that the more often a key is used, the more likely it is that it can be captured and misused. In the case of a credit-card company, the company may need to go in for a change of all keys once a week. The other frequencies mentioned won't work. Changing them thrice a day is an overkill and once a month or a quarter is too infrequent. [Cryptography]

4. D - Extreme programming meets the criteria listed. Typically, this model works best for small-size teams of less than 12 people. It relies on sub-projects of limited and clearly-defined scope. [Software Development Security]

5. D - This is a deterrent access control. Users are discouraged from using sniffers because they are aware of the potential punishment they may receive, if detected. [Access Control]

6. C - With clustering technology, multiple servers are connected to form a "cluster" of computers. Clustering prevents the failure of a single file server from denying access to data and adds computing power to the network for a large number of users. [Security Operations]

7. A - Such acts would normally be tried under criminal law since information was stolen and misused. The other types of law would not apply in this case since a crime has been committed. [Legal, Regulations, Compliance and Investigations]

8. B - This is termed as database partitioning and makes it very hard for an unauthorized individual to obtain access to the complete set of data. [Software Development Security]

9. C - Electronic vaulting is a good option for companies which use off-site locations for their backups and have an RTO of 3 to 5 days. [Business Continuity and Disaster Recovery Planning]

10. D - Management testing is not an assessment used in vulnerability

testing. The other choices are valid. [Access Control]

11. C - Developers should only have access to the development environment and should not be able to access the quality assurance and production environments. This will ensure that these two environments are protected from accidental changes as well as malicious attacks. [Software Development Security]

12. A - This would happen in a Mandatory Access Control System. In spite of the owner of the data clearing users, the system still determines whether they should or not have access. [Access Control]

13. B - As a best practice, doors should be designed to open outwards. This will prevent them from damaging equipment that may be inside. Doors should also have at least three hinges per door and be fixed to adjoining walls securely. [Physical (Environmental) Security]

14. D - Using identity values or userids that represent a user's role or task is a poor practice. Userids such as 'operator', 'purchasemanager', 'administrator' etc should be avoided. This is to ensure that the purpose of an account is not revealed in the identity value. A standard nomenclature such as lastname.firstname is often used for userids. [Access Control]

15. A - In a Hash based algorithm, the receiver can compare a hash of the message digest with the value that was transmitted with the message. If these are different, he/she will know that the message was modified. [Cryptography]

16. B - Elliptic Curve Cryptosystems (ECC) require a much smaller percentage of the resources used by other algorithms and RSA. ECC provides similar levels of protection as RSA with a key size that is shorter. Hence it is preferred for wireless device or cellular telephone applications. [Cryptography]

17. B - Electronic Code Book mode (ECB) is the fastest and easiest mode to use. It is typically used only for encrypting small amounts of data like PIN numbers or keys because it produces the same block of ciphertext given a block of plaintext and for a given key. [Cryptography]

18. B - Grinding the data side of the optical disk such that the media is rendered unreadable is a very effective way of destroying it. At a minimum, the grinding can be used to scratch the surface to such an extent that the media is rendered unreadable. [Security Operations]

19. B - Token ring technologies do not have the issue of collisions since in a token ring, only the computer which has the 24-bit token can transmit data. However, this is achieved at the cost of speed and token rings are slower compared to Ethernet. [Telecommunications and Network Security]

20. A - Two common problems which occur with processes using multi-threading are deadlocks and blocking. Deadlocks occur when two processes vie for the same resource. Blocking occurs when a process attempts to perform a read or a write on an input-output device and is not able to successfully exit. [Security Architecture and Design]

21. D - Planting of bushes in front of fences may not be good practice. Over a period of time they could damage the fencing. It is also possible that the integrity of the fencing could be impacted. [Physical (Environmental) Security]

22. C - The Bell-LaPadula model was primarily designed to address confidentiality and does not address the integrity of the data. [Security Architecture and Design]

23. D - Such situations can be avoided by implementing parameter checking. This would involve checking input for length, matching data-type, format and forbidden characters. [Software Development Security]

24. A - When an employee is being considered for a more sensitive role, it may be required to perform a more detailed background check since the earlier one was a regular one, probably at a lower-level. Longevity in the company may be a parameter as well, however 1 year is not sufficient to do away with the more detailed background check. [Information Security and Risk Management]

25. A - In hardware segmentation of memory, memory is physically separated instead of just being logically separated. As a result, this adds a high level of protection and prevents a lower-privileged access from modifying memory used by a higher-privileged access. [Security Architecture and Design]

26. C - Behavior blocking techniques analyze sequences of code in advance and can potentially identify malicious viruses. It is considered a proactive technique. Heuristic detection is another proactive technique. [Software Development Security]

27. C - Keystroke monitoring is associated with privacy issues. Of the choices listed, this is the choice that is most likely associated with criminal and civil liabilities. This may happen if employees are not properly informed that they are being monitored or liable to be monitored. [Access Control]

28. B - In symmetric cryptography, each set of users would need to use a separate set of keys. Therefore, the total number of keys required would be 45. This is given by the formula Total number of keys = n x (n-1) /2 where n is the total no. of people communicating. For ex: If 2 people communicate, you require 2 x (2-1)/2 = 2 keys and if 10 people communicate, you require 10 x (10-1)/2 = 45 keys [Cryptography]

29. C - The network and security administrator have different responsibilities although there is a tendency to overlap. The network administrator is responsible for network or resource availability and for responding to user needs for functionality. In contrast a security administrator may actually introduce processes and checks and balances, which decrease performance. [Security Operations]

30. D - All evidence in a cyber-crime should be properly labeled with information indicating the person who secured and validated it. This is one of the steps required in providing strong evidence of the crime and proper handling of the evidence. [Legal, Regulations, Compliance and Investigations]

31. B - Contamination of data can occur in multiple ways - while going into or out of a system. Error detection and correction is an input control and the Golay code can be used for this. The Golay code is a highly reliable one and is used for applications involving satellite / digital communications. [Software Development Security]

32. D - The Clark-Wilson model outlines how separation of duties is to be incorporated in an application. For example, if a user requires to do a certain approval that exceeds a certain value, the system may require this to be routed via a supervisor first. [Security Architecture and Design]

33. A - In order to ensure that there is no undue effort and security around protecting non-essential information, the information should be de-classified in an orderly manner. [Security Operations]

34. A - IPv6 is the next generation of IP addressing and has a very large address space, addressing the limitations of IPv4 addressing. However, its implementation has been very slow because of interoperability issues. [Telecommunications and Network Security]

35. A - Cryptography does not provide nonrepudiation (or authenticity). It only provides confidentiality of a message between two users. [Cryptography]

36. B - If UTP cable is used, the maximum cable segment it can be used for is 185 meters. After this attenuation occurs. So, the network administrator will need to use a repeater or an amplifying device for lengths beyond 185 meters. This is likely to be the issue. [Telecommunications and Network Security]

37. B - It is highly unlikely that virtual memory on hard disk overwrites any good data on the hard disk. The virtual memory and page swapping process is tightly controlled. The other three scenarios listed are security issues associated with the use of virtual memory. [Security Architecture and Design]

38. C - SESAME is a European Research and Development project intended to address some of the limitations of Kerberos. It is an extension of Kerberos and components are accessible via Kerberos v5 protocol. The other choices are attributes of SESAME. [Access Control]

39. B - Information within the company can be classified as public, sensitive, confidential or private. In the case of such financial information related to a company's quarterly results, it would typically be classified as sensitive, prior to the declaration of results. [Information Security and Risk Management]

40. C - Security is always an important consideration in application development. It is the responsibility of software developers to focus on both application functionality as well as security of a program. [Software Development Security]

Domain Area Test: Legal, Regulations, Compliance and Investigations Practice Questions

Test Name:
Domain Area Test: Legal, Regulations, Compliance and Investigations
Total Questions: 15
Correct Answers Needed to Pass: 11 (73.33%)
Time Allowed: 25 Minutes

Test Description

This practice test specifically targets your knowledge of the Legal, Regulations, Compliance and Investigations domain area.

Test Questions

1. What criterion must evidence meet to be admissible in a court of law?

   A. It must be insufficient and intangible

   B. It must be relevant and reliable

   C. It must be indisputable and intangible

   D. It must be corroborative and conclusive

2. Which of the following is not an ethical fallacy?

   A. Survival of the fittest includes accidentally receiving an internal price list from a competitor.

   B. Hackers are only trying to learn and do not make a profit by entering in to private systems. They should not be penalized.

   C. One may encrypt personal information with AES to prevent information theft or tampering.

   D. The creation of computer viruses is an expression of free speech, and protected by the US Bill of Rights.

3. There are various types of evidence that can be used in a court of law. What type of evidence is considered incidental?

   A. Circumstantial

   B. Hearsay

   C. Real

   D. Opinion

4. There are various types of evidence that can be used in a court of law. What type of evidence cannot be used on its own, but may be

admissible to prove other, more substantial evidence?

A. Circumstantial evidence

B. Opinion evidence

C. Hearsay evidence

D. Corroborative evidence

5. Alice is the network security administrator for her company. She detects a real-time attack on a server containing valuable and private records. Which of the following should she do first?

    A. Backup the server

    B. Turn off the server

    C. Disconnect the server from the network

    D. Unplug the electrical connection to the server

6. When investigating business risks, a company exercises _____, but when the company does all it reasonably can to mitigate the risks, the company exercises _____.

    A. Due Care / Due Burden

    B. Due Diligence / Due Care

    C. Due Care / Due Diligence

    D. Due Burden / Due Care

7. A manufacturing design firm comes up with a revolutionary and cost-effective process to manufacture an item. A few weeks later a competitor comes up with the same process by using documents recovered from refuse. This type of industrial espionage is known as:

    A. Social Engineering

    B. Dumpster Diving

    C. Phreaking

    D. Black Boxing

8. Nancy is the Chief Information Officer of a bank. In order to deal with suspicious network, internet, and cyber events; she creates a team of experts. This team will be responsible for dealing with these events. She assigns personnel from the WAN group, LAN group, Systems, Network Security, and Development. What is such a team traditionally called?

    A. Cyber Access Team

    B. Issue Response Team

C. Standards Drafting Team

D. Incident Response Team

9. A company had to resort to a lawsuit against a former employee who, it claimed, had stolen a very confidential set of procedures and leaked it to a competitor after he was fired. In retrospect, how could they have prevented him from stealing the procedure?

A. By implementing separation of duties

B. By use of CCTV cameras

C. By asking the employee to sign a non-disclosure agreement.

D. By applying for a patent.

10. Which of the following information gathering techniques is generally regarded as legal (although questionable)?

A. Firewall Hacking

B. Phishing

C. Dumpster Diving

D. Social Engineering

11. Samuel is a US citizen. He creates a new application that is based upon an incredibly powerful, new, 512-bit encryption methodology. Where may he market such a product freely?

A. Within the US and Canada

B. World-wide

C. Within the US and 23 specific other countries

D. Within the US only

12. As part of proper collection of evidence, an attacked system must be properly handled. The correct sequence of steps would be to:

A. Isolate the system from the network, power down the system, take a memory dump and make a copy of the attacked system's disk drives.

B. Isolate the system from the network, take a memory dump, power down the system and make a copy of the attacked system's disk drives.

C. Power down the system, isolate the system from the network, make a copy of the attacked system's disk drives and take a memory dump.

D. Power down the system, isolate the system from the network, take a memory dump and make a copy of the attacked system's disk drives

13. A software product manufacturer wishes to protect a complex algorithm that he developed. What steps should he take to have complete control over who else uses the algorithm?

    A. He should trademark the algorithm.

    B. He should have every user of the product sign an End User Licensing Agreement (EULA).

    C. He should obtain a patent for the algorithm.

    D. He should file the algorithm as a trade secret.

14. What law protects company logos from illegal duplication?

    A. Trademark

    B. Patent

    C. Copyright

    D. Trade secret

15. A CISSP violates the (ISC)2 Code of Ethics for CISSPs. Another CISSP, who is his peer, reports this to (ISC)2. What is the next step that may happen?

    A. (ISC)2 will give the alleged violator a warning and inform him that the next occurrence could result in his losing his certification.

    B. (ISC)2 will subject the alleged violator to a peer review panel to determine whether he knowingly or unknowingly committed the violation.

    C. (ISC)2 will send the alleged violator an official communication informing him that his CISSP certification is invalidated.

    D. (ISC)2 will place the alleged violator's name on a black-list and inform him that his certification is no longer valid.

Domain Area Test:
Legal, Regulations, Compliance and Investigations
Answer Key and Explanations

1. B - All evidence placed before a court of law must have a significant bearing on a material fact. This data should be reliable and contribute to the proving or disproving of the disputed issue. [Legal, Regulations, Compliance and Investigations]

2. C - Encryption of personal data is the only choice listed that is not an ethical fallacy. [Legal, Regulations, Compliance and Investigations]

3. A - Circumstantial evidence is incidental evidence that may become significant only when considered along with other facts. [Legal, Regulations, Compliance and Investigations]

4. D - Corroborative evidence may support other evidence in order to prove a theory or idea. This type of evidence is not admissible on its own, but may supplement a more credible piece of evidence. [Legal, Regulations, Compliance and Investigations]

5. C - Disconnecting from the network is the best course of action. Anything that might interrupt the power to machine will destroy evidence in cache and RAM. A backup is useless once the damage is done. [Legal, Regulations, Compliance and Investigations]

6. B - Due Diligence involves investigating the company's weaknesses and vulnerabilities whereas due care refers to using reasonable business judgment to mitigate those possibilities. [Legal, Regulations, Compliance and Investigations]

7. B - Dumpster diving is the specific term used for this action. Social engineering was not used here. Phreaking is a type of telephone hacking to make free calls, and black boxing is a specific type of phreaking [Legal, Regulations, Compliance and Investigations]

8. D - Such a team is usually called the Incident Response Team. This team works with a set of procedures to be carried out in the event of actual or suspected incidents. [Legal, Regulations, Compliance and Investigations]

9. A - Implementation of separation of duties could have ensured that no single individual had access to all aspects of the sensitive procedure. The other choices do not prevent the ex-employee from possessing critical information that he leaked. [Legal, Regulations, Compliance and Investigations]

10. C - In many cases, such as California vs. Greenwood, it has been upheld in court that there is no expectation of privacy for discarded materials. [Legal, Regulations, Compliance and Investigations]

11. C - In October 2000, the US Department of Commerce named a list of 15 European Union countries and 8 additional US trading partner countries to which high-strength encryption algorithms could be exported. Export outside of these countries would be a violation of law. [Legal, Regulations, Compliance and Investigations]

12. B - The correct sequence of events would be to: Isolate the system from the network, take a memory dump, power down the system and make a copy of the attacked system's disk drives. Since primary memory is volatile, its contents will be lost if the system is powered down. Hence it has to be copied first. [Legal, Regulations, Compliance and Investigations]

13. C - The software product manufacturer should acquire a patent so that he has full control over the algorithm and who can use it in their products. This will be typically valid for a specific period of time. [Legal, Regulations, Compliance and Investigations]

14. A - Trademarks are a means of identifying and distinguishing a company's product or goods. A trademark can be a color, device, name, shape, sound, symbol, word, or a combination of these elements. A company's logo is an example of a trademark. [Legal, Regulations, Compliance and Investigations]

15. B - When a CISSP violates the (ISC)2 Code of Ethics, (ISC)2 will form a peer review panel to determine whether he knowingly violated the Code of Ethics. Subsequent actions are decided based on the recommendations of this panel. [Legal, Regulations, Compliance and Investigations]

CISSP Mock Exam (LITE) - 11
Practice Questions

Test Name:
CISSP Mock Exam (LITE) - 11
Total Questions: 40
Correct Answers Needed to Pass:
30 (0.00%)
Time Allowed: 60 Minutes

Test Description

This is a cumulative CISSP Mock Exam which can be used as a benchmark for your CISSP aptitude. This practice test includes questions from all ten domains of the CISSP CBK.

Test Questions

1. All users in a system have security clearance to access the information in the system but do not necessarily have a need to know all the information processed in the system. This is typical of:

   A. System High-Security Mode

   B. Compartmented Security Mode

   C. Multi-level Security Mode.

   D. Dedicated Security Mode

2. An organization is located in the US. In which of the following situations is the organization better suited to handle a disaster and ensure continuity of operations?

   A. Multiple offices located in different parts of the US.

   B. Multiple buildings on the same campus

   C. Multiple offices in the same city.

   D. Multiple floors in the same building.

3. An operating system is designed such that it can handle requests from several different processes loaded into memory concurrently. This type of operation is called:

   A. Multitasking

   B. Multiprocessing

   C. Multithreading

   D. Multiprogramming

4. If data hiding is a key feature that you are looking for in an operating system, what type of operating system should you look for?

   A. Multiprocessing operating systems

   B. Flat operating systems

C. Monolithic operating system

D. Layered operating system

5. Sally is heading a risk assessment team for her company. She is looking at the various methodologies that she can choose from. Which of the following will not be part of her list of choices?

A. PRISM

B. NIST SP 800-30

C. CRAMM

D. OCTAVE

6. A disaster struck a company but the company was effectively prepared and put its disaster recovery plan into place and moved to a backup site. The original facility was destroyed and had to be rebuilt over a period of 3 months. Which of the following functions should be moved first to new facility?

A. The most critical function

B. The least critical function

C. Move all functions simultaneously

D. None. Operate out of the backup location for at least 1 year before moving.

7. The biggest disadvantage of Pretty Good Privacy (PGP) is:

A. Standardized functionality is not easy to accomplish. For example, if a user were to lose his private key, he needs to inform everyone else trusting his public key that his private key can no longer be trusted.

B. It is a proprietary software, very expensive and is not as popular as some other options available.

C. Once a user is fixed at a certain trust level, it can never be changed. This causes a hierarchy of trust and becomes unmanageable.

D. It has a central leader and all changes need to pass through this central leader. This makes it cumbersome to handle changes.

8. A user wishes to inappropriately access an object to which he has no access. He does this by accessing another program to which he has access, which in turn has access to the object, and manages to get at some confidential data. This kind of a situation can be avoided by:

A. One-way access rule

B. Control of environment

C. Adequate granularity of controls.

D. Separation of duties

9. Which of the following is a type of urban camouflage that makes it difficult for attackers to target a company?

A. Use of padlocks

B. Limited or no use of flood lights

C. Small or no logo on building

D. Use of fake signboards

10. As a vendor, you need to provide periodic patches or updates to a product. Your customers would like to be sure that they are downloading the patches from the legitimate site. Further, they would like to ensure that the integrity of the download has not been compromised. An effective way to do this is through the use of:

A. Symmetric cryptography

B. Digital signatures.

C. Asymmetric cryptography

D. PGP

11. An administrator found that there were numerous telnet calls to computers on the network and wanted to ensure that this was turned off. Which port needs to be disabled to prevent telnet connections?

A. Port 23

B. Port 21

C. Port 25

D. Port 80

12. You are assigned the responsibility of performing a risk analysis to ensure that security is properly addressed in your organization. The first step would be to:

A. Perform asset valuation

B. Prepare a cost/benefit comparison.

C. Carry out project sizing

D. Prepare a contingency plan

13. A programmer wrote poor code that resulted in multiple tuples (rows) in a database having the same primary

key value. What kind of integrity does this violate?

A. Semantic integrity

B. Program integrity

C. Referential integrity

D. Entity integrity

14. As part of an application development project, the project did an analysis related to the risk of the project failing. This would be termed as:

A. Security risk analysis

B. Project risk analysis

C. Project success analysis

D. Application failure analysis

15. Which of the following Wide Area Network (WAN) technologies avoids the problem of using a CAT-3 cable?

A. ADSL

B. Cable modem

C. RADSL

D. PSTN

16. Redundancy planned for a system required data storage in excess of five hundred terabytes and mostly needed to carry out a write operation. An effective option in this case would be to use:

A. SAN

B. MAID

C. RAIT

D. RAID

17. Virtual memory usually refers to the hard-disk being used as swap space. This is typically the slowest of the types of memories used. Which one is the fastest?

A. Secondary memory

B. Cache memory

C. RAM

D. Main memory

18. A redundancy option using only hard disks proves very expensive, while use of tapes makes it a very slow option. Which of the following provides an effective solution combining the two technologies?

A. Redundant Array of Independent Tapes (RAIT)

B. Random Storage Management (RSM)

C. Hierarchical Storage Management (HSM)

D. Direct Access Tape Storage (DATS)

19. Jon is an administrative assistant in the corporate department of a company. His role involves printing out company reports. What sort of access rights should Jon be given to the LAN server where the files reside?

A. Execute privileges

B. Write privileges

C. Read, write and execute privileges

D. Read privileges

20. In order to achieve a Recover Time Objective (RTO) of zero or near-zero, what sort of a backup site should be planned?

A. Cold site

B. Reciprocal arrangement

C. Hot site

D. Warm site

21. Which of the following will be a very important consideration for the management team of a company that is currently doing business continuity and disaster recovery planning for its operations?

A. Cost/Benefit analysis

B. Regulatory issues

C. Minimizing cost

D. Legal issues

22. You receive an emergency call that a server has been compromised. What is the first step that you would advise to be done?

A. Power down the server

B. Isolate the server from the network

C. Backup the data on the server

D. Re-install the data on the server from the most recent backup.

23. A security professional has shortlisted various options for access control. Which of these has a high degree of security, is tamper-

resistant, and can store personal information?

A. Smart cards

B. Retinal scanners

C. Iris scanners

D. RSA cards

24. The risk analysis team has come up with a set of findings and identified certain threats. The information security team puts up a contingency plan in place so that the company can continue to function if that threat takes place. This would be termed as:

A. Risk acceptance

B. Risk reduction

C. Risk mitigation

D. Risk transfer

25. When IPSec is used in transport mode, what is the only part of the message that is encrypted?

A. Authentication Header

B. Routing Header

C. Symmetric Public Payload

D. Payload

26. An initialization vector is used as the initializing input algorithm to encrypt a cleartext sequence. The initialization vector would be considered as:

A. Non-secret

B. Non-secret but private

C. Secret

D. Secret, but known between the two communicating parties.

27. For the highest level of protection using IPSec, which mode would you use?

A. Secure mode

B. Tunnel mode

C. Transport mode

D. Network mode

28. While setting up security measures and controls, what should be the level of transparency of these measures to users?

A. Security controls and measures should not be transparent. The users should be completely aware of their existence.

B. Security controls and measures should be completely transparent. The users should not be aware of their existence.

C. Security controls and measures should be transparent only to a degree. The users should be aware of their existence.

D. Security controls and measures should be completely transparent but the users should be aware of their existence.

29. Network systems personnel in a company notice that the system performance has degraded considerably. They attribute this to cross-talk. Which of the following cabling would be the first suspect?

A. Shielded cables

B. UTP cables

C. Co-axial cables

D. Optic fiber cables

30. A network may come under denial-of-service attack and get overloaded due to the excessive traffic generated. Which of these following

options will not work as a countermeasure against such attacks?

A. Shifting of IP address by the target.

B. Load balancing

C. Redundant network

D. Installation of a DMZ

31. Testing out a business continuity/disaster recovery plan is a very important aspect of the planning. What kind of testing should be carried out to verify that the alternate facility actually works, without impacting current operations?

A. Walk-through testing

B. Full-Interruption testing

C. Simulation testing

D. Parallel testing

32. Which protocol relies on a "web of trust" for its key management approach instead of a hierarchy of certificate authorities?

A. SSL

B. PGP

C. RSA

D. Deffie-Hellman

33. A wireless network can be a vulnerability and allow unauthorized users to access a company's networks. What should be the first point of defense/action in preventing unauthorized users from getting into the network?

A. Strong perimeter security

B. The access point's signal should be hidden.

C. Weak signal strength

D. Authentication

34. The landscaping of a company's premises often includes furnishings such as benches and tables placed outdoors. What is the purpose of these furnishings?

A. Such furnishings encourage people to 'lounge' and watch what is going on around them. This deters criminal activity.

B. Such furnishings can be used to install concealed cameras. This deters criminal activity.

C. This is usually a HR program that allows employees to take a

break from work in a secure setting.

D. It is mandated by city laws that all companies need to provide for such furnishings.

35. Collusion is a threat in which two people within an organization work together to defraud the company. Which of the following controls will be ineffective against such a threat?

A. Use of confidentiality agreements

B. Rotation of duties

C. Supervision

D. Pre-employment background checks

36. One of the protective mechanisms implemented by CPUs is use of different execution modes. By doing so, the operating system can ensure that certain types of instructions may not be executed in a lower execution mode. Which of the following would typically operate in the lowest execution mode?

A. Kernel mode

B. User mode

C. Supervisor mode

D. Privileged mode

37. Which of the following techniques would you not consider while performing qualitative risk analysis?

    A. Checklists

    B. Surveys

    C. Cost / benefit analysis

    D. Delphi technique

38. An IDS software was not properly configured. As a result, the IDS continually identified many activities as suspicious and the workload became unmanageable for the administrator. What can be done to manage this situation better?

    A. The administrator should set a clipping level. The IDS should raise alerts only if the clipping level is crossed.

    B. The administrator should set a beeping level. The IDS should raise alerts only if the beeping level is crossed.

    C. The administrator should set a lower level. The IDS should raise alerts only if the lower level is crossed.

    D. The administrator should set a tripping level. The IDS should raise alerts only if the tripping level is crossed.

39. Which of the following determines whether a strong encryption method should be used?

    A. The sensitivity of the data being encrypted.

    B. The algorithm

    C. The length of the key

    D. The initialization vectors

40. A risk assessment team has just performed quantitative risk analysis on the assets of a company. The team found that the annualized rate of occurrence (ARO) values were 0.01, 0.1, 0.99 and 1.01 respectively for four of the assets. To which of these assets should the company give the highest priority?

    A. The data provided is insufficient to determine which asset is the highest priority.

    B. The asset with the ARO of 1.01

    C. The asset with the ARO of 0.01

    D. The asset with the ARO of 0.99

CISSP Mock Exam (LITE) - 11
Answer Key and Explanations

1. A - This is typical of System High-Security Mode. This mode requires all users to have a very high level of clearance since they can access all data on the system. [Security Architecture and Design]

2. A - From a disaster recovery angle, the best option is to have multiple offices in different parts of the US. This addresses the issue of business availability, and it is easier to service customers. Having multiple floors in the same building, or using a different building on the same campus, or another office in the same city has the risk that they may also be struck by the same disaster. [Business Continuity and Disaster Recovery Planning]

3. A - If an operating system is able to handle requests from different processes that are loaded in memory, it is referred to as multitasking. [Security Architecture and Design]

4. D - Data hiding is achieved in layered operating systems where the instructions and data at various layers do not have direct access to instructions and data of other layers. [Security Architecture and Design]

5. A - All the choices listed are valid risk assessment methodologies

except PRISM. [Information Security and Risk Management]

6. B - It is preferred that the least critical function be moved into the rebuilt facility first. Any problems in configurations, setup, network connectivity can be thoroughly investigated first, before moving in the critical functions. [Business Continuity and Disaster Recovery Planning]

7. A - The biggest disadvantage of PGP is that standardized functionality is difficult to achieve. For example, if a user were to lose his private key, he needs to inform everyone else trusting his public key that his private key can no longer be trusted. [Cryptography]

8. C - Such access control issues can be addressed by introducing adequate granularity of controls. These will then address both the program and the user and their access requirements. [Software Development Security]

9. C - Using a very small logo or no identification at all on a building serves as a type of urban camouflage. This makes it harder for attackers to target a building. The other options do not necessarily provide any camouflage. Use of fake signboards may be prohibited by law. [Physical (Environmental) Security]

10. B - Digital signatures are used for this purpose and can be used to ensure both integrity of a download and legitimacy of the site from which it was downloaded. [Cryptography]

11. A - The Telnet port is 23 and can be disabled to prevent telnet sessions from being established. The other ports given represent the following protocols: SMTP - 25, HTTP - 80, and FTP -21. [Telecommunications and Network Security]

12. C - The first step in carrying out a risk analysis would be to carry out a project sizing. This is a very essential step and can mean the difference between project success and failure. It helps understand what assets and threats should be looked at and evaluated. If this step is not done properly, the project could end being budgeted wrongly. It may appear that the first step is to prepare a cost/benefit comparison, but that is a later step. [Information Security and Risk Management]

13. D - This violates entity integrity which necessitates that no two rows or tuples in a database table can have the same primary key values. [Software Development Security]

14. B - This is an instance of project risk analysis. This is different from security risk analysis which is more concerned with risks and consequences that a customer may face when using a particular product being developed. [Software Development Security]

15. B - A CAT-3 cable is a copper cable that connects phones to a central office (CO). PSTN, RADSL and ADSL technologies ride on the copper cable to connect to a network. The cable modem based network uses a different technology. [Telecommunications and Network Security]

16. B - A Massive array of inactive disks (MAID) suits this requirement. A MAID is especially suited for a requirement that involves write operations for the most part and has storage requirement in excess of hundreds of terabytes. [Security Operations]

17. B - Among the choices listed, cache memory is the fastest in operation. Cache memory is very fast and is the place where information needed by a processor can quickly be retrieved. The memory manager component of an operating system manages the memory and ensures proper access control so that processes are able to only access memory that they have access privileges to. [Security Architecture and Design]

18. C - Hierarchical Storage Management (HSM) is a technology which combines expensive hard drives and slower tape drives in a

very effective manner and provides a cost-effective solution. [Security Operations]

19. D - Jon should be given Read privileges to the files. This will ensure that Jon cannot alter the files in any way or obtain a copy of it. If Jon is given write / update access, then he could maliciously or inadvertently alter/delete the files. This is in line with the least-privilege principle of access control. [Access Control]

20. C - An RTO of near zero means that the company should be able to shift operations very quickly and start at the new site. This can be achieved by using a hot site. [Business Continuity and Disaster Recovery Planning]

21. A - Management is primarily concerned with looking at Cost/Benefit considerations and would like to ensure that the expenditure on business continuity and disaster recovery activities is a trade-off. On legal and regulatory issues, the company will not have much choice but to comply with them. [Business Continuity and Disaster Recovery Planning]

22. B - The first step is to take the server offline and isolate it from the network. The next steps should be to preserve the evidence. [Legal, Regulations, Compliance and Investigations]

23. A - The correct response is smart cards. They have a high degree of security, are tamper-resistant, and can store personal information very effectively because of a microprocessor and integrated chip embedded in the card. [Access Control]

24. B - This would be termed as risk reduction. A contingency plan will reduce damages if a threat actually takes place. [Information Security and Risk Management]

25. D - When IPSec is used in transport mode, only the payload portion of the message is encrypted. [Cryptography]

26. A - The initialization vector is usually non-secret and increases security by introducing additional cryptographic variances. [Cryptography]

27. B - IPSec works in either tunnel mode or transport mode. Tunnel mode is very secure since the payload along with routing/header information are all protected by encryption. An attacker will be unable to view any of the information. [Cryptography]

28. C - Security controls and measures should be transparent to a certain degree. The users should be aware of their existence but should not know the complete details. This will prevent them from working out a strategy to counter the controls. [Security Operations]

29. B - UTP cabling is very vulnerable to cross-talk. This is because it lacks the extra layers of shielding that the other cables have. Hence any electrical impulses being transmitted through UTP can interfere with those being transmitted in adjacent cables. This will result in degraded performance. [Telecommunications and Network Security]

30. D - A DMZ will prevent inbound connections if the firewall is properly setup. However, it cannot counter against denial-of-service attacks which strikes at network availability by generating excessive traffic. [Telecommunications and Network Security]

31. D - A parallel test should be carried out to verify that the alternate facility actually works, without impacting current operations. This can be followed by appropriate tweaking or adjustments to the alternate site and processes. [Business Continuity and Disaster Recovery Planning]

32. B - PGP is used as an e-mail security program and relies on a "web of trust" for its key management approach instead of certificate authorities. Users will generate and distribute their own public keys and they will sign each other's public keys

to determine who will trust each other. With a certificate authority hierarchy, no one trusts each other. They only trust the CA. [Cryptography]

33. D - The first strong defense employed by a company against unauthorized people getting in through a wireless network is authentication. The other options are not solutions to address the vulnerability of wireless networks. [Telecommunications and Network Security]

34. A - Such furnishings encourage people to 'lounge' and watch what is going on around them. This puts off criminals since they feel their actions are likely to be watched. [Physical (Environmental) Security]

35. A - Use of confidentiality agreements may not deter employees from colluding. All the other controls mentioned will help prevent collusion. [Physical (Environmental) Security]

36. B - User mode typically would have the least privileges and operate in the lowest execution mode. Operating systems are designed such that they execute user programs in a lower privileged mode, ensuring that some of the CPU's instructions are not available to the application. [Security Architecture and Design]

37. C - Cost/benefit analysis is a quantitative technique and would not be considered while performing qualitative risk analysis. [Information Security and Risk Management]

38. A - The baseline level which an administrator sets up is called the clipping level. The administrator can set this up on the IDS such that the IDS will notify the administrator of any detections beyond the threshold of the clipping level. [Security Operations]

39. A - Selection of a strong encryption method will be influenced by the nature of the data. Hence, a stronger method will be used for very sensitive data. [Cryptography]

40. A - The annualized rate of occurrence (ARO) is a number that represents the frequency with which a particular threat will occur in a given year's time-frame. Knowing the ARO values for a set of assets is not sufficient to determine which asset is to be given priority. The single loss expectancy (SLE) is required to arrive at the annualized loss expectancy (ALE). This can then drive the company's priorities. [Information Security and Risk Management]

CISSP Mock Exam (LITE) - 12 Practice Questions

Test Name:
CISSP Mock Exam (LITE) - 12
Total Questions: 40
Correct Answers Needed to Pass:
30 (75.00%)
Time Allowed: 60 Minutes

Test Description

This is a cumulative CISSP Mock Exam which can be used as a benchmark for your CISSP aptitude. This practice test includes questions from all ten domains of the CISSP CBK.

Test Questions

1. A bank's online banking software is a product from an established product vendor. The bank has a requirement of high availability for the online system and it is extremely concerned that a crisis may arise in case the product vendor is unable to support it (the bank). What is a possible solution to this?

   A. Use of a software escrow service so that the bank can get access to the source code in case of any issues with the product vendor.

   B. The bank should purchase the source code from the product vendor with a right to only make changes within their systems.

   C. The bank should identify an alternative vendor and come out with a backup implementation plan in case of such a situation.

   D. This is an unnecessary concern for the bank. The bank should sign an agreement with the product vendor and include a clause which states that they can have access to the source code if required in an emergency.

2. As part of an intensive anti-piracy drive, a company puts up a web-page on the internet. This web-page contains a link to a second webpage which promises them an illegal copy of the software, but in reality doesn't lead anywhere. The company intends to prosecute all those who clicked the link on the first page. Your view on this would be:

   A. Software downloads on the internet are protected by Internet laws.

   B. The company has a strong case and can prosecute under anti-piracy laws.

   C. The company will not have a case. Clicking on the link does not prove a crime was committed.

D. The company has a strong case of successful entrapment.

3. A company had a competitive edge by virtue of some of its business processes. This information leaked out into public domain and a number of its competitors started using similar processes. The company went to court to prevent its competitors from doing so. What would your comment be?

A. The company has a strong case. Copyright laws would prevent other companies from using the business processes in their companies.

B. The company has a strong case. The business processes can be considered as trademarks and the company can go to court to prevent other companies from using the business processes in their companies.

C. The company does not have a valid stance. Trade secrets are protected as long as the owner of the information (ex: business processes) takes steps to keep it secret. If it is leaked out into public domain, other companies cannot be prevented from using the information.

D. The company's case is quite weak. This type of information comes under the category of patents which grants ownership and exclusive rights to the owner to use the processes.

4. A company placed certain sensitive data on a server that was accessible to all employees. The company clearly informed its employees that the files were confidential. If an employee copies the files onto a USB flash drive and uses it outside the company, what would the company's position be?

A. The company is appropriately covered since the information was stored on its property.

B. The company will not be covered under criminal laws since this is a matter internal to the company.

C. The company will not be properly covered by criminal laws since it did not practice due care.

D. The company is covered properly under criminal laws since it informed its employees that the files were confidential.

5. A company was hesitant to bring in law-enforcement agencies after a security breach at the company and

after much deliberation, decided not to do so. Which of these would NOT have been a major factor in the company's decision?

A. The company was worried that it would lose control over the investigation if the authorities were brought in.

B. The company was worried that it would take three years to go to court with the case.

C. The company was worried that knowledge of the breach would become public and tarnish its reputation.

D. The company was worried about reactions of its shareholders and customers.

6. The risk analysis team is evaluating the functionality and effectiveness of countermeasures that they propose to apply. Which of the following characteristics is undesirable for a countermeasure?

A. Resetting the asset to its original settings should be as difficult as possible and the countermeasure mechanism should not permit easy resetting.

B. The countermeasure should not provide any backdoors or covert channels.

C. An administrator should have override facility over the countermeasure, if necessary.

D. Users should have as few permissions as possible to configure or disable the protection mechanism of the countermeasure.

7. A user was unauthorizedly able to access certain information. The audit logs revealed that the data had been accessed, but was unable to provide details of who accessed them. This turned out to be due to poor application programming of the in-house developed application (which did not capture details of the user who accessed the data, in the audit log). Who would hold the bottom-line responsibility for this situation?

A. Software quality control

B. The data owner

C. The application programmer

D. The security administrator.

8. An employee notices that the photograph on the ID card worn by a contractor on the campus does not match his appearance. The ID seems to be valid and has the company logo

and other details clearly listed. What should the employee do?

A. The employee should check with other people in the vicinity if they are aware of who the person is and whether his ID is valid.

B. Nothing needs to be done in this case. As long the other individual has a valid ID card, it is sufficient. It is possible that the individual's appearance has changed since the time the photograph was taken.

C. The employee should make a note of details such as the location of the individual, and inform security immediately.

D. Nothing needs to be done. It is the responsibility of the security department to detect such cases.

9. A software vendor discovered that a company was using illegal copies of its software. An employee had copied the installation disks and installed the software on the company's server. Who would be held primarily responsible for this?

A. The employee who copied the software.

B. The security officer in charge.

C. The legal department of the company.

D. The manager of the employee who copied the software.

10. A Trusted Computing Base (TCB) addresses the level of trust that a system provides. What components does it address?

A. The firmware

B. The hardware

C. The software

D. The hardware, software and firmware

11. Asset management will typically not include details on:

A. The firmware used in the company.

B. The number of users in the company

C. The software used in the company.

D. The hardware used in the company.

12. As part of a cost-saving initiative, the security and network team decided to

handle all security awareness and specialized security training in-house. Management questioned the team on whether paid outside training was required but the security officer indicated that she was comfortable with doing the training in-house itself. A month later, a breach occurred and some important information was stolen. Who is likely to be held responsible for this?

A. The in-house trainer

B. Management

C. The security officer

D. The network department

13. Multiple vendors have developed their own networking frameworks. How do they ensure that layers within their frameworks are interoperable with those developed by other vendors?

A. By using network modulators

B. By implementing polymorphism of the layers

C. By modularization of the network layers

D. By using a common voltage level

14. Data backup is a crucial activity in organizations. Which of the following teams should define what data gets backed up and how often?

A. The legal team

B. The management team

C. The security team

D. The operations team

15. Lin would like to use a hybrid encryption method using both symmetric and asymmetric encryption methods. How would he go about this?

A. The message sent would be encrypted using a public key and the key used would be encrypted using a symmetric algorithm.

B. The message sent and the key would be encrypted using a symmetric algorithm and the receiver would decrypt this using his private key.

C. The message sent would be encrypted using a symmetric algorithm and the key used would be sent using an asymmetric encryption.

D. The message sent would be encrypted using an asymmetric algorithm and the key used would be sent using a symmetric encryption.

16. A software company provides software services to financial companies and also has a product division that has a financial product in the market. Employees working on services for other financial companies could potentially be working on products that compete in the market with the company's own product. This type of conflict of interest is well-handled by:

A. The Noninterference model

B. The Brewer and Nash model

C. The Graham and Denning model

D. The Lattice model

17. An administrator discovered that there were certain default system accounts in an application. It was not clear what they were used for. What is the best way to handle this?

A. The security administrator should send out an email with the list of the accounts to all senior managers to find out who uses them.

B. The best way is to leave the accounts since they will be required by users.

C. The security administrator should wait for a minimum of 30 days before deciding to disable the accounts.

D. The best way is to disable these accounts first and then determine who uses them, if at all.

18. Robert is a systems engineer and was called in to preserve certain evidence in a cyber-attack on the company. Robert isolated the hard disk but inadvertently made some changes to the hard disk. This seriously compromised the company's case. Who is responsible for actions taken with digital evidence?

A. The security officer

B. The company

C. The supervisor of the individual handling digital evidence.

D. The individual handling the digital evidence (Robert)

19. An organization opts for disk shadowing to provide a fault-tolerant solution. Which of the following is incorrect with regard to a disk shadowing solution?

A. Disk shadowing is a very expensive solution.

B. The company will need to perform periodic offline manual backup of the data.

C. The shadow set can carry out multiple reads in parallel.

D. Multiple paths are provided to duplicate data

20. One of the biggest challenges in successfully taking a cyber-criminal to court is:

A. Current technology is still not advanced enough to properly seize and control evidence of such crimes.

B. There are not enough security devices available to prevent a cyber-crime.

C. There are an insufficient number of lawyers to handle such cases.

D. Companies are unwilling to come forward with evidence.

21. A team that is doing risk analysis pegs the exposure factor (EF) of a large storage warehouse at 10%. How would this be interpreted?

A. This means that 10% of the warehouse would be specially protected with fire controls and other means to protect the goods in that area.

B. This means that if a fire or untoward incident were to occur, only 10% of the warehouse is expected to be lost.

C. This means that items which are the highest in value would be stored in a space that occupies no more than 10% of the warehouse.

D. This means that if a fire or untoward incident were to occur, only 10% of the warehouse is expected to be saved.

22. An attacker took advantage of a vulnerability in an application system. Once a process validated the authorization of a user for a noncritical file, the attacker substituted the noncritical file with a critical one and managed to obtain access to it because the file access was carried out by a second process. What type of attack is this?

A. Time of check / Time of use attack

B. Time of authorization / Time of access attack

C. Time of use / Time of check attack

D. Time of validation / Time of Input-output attack

23. A company plans to step-up its monitoring activities and decides to implement a CCTV monitoring system. The best way to install the CCTV cameras is:

A. To install them within fittings for lighting.

B. To discretely mount them behind other fittings

C. To completely conceal them.

D. To mount them In full view

24. When dealing with physical safety, to what should a company give the highest priority?

A. To have a proper procedure in place to deal with crimes if and when they occur.

B. Installation of CCTV cameras

C. To prevent the occurrence of crimes.

D. To prevent crimes and disruptions to the company's operations, but also plan to deal with them if and when they occur.

25. A very poorly written application makes periodic calls to the operating system to allocate memory, and does not release the memory. The result is that the operating system often gets starved for memory and even crashes. What is a solution to this?

A. To use a trash collector

B. To use a garbage collector

C. To use a disk cleaner

D. To use a memory manager

26. A hacker uses a new signature pattern to launch an attack. Which of these intrusion detection systems will be unable to detect this attack?

A. Pattern matching IDS

B. Protocol anomaly-based IDS

C. Traffic anomaly-based IDS

D. Statistical anomaly-based IDS

27. A Local Area Network (LAN) needs to be designed to be resilient and impervious to failures of single nodes. Which of the following topologies would you recommend?

A. Tree topology

B. Ring topology

C. Star topology

D. Linear bus topology

28. You are implementing an Intrusion Detection System (IDS). Which of these problems would you expect to run into often?

    A. False-negatives

    B. False-positives

    C. True-positives

    D. True-negatives

29. A number of changes were made to an application system. What kind of testing now needs to be done to ensure that the functionality and existing security has not been compromised?

    A. Acceptance testing

    B. Unit testing

    C. Regression testing

    D. Integration testing

30. The Information Technology Security Evaluation Criteria (ITSEC) is a single standard for evaluating security attributes of computer systems. It is primarily used in which regions?

    A. United States and Europe

    B. United States Only

    C. Europe Only

    D. United States and Canada

31. You are involved in the selection of material for windows in a facility. You are aware that there have been a number of burglaries in the area and would like to prevent would-be thieves from breaking windows and getting into the facility. If cost is not an issue, what material should you choose?

    A. Standard glass

    B. Laminated glass

    C. Untempered glass

    D. White glass

32. Stateful firewalls provide an additional level of protection. However, they are also vulnerable to some attacks. Which of these is a possible attack on a stateful firewall?

    A. Denial of Service (DOS) attack.

B. Phishing attack

C. URL service attack

D. Phreaker attack

33. In a symmetric key cryptographic system for a fax software, one of the users also sent the cryptographic key via a fax message. What would you comment on this?

   A. Use of a fax is unreliable since the maximum speed of transmission is 56.4 kbps.

   B. Use of the fax will ensure that the cryptographic key is not available to anyone else but the recipient.

   C. Usually, a fax does not need to be encrypted since it is targeted at an individual machine and is safe by definition.

   D. The cryptographic key should have been sent using an out-of-band transmission method.

34. Which of these is a preferred security practice in handling accounts?

   A. Assigning of individual accounts to groups

   B. Use of group IDs for better accountability

   C. Use of group accounts for better accountability

   D. Use of shared accounts for common responsibilities.

35. A key security concern in an organization is that unattended laptops on the desks of employees may be stolen. What can the company do as a preventive measure?

   A. Use slot locks.

   B. Use cable traps.

   C. Use port locks.

   D. Use switch controls

36. A security officer receives complaints that hardware in the company such as disk drives, I/O devices and memory are periodically being stolen. What preventive measures can he take?

   A. Use device locks to protect hardware.

   B. Provide stiff penalties including removal from service for employees caught in the act.

   C. Install CCTV cameras to cover all workstations.

D. User circumventing locks to protect hardware.

37. A systems analyst is designing a new application which should have restricted access. Which of the following would be best suited for the application?

    A. Multi-factor authentication

    B. Anonymous authentication

    C. UserID/Password based authentication.

    D. Shared Secret authentication

38. As part of its final report, a team assigned monetary values to assets. This is likely to have been the output of:

    A. Vulnerability analysis

    B. Threat analysis

    C. Risk analysis

    D. Asset analysis

39. An eavesdropper finds out the algorithm being used between two people for their encrypted communication. What will be the result if he now manages to capture a message between the two encrypted using that algorithm?

    A. When an eavesdropper intercepts a message, the communication will get terminated. The communication software will recognize that the message was intercepted and initiate this action.

    B. The message is in encrypted format, so he would unable to decipher its contents.

    C. The eavesdropper knows the algorithm used and can now decipher the message even though it is encrypted.

    D. It is not possible for the eavesdropper to capture the information.

40. Samantha works for an accounting firm with the responsibility of traveling to client sites to assist in SOX compliance checking. Which of the following accurately describes this work?

    A. External Audit

    B. Blackbox Penetration Testing

    C. Internal Audit

    D. Whitebox Penetration Testing

CISSP Mock Exam (LITE) - 12
Answer Key and Explanations

1. A - In such an instance where the operations of the bank are very critical, the bank can look at using the services of third party software escrow services. Various clauses are clearly defined and can come into effect if the product company is unable to service the bank for any reason. [Business Continuity and Disaster Recovery Planning]

2. C - The company does not have a strong case. Merely clicking on the link that promised illegal software does not prove that a crime was committed. [Legal, Regulations, Compliance and Investigations]

3. C - The company does not have a strong position. This type of information is considered as a trade secret since it gives the company a competitive edge over others. Trade secrets are protected as long as the owner of the information (ex: business processes) takes steps to keep it secret. If it is leaked out into public domain, other companies cannot be prevented from using the information. [Legal, Regulations, Compliance and Investigations]

4. C - Although the company informed its employees that the information was confidential, it did not practice due care in ensuring that the server was accessible only to those who required access. Hence, it may not be properly covered under criminal law. [Legal, Regulations, Compliance and Investigations]

5. B - One of the considerations that a company will be concerned about is the duration it takes to go to court. However, the figure indicated (three years) is on the higher side. Typically a company should be able to go to court within a year's time. Hence this would not have been a likely consideration. [Legal, Regulations, Compliance and Investigations]

6. A - The countermeasure should be such that it can be easily reset and restored to original settings without affecting the asset it is protecting. [Information Security and Risk Management]

7. D - The security administrator has the bottom-line responsibility for this. During the application development phase, the security administrator should have been involved in the process and laid out the requirements for the audit log files. This should have also been captured during testing. A failure in this process will be the security administrator's responsibility. [Security Operations]

8. C - All such incidents need to be brought to the notice of security personnel as soon as possible. There

could be valid reasons for the photograph looking different. However, the primary purpose of an ID is to authenticate an individual, so it is important to have a recent photograph if the individual's appearance has changed. [Security Operations]

9. B - It is usually the responsibility of the security officer in-charge to ensure that only legal copies of software are used within the company. There need to be appropriate procedures in place to control the copies of software installed on various machines in the company, and the security officer is held responsible for this. [Legal, Regulations, Compliance and Investigations]

10. D - The TCB all three components of hardware, firmware and software because each has the ability to impact a computer's environment positively or negatively. [Security Architecture and Design]

11. B - Asset management typically does not include details of how many users are there in the company. It focuses on hardware, software, firmware, application software and software libraries. [Security Operations]

12. B - Management is responsible. Although it may have been the ineffectiveness of training that lead

to poor patch deployment, it is always management who is held responsible for security breaches. [Information Security and Risk Management]

13. C - The modularization of layers enables the functionality within a layer to be interoperable with protocols developed by other vendors. [Telecommunications and Network Security]

14. D - It is the responsibility of the operations team to define what data gets backed up and the periodicity of the backup. [Business Continuity and Disaster Recovery Planning]

15. C - Symmetric algorithms are very fast but the keys are difficult to manage. On the other hand, asymmetric algorithms are slow but key management is easier. A hybrid approach is one in which the message is encrypted using a symmetric algorithm. The symmetric key is then encrypted using an asymmetric algorithm and sent to the recipient. [Cryptography]

16. B - This type of conflict of interest is handled well by the Brewer and Nash model. The software company could implement a product that tracks its employees' activities and ensures that certain types of accesses would be disallowed due to conflicts of interest. [Security Architecture and Design]

17. D - Typically, systems will contain a number of default system accounts and these could turn out to be security loop-holes. If it is not possible to determine who or what system accounts are used for, they should be disabled first. Re-enabling them can be a decision based on subsequent information obtained. [Security Operations]

18. D - According to general principles for handling evidence involving computer crimes, the individual handling digital evidence is responsible for it as long it is in his possession. [Legal, Regulations, Compliance and Investigations]

19. B - Disk shadowing is a very effective, expensive option. However, if it is employed, the company can likely dispense with its offline manual backup operations or perform it in a very reduced manner. [Business Continuity and Disaster Recovery Planning]

20. A - Currently, the biggest hurdle in bringing cyber-criminals to book is the lack of technology to seize and control evidence of such crimes. The courts of law require conclusive evidence and it is still a difficult to task to obtain evidence that can hold up to a court of law. [Legal, Regulations, Compliance and Investigations]

21. B - The exposure factor (EF) is the percentage of loss that a threat (which actually occurs) could have on a certain asset. Hence an EF of 10% means that it is expected that not more than 10% of the warehouse is expected to be lost due to a fire or other incident. [Information Security and Risk Management]

22. A - This is called a time of check / time of use (TOC/TOU) attack. This can happen due to poor coding of an application which permits process 2 to access a critical file even though process 1 authenticated the user for a non-critical file at a different time. [Security Architecture and Design]

23. D - The recommended way to mount CCTV cameras is to mount them in full view. This will act as a deterrent to criminals by announcing that the environment is being monitored. In addition, there should be prominent displays indicating that the system / facility is under surveillance. [Physical (Environmental) Security]

24. D - When dealing with physical safety, a company should give the highest priority not only to the prevention of crimes and disruptions to business, but also to procedures to properly deal with them when they occur. [Physical (Environmental) Security]

25. B - A garbage collector can be used to help alleviate the problem. This is a special software which runs an algorithm to identify unused memory allocated to application programs. The program then informs the operating system that the memory is now available for reuse. [Security Architecture and Design]

26. A - A pattern matching IDS is a signature based IDS and has thousands of signatures that are compared to traffic streams. If an attacker uses a new signature, the pattern matching based IDS will not be able to detect the attack. [Access Control]

27. C - Both ring and bus topologies (tree/linear bus) suffer from the disadvantage that there are single points of failure which can cause the entire network to fail. The Star topology is more resilient. [Telecommunications and Network Security]

28. B - A very common problem that IDS suffers from is false-positives. This happens when normal or expected behavior gets classified as a potential problem. An administrator needs to be aware of this and be able to handle this appropriately. [Security Operations]

29. C - When changes have been made to an application, regression testing is required to ensure that none of the existing functionality and security features have been compromised. [Software Development Security]

30. C - The ITSEC is only used in Europe. The United States uses the Orange book. However most regions are now moving to Common Criteria. [Security Architecture and Design]

31. B - Among the choices listed, laminated glass provides the best security from break-ins. They are made with two sheets of glass and a plastic film in between. This makes them extremely difficult to break. They come in different depths and the greater the depth, the greater the security. [Physical (Environmental) Security]

32. A - Although a stateful firewall provides an additional level of protection, it is unable to fend off Denial-of-Service attacks. If the state table of the firewall is flooded with bogus information, it consumes memory and hard disk space. The firewall could then require to be rebooted. [Telecommunications and Network Security]

33. D - In a symmetric cryptosystem, the cryptographic key should always be sent using an out-of-band transmission method. Since the primary communication is going to happen over the fax system, the key should have been sent using a channel   other   than   fax. [Cryptography]

34. A - As a security practice, group IDs are best avoided since they cannot provide accountability. A good practice though is to assign individual users to groups or roles. This makes it efficient to administer the groups or roles. [Security Operations]

35. A - Slot lock are used to secure laptops. The consist of steel or tough metal cables. These are used to fasten laptops to desks or other immovable objects. [Physical (Environmental) Security]

36. A - Pilferage of hardware (especially smaller components) affects companies quite a bit. Device locks are quite effective and can be used to prevent such occurrences. [Physical (Environmental) Security]

37. A - An application which should have restricted access should use multi-level authentication. This will ensure better access control because of the extra level of authentication. [Access Control]

38. C - One of the key outputs of a Risk Analysis is that monetary values are assigned to assets. This allows the team to calculate the necessary costs to mitigate risks to these assets. [Information Security and Risk Management]

39. B - A key is required to decipher a message. Hence, if an eavesdropper intercepts a message, he will only be able to view the encrypted message and this will be useless to him. He will be unable to decipher it without the key. [Cryptography]

40. A - An external auditor is hired to assist an organization. This can take the form of an on-going contractor engagement, or a brief spot-check. [Security Operations]

Domain Area Test: Multi Domain Practice Questions

Test Name:
Domain Area Test: Multi Domain
Total Questions: 20
Correct Answers Needed to Pass:
15 (75.00%)
Time Allowed: 30 Minutes

Test Description

This domain area test focuses on many of the more difficult domains; including Cryptography, Legal, and Security Architecture.

Test Questions

1. Data Encryption Standard (DES) is a symmetric algorithm that was a standard for many years. However, with the increase in availability of computing power to break algorithms, this standard has now been replaced. Which of these is the replacement for DES?

   A. International Data Encryption Algorithm (IDEA)

   B. Triple DES

   C. Advanced Encryption Standard (AES)

   D. Secure and Fast Encryption routine (SAFER)

2. When working with asymmetric algorithms, which of these principles regarding open / confidential messages is correct?

   A. Confidential messages are encrypted with the public key whereas open messages are encrypted with the private key.

   B. Confidential messages are encrypted with the private key whereas open messages are encrypted with the public key.

   C. Both open and confidential messages are encrypted with the public key.

   D. Both open and confidential messages are encrypted with the private key.

3. Which of these is the correct way to digitally sign a message?

   A. Encrypt the message using a symmetric algorithm and then encrypt the hash of the result with the sender's private key.

   B. Encrypt the message using a symmetric algorithm and then encrypt the hash of the result with the sender's public key.

C. Encrypt a hash of the message with the sender's private key and append it to the message.

D. Encrypt a hash of the message with the public key of the sender and append it to the message.

4. Key management is a very important aspect of a cryptographic implementation. What is multiparty key recovery in the context of key management?

A. In case the private key is lost, multiple parties are contacted and a new key is generated using the public information.

B. The private key is broken up into multiple parts and these are handed out to various trusted people within an organization. In case of loss of the key, these people are grouped together and the key is reconstructed.

C. The private key is given to multiple trusted people. In case of loss of the key, any one of these people can be approached to obtain the key.

D. The private key is locked in a safe whose combination is known only to one individual. In case of loss of the key, this person may be contacted to open the safe.

5. There are 20 people in an organization. How many keys does this organization need to manage if they use symmetric algorithms?

A. 190

B. 400

C. 20

D. 40

6. An information security team is doing a threat-agent vs. threat analysis. Which of the following categories of threat agents would be the first candidate for suspicion in case of a loss of valuable trade secrets in the company?

A. User

B. Contractor

C. Employee

D. Janitor

7. A company would like to use a process to determine chronic failure and where exactly it is likely to happen. Which of the following will allow such an analysis to be performed?

A. Ishikawa analysis

B. Facilitated risk analysis process (FRAP).

C. Failure modes and effect analysis (FMEA)

D. Analysis Tree

8. An approval system was designed such that all purchase orders of value greater than $ 100 needed to be approved by an immediate supervisor and orders of value greater than $ 1000 needed to be approved by the higher up manager. This is an example of:

A. Job position sensitivity

B. Separation of duties

C. Least privilege

D. Job rotation

9. A company has a very effective background check program in place. How often should background checks be done on employees in a company?

A. Prior to their joining work and every two years.

B. Prior to their joining work and every three years.

C. Prior to their joining work and as required.

D. Prior to their joining work and every year.

10. The annualized loss expectancy (ALE) for an asset is $ 10,000. A security officer decides to apply a countermeasure for the risk. If the countermeasure can be used for a period of 5 years, what is the maximum countermeasure cost that the company can spend?

A. $2,000

B. $20,000

C. $10,000

D. $50,000

11. You would like to ensure that the operating system you are running is capable of loading more than one program in memory at the same time and can handle requests from different processes at the same time. What capabilities does this operating system need to have?

A. Multiprogramming, multitasking

B. Multiprogramming, multithreading

C. Multiprocessing, multitasking

D. Multiprogramming, multiprocessing

12. Integrity models primarily need to prevent unauthorized users from making changes, authorized users from making improper changes and maintain both internal as well as external consistency. Which of the models satisfies all three goals?

A. Clark-Wilson model

B. Bell-La Padula model

C. Biba model

D. Clark-Frost model

13. In a security model that you are analyzing, the commands and activities performed at a particular security level are not seen by objects at another security level. What model is this?

A. The information flow model

B. The Brewer and Nash model

C. The access control matrix model

D. The noninterference model

14. Systems operate in different security modes of operation. In which mode can all users access all the data?

A. System high security mode

B. Dedicated security mode

C. Multi-level security mode

D. System high security mode

15. In which of the following models is an evaluation carried out on a product and an Evaluation Assurance Level (EAL assigned)?

A. ITSEC model

B. Common criteria model

C. Specific criteria model

D. TCSEC model

16. A hacker committed a computer crime in an organization. During investigation, a trained employee from the information security department took custody of one of the computers that was part of the crime. While the computer was in his custody, the computer got damaged. As per generally accepted principles, who is likely to be held responsible for the computer damage?

A. The chief security officer

B. The hacker

C. The employee

D. The employee's supervisor

17. In which of the following legal systems are court decisions governed by previous court rulings and generally use an adversarial approach to litigation?

   A. Civil law

   B. Common law

   C. Tort law

   D. Criminal law

18. An organization is using a commercial off-the-shelf software to perform some of its daily operations. On whom does the onus lie to make sure the software is a legitimate, licensed copy?

   A. The end-user

   B. The software product manufacturer

   C. The end-user's supervisor

   D. The company

19. A hacker hacked into a system to access confidential data in an unauthorized manner. In order to prevent being tracked, he manually changed the IP address on the packets to show a different IP address than the actual one. This is called:

   A. Phishing

   B. IP masking

   C. IP spoofing

   D. IP hacking

20. The chief executive officer (CEO) of a publicly traded company was prosecuted due to major inaccuracies in the financial information presented by the company. Under what act would this likely have been done?

   A. The Federal Privacy Act

   B. The Sarbanes-Oxley Act (SOX)

   C. The Computer Fraud and Abuse Act

   D. The Gramm-Leach-Bliley Act (GLBA)

Domain Area Test: Multi Domain Answer Key and Explanations

1. C - With computing power becoming more easily available, the need was felt to have a more efficient and secure system than DES. Advanced Encryption Standard (AES) was developed for this purpose. Triple DES is an intermediate solution. [Cryptography]

2. A - Confidential messages are encrypted with the public key. This allows only the holder of the private key to decrypt them. Open messages are encrypted with the private key of a sender. They can be decrypted by anyone having the corresponding public key. [Cryptography]

3. C - A hash value is obtained by running a one-way hashing function on the message. The hash value is then encrypted with the private key of the sender and appended to the message. [Cryptography]

4. B - In multiparty key recovery, the private key is broken up into parts and given to various trusted people across the organization. One single individual will not be able to construct the key. In case of loss of the key, all of these people would report to a common party and the key would then be reconstructed. [Cryptography]

5. A - The general formula to compute the number of keys required for 'n' users is n x (n-1) / 2. For 20 users, this works out to 20 x (20-1)/2 = 10 x 19 = 190. [Cryptography]

6. B - Contractors work within organizations and often have access to trade secrets. Hence appropriate precautions need to be taken care to ensure that the trade secrets are guarded. The other choices mentioned could also be involved in stealing trade secrets, but the probabilities are lower. [Information Security and Risk Management]

7. C - Failure modes and effect analysis is a method that helps identify failures, assesses the failures and looks at the effects of the failure in a structured manner. It is extremely useful in determining where a vulnerability exists and the scope of the vulnerability. [Information Security and Risk Management]

8. B - This is an example of separation of duties and ensures that for larger value orders, an individual will himself be unable to approve a purchase order. Hence, the possibility of malpractice is reduced. [Information Security and Risk Management]

9. C - The best time to do background checks is prior to an employee joining the company. Subsequent reinvestigation can be done depending on the sensitivity of their positions. Once an employee has joined a company, it is usually not necessary to reinvestigate and do a background check without a valid cause. [Information Security and Risk Management]

10. D - The general rule is that no countermeasure should be greater in cost than the risk it mitigates. To make a comparison with the cost of the risk (ALE), the countermeasure cost per year is calculated. This is the cost of the countermeasure divided by the years of its use within the organization. Hence, maximum countermeasure cost per year = cost of risk = $ 10,000. Total cost of the countermeasure = 10000 x 5 = $ 50,000 (given that the countermeasure can be used for 5 years). [Information Security and Risk Management]

11. A - Multiprogramming refers to the capability to load more than one program in memory at the same time while multitasking means the operating system can handle requests from several different processes loaded in memory at the same time. [Security Architecture and Design]

12. A - The Clark-Wilson model addresses all the three objectives listed whereas the other models (Biba and Bell-LaPadula) address only one of the objectives listed.

Clark-Frost is not a valid model. [Security Architecture and Design]

13. D - The noninterference model ensures that any actions taking place at a lower or higher level do not interfere with those taking place at a different level. The focus here is not the data itself, but what a subject knows about the state of the system. [Security Architecture and Design]

14. B - In dedicated security mode, all users have clearance to access data within a system. A single classification level of information is handled by the system. An example of this is military systems. [Security Architecture and Design]

15. B - An evaluation is carried out on a product in the Common criteria model. It is assigned an Evaluation Assurance Model (EAL) ranging from EAL1 to EAL7 corresponding different assurance levels. [Security Architecture and Design]

16. C - As per the generally accepted principles for computer forensics and digital evidence, an individual is responsible for all actions related to any digital evidence while it is in his possession. Hence, the trained employee would be held accountable for the damage to the computer. [Legal, Regulations, Compliance and Investigations]

17. B - This is the case in common law. Common law is based on the notion of legal precedence, past decisions and societal traditions. This framework can be found in many parts of the world which were once colonies or territories of the British empire. [Legal, Regulations, Compliance and Investigations]

18. D - It is the company's responsibility to ensure that all copies of software being used for its operations are legal copies. It is also the responsibility of the company to keep track of all copies of software, and the licenses involved. Ignorance cannot be used as an excuse as far as compliance is concerned. [Legal, Regulations, Compliance and Investigations]

19. C - This is called IP spoofing. Attackers spoof their IP addresses so that it becomes difficult, if not impossible for the victim to track them down. [Legal, Regulations, Compliance and Investigations]

20. B - The Sarbanes-Oxley Act (SOX) applies to any company that is publicly traded on the US stock markets. This law governs accounting practices and directs how the company needs to report on their financial status. It provides requirements on how they must track, manage and report financial information. Non-compliance of this can lead to prosecution and stiff penalties for the CEO, CFO and others. [Legal, Regulations, Compliance and Investigations]

CISSP Mock Exam (LITE) - 13
Practice Questions

Test Name:
CISSP Mock Exam (LITE) - 13
Total Questions: 40
Correct Answers Needed to Pass:
30 (75.00%)
Time Allowed: 60 Minutes

Test Description

This is a cumulative CISSP Mock Exam which can be used as a benchmark for your CISSP aptitude. This practice test includes questions from all ten domains of the CISSP CBK.

Test Questions

1. A company is concerned that log files may be tampered or manipulated by users who have access to it. This could then seriously compromise the validity of the log files. What strategy can a company employ during the process of review of logs to prevent this?

   A. Monitoring

   B. Background check

   C. Strong security policy

   D. Separation of duties

2. Which of these chemicals used in older fire extinguishers is dangerous for humans and has also been found to damage the ozone layer?

   A. Halogen

   B. Nitron

   C. Halon

   D. Argon

3. Network Information System (NIS) and NIS+ enable users and applications to locate network resources. Which of the following describes NIS+ rather than NIS?

   A. Hierarchical naming structure

   B. No security

   C. Flat naming structure

   D. Data stored in two-column maps

4. You are analyzing an application that was developed 20 years ago. To access certain data, you need to start at a particular branch and go through different layers before reaching the data you need. What database model will this likely be?

   A. Hierarchical

B. Quasi-relational

C. Object-oriented

D. Relational

5. You are part of a business continuity planning team. The team comes up with an elaborate continuity plan that requires a large budget. During an interim meeting, team members are asked to present their views on the budget: Your view would be that:

A. Obtaining funds for BCP activities is usually quite tough. The activities are mostly unnecessary, so management doesn't support this.

B. Large budgets are fine. Management is usually co-operative in authorizing funds for BCP work.

C. Obtaining funds for BCP activities is usually quite tough. The team needs to cut down the cost as much as possible even thought continuity planning is very important.

D. Large budgets are fine. Management usually has a special fund for this purpose with visibility right up to the CEO of the company.

6. Fire drills, evacuation drills etc need to be periodically conducted to ensure that the procedures in place work, and to identify issues. The recommended frequency is to carry these drills out at least:

A. Once a year

B. Once in 2 years

C. Once a month

D. Once in 3 months

7. A company plans to procure a new product to improve its operations. Which of the following types of evaluation will help assure that the product conforms to certain clipping level configurations?

A. Functionality assurance

B. Parametric assurance

C. Life-cycle assurance

D. Operational assurance

8. An airline ticket booking application is accessed by users across the internet or via dedicated networks. Given a scenario where multiple users are accessing the system at the same time, which of the following is a key issue in such a ticket booking application?

A. Aggregation of data

B. Performance

C. Overloading of the network

D. Concurrency of data

9. Which among the following forms of authentication will be relatively tougher to attack?

A. PIN number

B. Passphrase

C. Passcode

D. Password

10. A major project has just been approved. This project will require access to a number of internal company systems. What kind of controls are used to provide such access?

A. Directive controls

B. Compensatory controls

C. Preventive controls

D. Technical controls

11. What type of control is review of violation reports, log files, Intrusion Detection systems (IDS), or use of CCTV?

A. Preventive controls

B. Recovery

C. Deterrent

D. Detective

12. A company is classifying data within the company. How it would classify trade secrets?

A. Confidential

B. Public

C. Blocked

D. Sensitive

13. In a wormhole attack, two attackers are involved, one at each end of the tunnel (called wormhole). This typically takes place on wireless networks (but can be done on wired networks too). What is the countermeasure to this?

A. A leash

B. A collar

C. A restraint

D. A tie

14. While auditing a set of business continuity and disaster recovery programs, you review a list of preventive measures that the company has undertaken. Which of the following would incorrectly be classified as a preventive measure?

A. Purchase of a redundant server.

B. Purchase of a UPS.

C. Purchase of insurance.

D. Purchase of additional network bandwidth on an existing link.

15. As part of acceptance testing, an independent group performed a security test on an application. What kinds of test data should the team use?

A. Data in the acceptable range, outside the acceptable range, random data and data on the boundary.

B. Data on the boundary and outside the acceptable range.

C. Random data

D. Data in the acceptable range.

16. At a software development facility, the security personnel found that there were a lot of incidents involving stolen laptops. Users found that when they left desks for extended periods of time, their laptops were missing on their return. What can be done to prevent this?

A. Introduce additional CCTV cameras.

B. Use slot locks

C. Use port controls

D. Replace laptops with desktop computers

17. A large retailer has been told that there are numerous risks associated with doing business on the internet. As a result, the retailer decides to stay away from doing business on the internet. This is an example of:

A. Risk avoidance

B. Risk Transfer

C. Risk mitigation

D. Risk acceptance

18. An administrator wants to separate out some of the departments into logical groups such as HR, payroll, production and research. Which of the following will allow this to be done?

A. SLANs

B. RLANs

C. VLANs

D. XLANs

19. Which of the following can speed up the performance of the CPU by reducing memory access time?

A. RAM

B. ROM

C. Cache memory

D. SDRAM

20. Wireless device and cellphone encryption needs to be as efficient as possible so as to conserve bandwidth. Which of the following asymmetric algorithms is used for such devices?

A. DES

B. International Data Encryption Algorithm (IDEA)

C. RSA

D. Elliptic curve cryptosystems (ECC)

21. Financial fraud committed by one of the company's junior officers came to light during a review of certain data. The officer in question had obtained access in excess of his requirements and managed to commit the crime. Which of the following could have helped prevent or avoid this situation?

A. User authentication

B. Single sign-on

C. Digital identity

D. User provisioning

22. There is no specific standard but almost every computer has the same port mapped to the same protocol. If a network programmer is referring to port 25, he is likely referring to which protocol?

A. Telnet

B. FTP

C. SMTP

D. HTTP

23. An auditor finds that the business continuity plan in an organization was last tested 6 months ago. He notes this down as an issue. However, the continuity planning team does not agree. What is your view on this?

A. The auditor is right. A BCP should be tested once every 3 months.

B. The auditor is right. A BCP should be tested at least once in 6 months.

C. The auditor is wrong. A BCP should be tested once in 2 years.

D. The auditor is wrong. A BCP should be tested at least once a year.

24. Which of the following is not true about keypad or pushbutton locks?

A. The combination relates to the lock rather than an individual

B. Accountability is lower in case of keypad locks.

C. These locks require a combination of numbers to be learned and secured.

D. The keypad usually needs to be changed once in 5 years

25. A connection between two machines dropped. However, before this link failure was detected, an attacker managed to attach to one of the ports and pretended to be the trusted machine, thus gaining unauthorized access. What is the counter against this?

A. The counter to this is to forcibly log out the user periodically.

B. The counter to this is to use a fire-wall.

C. The counter to this is to use SSL.

D. The counter is to have some form of authentication constantly performed on the line.

26. The management of a company decided to cut down on training budgets due to a crunch of funds. A few months later, a hacker broke into one of the servers of the company and stole some valuable information. This could have been prevented if the employee monitoring the intrusion detection system had been trained to monitor and interpret the logs. Who is held responsible in this case?

A. The employee

B. The employee's supervisor

C. Management

D. The manufacturer of the intrusion detection system

27. One of the employees in an organization illegally installed a software and started using it. The software manufacturer detected this and took the organization to court over this. The organization is of the view that this is a matter between the employee and the software manufacturer. What is your view on this?

A. The organization is correct. This is a matter between the employee and the software manufacturer. However, the organization may ask the employee to delete the software.

B. The organization is responsible for all software that is installed on its premises.

C. The organization is correct. This is a matter between the employee and the software manufacturer.

D. The software manufacturer has no case. What goes on within an organization is an internal matter.

28. In the OSI model, which of the following layers will contain a data

packet that also has information added by each of the 7 layers?

A. The Application layer

B. The Transport layer

C. The Physical layer

D. The Data link layer

29. Outermost perimeter in the context of physical security usually refers to the farthest extent that an organization can patrol. How is physical security managed for the outermost perimeter?

A. Through creation of security zones.

B. Through hard control logic

C. Through procedural controls

D. Through soft control logic

30. Process isolation needs to be enforced to ensure that individual processes do not affect other processes' performance. This can be done by any of the following except:

A. Encapsulation of objects

B. Naming distinctions

C. Underloading of objects

D. Time multiplexing of shared resources

31. The physical security team of a company did a risk analysis and came up with a set of criteria outlining the level of protection required for its security program. What should be the objective of the first level of control of a security program?

A. To detect intruders

B. To deter intruders

C. To capture intruders

D. To delay intruders

32. A computer programmer came up with a brilliant algorithm to perform a certain calculation. Such an algorithm would most likely be protected by:

A. Trade secret laws

B. Trademark laws

C. Copyright laws

D. Patent laws

33. A company uses a number of legacy computers and hardware. During business impact analysis, this is flagged as one of the potential areas of concern. As part of continuity and disaster recovery planning what can the company do to minimize the impact if a disaster strikes?

A. Identify legacy devices and plan for commercial off the shelf products, if possible.

B. Train additional personnel in the use and maintenance of the legacy systems

C. Duplicate the legacy systems and place orders for new equipment while they are available.

D. Strengthen the backup around the legacy systems.

34. Which of the following represents the correct order in of activities in response to an incident?

A. Triage, Repair, Recovery

B. Triage, Analysis, Tracking

C. Triage, Reaction, Follow-up

D. Triage, Containment, Tracking

35. A security officer is auditing the operations of a computer center. She finds that downtime is high for a particular server. She looks up the operations log and finds a comment

that the server often reboots on its own and works fine after that. What would the security officer recommend?

A. Upgradation of the server capacity since it is unable to withstand the load.

B. Monitoring of the server for another 3 months after which a new one needs to be installed.

C. Upgradation of the memory on the server since it is unable to withstand the load.

D. An investigation as to why the server is rebooting on its own often.

36. Which of the following methods are most commonly used to ensure that an end-user has read and accepts a licensing agreement (EULA)?

A. Use of a click through or radio button which the user must click on to signify acceptance of the terms, before being able to click on the Install button.

B. Use of a licensing agreement, provided as a separate document which the user must read after installation.

C. Use of a hardcopy which the end-user must sign and mail back to the software manufacturer.

D. Use of an email which will get sent over the internet once an end user has accepted the terms and conditions of the license.

37. Which of the following is not a recommended security practice?

A. Assignment of group accounts to be shared by multiple individuals.

B. Assignment of individual accounts into groups or roles.

C. Use of automated password reset methods

D. Assignment of temporary passwords when a new user is created in the system.

38. A hardware vendor would like to ensure that he need not replace an entire product in case of a firmware change. Which of the following can help in achieving this?

A. Use of a PROM

B. Use of an EEPROM

C. Use of ROM

D. Use of cache memory

39. A continuity planning team came up with a detailed analysis of the current state of readiness, the gaps and the action areas for a company. The team is concerned that there could be areas that they have not considered. What would be a good way to innovate practices in this area?

A. Through standardization

B. Use of readily available software packages

C. Through benchmarking

D. Use of continuity planning workshops

40. Routers and firewalls are implemented with failover equipment as secondary devices. These secondary devices take over when the primary fails. This type of hardware backup is known as:

A. Tepid spare

B. Warm spare

C. Hot spare

D. Cold spare

CISSP Mock Exam (LITE) - 13
Answer Key and Explanations

1. D - The company can use separation of duties to ensure that the individuals who have access to data are not the ones who have access to review the logs. This will ensure that a situation where an employee accesses logs to delete information about his unauthorized activities is avoided. [Access Control]

2. C - Halon has been banned since it damages the ozone layer. Companies with older fire extinguishers that use halon need to use a replacement FM-200 which is similar to halon but does not damage the ozone layer. [Physical (Environmental) Security]

3. A - NIS+ improved upon the performance and security issues that existed with NIS. The naming structure is hierarchical in case of NIS+. [Telecommunications and Network Security]

4. A - This will likely be a hierarchical database. They are found on older systems and follow a hierarchical structure. To reach a data entity, you need to traverse down layers on a particular branch. [Software Development Security]

5. C - Although BCP activities are very important, obtaining funds for this purpose is often quite difficult.

Hence it is important to keep costs as low as possible. [Business Continuity and Disaster Recovery Planning]

6. A - Fire drills, evacuation drills etc should be carried out at least once a year. Doing them less frequently than a year will entail additional costs, while 2 years is too far apart to be of significant value. [Physical (Environmental) Security]

7. C - Life-cycle assurance deals with the standards and expectations a product must meet before it can be considered a trusted product. Design specifications and clipping-level configurations are part of these standards. [Security Operations]

8. D - When multiple users are trying to access the same data, it is possible to run into concurrency issues that violate the integrity of the data. For example, if multiple users are trying to make reservations for the same flight on a given day, the system should be able to resolve the situation. [Software Development Security]

9. B - Passphrases are longer to enter and that makes them harder to attack. They are relatively easy for users to remember but given their length, an attacker will be unable to crack them easily. [Access Control]

10. B - Compensating controls are introduced to handle temporary situations such as new projects, business development, application testing etc. [Access Control]

11. D - Review of violation reports, log files, use of an intrusion detection system (IDS), CCTV are considered as detective type of controls since these provide information after the event. [Access Control]

12. A - Trade secrets would be classified as confidential. This type of data is for use within the company only. Unauthorized disclosure of confidential data could seriously affect a company. [Information Security and Risk Management]

13. A - The countermeasure to a wormhole attack is a leash. This is a data packet put into the header of individual packets and this restricts the packet's transmission distance either geographically or puts a limit on the lifetime of the packet. [Telecommunications and Network Security]

14. D - Increase in the bandwidth of an existing network link cannot be termed as a preventive measure since it will not be of any use when a disaster actually strikes. Each of the other choices listed will help in a specific way during a disaster. [Business Continuity and Disaster Recovery Planning]

15. A - While performing acceptance testing, all kinds of input data conditions should be tested. This includes data in the acceptable range, outside the acceptable range, random data and data on the boundary. [Software Development Security]

16. B - Slot locks are commonly used to secure laptops to a stationary component in the vicinity of the desk. This will help prevent them from being stolen. [Physical (Environmental) Security]

17. A - This is an example of risk avoidance. Such a decision will also likely have an impact on the company's revenues, and the company needs to have taken that into consideration while making the decision to stay away from the internet business. [Information Security and Risk Management]

18. C - VLANs stand for virtual LANs and enables administrators to group computers logically based on certain business needs. [Telecommunications and Network Security]

19. C - Cache memory is used to improve CPU performance. This is because cache memory is high-speed RAM. Data moves from the lower speed RAM to the faster cache and then to the CPU. An optimally designed cache can ensure higher processing speeds. [Security Architecture and Design]

20. D - Elliptic curve cryptosystems (ECC) are used as asymmetric algorithms. They use much lesser resources than other algorithms and hence they are used in wireless device and cell phone encryption. [Cryptography]

21. D - User provisioning could have helped prevent this. It controls how user privileges are created, maintained and deleted. Such a system would have placed checks on the level of access the officer had. One of the audits or reviews would also have revealed that the officer had excessive access and this could have potentially avoided the fraud. [Access Control]

22. C - Although there is no specific standard created for this purpose, all computers are usually mapped to the same ports. Port 25 is the port for SMTP (simple mail transfer protocol). [Telecommunications and Network Security]

23. D - Generally, a business continuity plan should be tested at least once a year. Such tests and drills prepare the team and management for the kinds of issues they may run into, and provide a controlled environment where they can learn the tasks to be done when a disaster actually strikes.

[Business Continuity and Disaster Recovery Planning]

24. D - The keypad needs to be changed more frequently. Due to repeated use, the keypad wears out and an astute criminal will be able to determine which keys are used to open the lock. [Physical (Environmental) Security]

25. D - The counter to an attack where the attacker attaches to one of the ports used in communication between two computers before the link failed is to have a form of authentication performed constantly on the line. The attacker will be unable to respond to this and appropriate action can be taken by the server or other computer to drop the connection. [Software Development Security]

26. C - Management is held responsible in this case. It is always their responsibility to protect the environment by properly training the staff. Although a budget crunch may have been a valid reason for cutting down on training, management needs to look at the impact of such decisions closely in the context of security. [Information Security and Risk Management]

27. B - Organizations are responsible for all software installed on their premises. In case an employee has installed an illegal copy of a software,

the organization is still responsible for it. [Security Operations]

28. C - In the OSI model, the physical layer is the lowest layer (layer 7) while the application layer is the highest (layer 1). Each of the layers in between add their own information to a data packet, so the physical layer contains information from all the layers since it is at the bottom. [Telecommunications and Network Security]

29. C - Environment boundaries and open spaces at the outermost perimeter are usually managed through the use of procedural controls. These include guard posts, checking and escorting visitors on site, and managing deliveries to the site. [Physical (Environmental) Security]

30. C - Underloading of objects is not a valid method. The other three methods (encapsulation of objects, time multiplexing of shared resources and naming distinctions) are used to carry out process isolation. Older operating systems did not enforce this as well as today's operating systems. [Security Architecture and Design]

31. B - The objective of the first level of control of a physical security program should be to deter intruders. The general psyche of an intruder is to go for easy pickings.

Hence a well implemented security program should make intruders feel it is not worth their while to break-in, and deter them. [Physical (Environmental) Security]

32. D - An inventor of an algorithm typically gets a patent to the algorithm and controls all rights on it. [Legal, Regulations, Compliance and Investigations]

33. A - During a disaster it is possible that replacements for legacy equipment can no longer be found. Hence, as part of continuity planning, the company should look at moving away from the legacy systems. The other choices are unrealistic. Training additional personnel or improving backup procedures will not help during a disaster since the issue is availability of replacement hardware. Duplicating the hardware may also not be practical. [Business Continuity and Disaster Recovery Planning]

34. C - The sequence in which an incident needs to be responded to is Triage, Reaction and Follow-up. Triage refers to the actual incident itself. Reaction is the action taken to contain and track the incident. Follow-up is the action done to avoid recurrence of the incident. [Legal, Regulations, Compliance and Investigations]

35. D - Incidents where a server or a computer reboots on its own without any apparent cause need to be investigated carefully. They could indicate a deeper problem such as a virus infection or a compromise in the security of the system by a hacker. [Security Operations]

36. A - The EULA is typically a click through or radio button that a user clicks on. This signifies that the user has gone through the terms and conditions of licensing. Only after this step has been done, the is the install button enabled. [Legal, Regulations, Compliance and Investigations]

37. A - As a general practice, sharing of a single group account by multiple individuals is not recommended. This is because there is no accountability and the group account can potentially be misused. The preferred approach is to assign individual accounts to groups or roles. [Security Operations]

38. B - Firmware that is stored in EEPROMs can be easily upgraded without changing the product. The hardware itself is not upgradeable, but the firmware can be upgraded easily. [Security Architecture and Design]

39. C - Benchmarking involves comparison with industry standards and covers the performance of the industry. Such peer or benchmarking techniques will allow the team to look beyond their company. A number of best practices can be learned from this activity and will allow the team to innovate practices. [Business Continuity and Disaster Recovery Planning]

40. C - Redundant hardware components that are already operating are called hot spares. Other examples of hot spares are when multiple power supplies are running in parallel. [Security Operations]

CISSP Mock Exam (LITE) - 14
Practice Questions

Test Name:
CISSP Mock Exam (LITE) - 14
Total Questions: 40
Correct Answers Needed to Pass:
30 (75.00%)
Time Allowed: 60 Minutes

Test Description

This is a cumulative CISSP Mock Exam which can be used as a benchmark for your CISSP aptitude. This practice test includes questions from all ten domains of the CISSP CBK.

Test Questions

1. As a security officer, you are reviewing the thickness of wire to use for the fences around your company. If you wish to have greater security, which of the following should you choose?

    A. 1 inch mesh, 11 gauge

    B. 2 inch mesh, 6 gauge

    C. 1 inch mesh, 9 gauge

    D. 2 inch mesh, 9 gauge

2. One of the team members of a security team was performing a random audit of a computer system and found signs that it had been tampered. This is usually indicative of:

    A. Forensic activity

    B. A hacker attack

    C. An insider attack

    D. An external attack

3. A user entered her userID, followed by her password. This authentication process to verify an individual's identity can be viewed as:

    A. An identification step and an authentication step, both involving private information

    B. An identification step involving public information and an authentication step involving private information.

    C. An authentication step involving private information and an identification step involving public information.

    D. An identification step involving private information and an authentication step involving public information.

4. Your company has installed an intrusion detection system that automatically turns on the lights in a specific area when it detects suspicious activity. This is referred to as:

   A. Backup lighting

   B. Standby lighting

   C. Active lighting

   D. Responsive area illumination

5. Which of the following norms governs how banks can protect themselves and prevent themselves from overextending / becoming insolvent?

   A. Base II

   B. Basel II

   C. Base I

   D. International Banking Act

6. Which of the following firewall architectures provides the highest security?

   A. Screened host

   B. Screened subnet

   C. Unscreened host

   D. Unscreened subnet

7. Which of the following power fluctuations is the most dangerous for hardware equipment?

   A. Surges

   B. Noise

   C. Blackouts

   D. Brownouts

8. Stream and block methods are used to encrypt data. Which of these statements about stream and block ciphers is not true?

   A. Stream-based ciphers are relatively stronger than block ciphers.

   B. Many stream-based ciphers are implemented in hardware, whereas block-based ciphers are implemented in software.

   C. Block ciphers are more expensive to implement than stream-based ciphers.

   D. Block ciphers require much more processing power than stream-based ciphers.

9. Buffer overflows, which used to be a key threat earlier have now been replaced by another type of threat. Which of the following is now considered the biggest threat to current web systems?

    A. Boot viruses

    B. Cross-site scripting (XSS)

    C. Server side scripting (SSS)

    D. Macro viruses

10. A programmer did not have access to a secure resource. However, he has been granted access to a program that has access to the secure resource. The programmer is able to bypass the security and obtain information from the secure resource. How can this be prevented?

    A. By implementing the concept of most privilege.

    B. By having a low granularity of control.

    C. By having high granularity of control

    D. By centralizing all requests related to access control.

11. Many companies define the scope of their business continuity plans to only cover larger threats. How are smaller threats handled in such cases?

    A. By independent departmental plans

    B. Smaller threats are ignored since their impact is lower.

    C. By mini-BCP plans

    D. By common departmental plans

12. Which of the following processes provides integrity of data but not data origin authentication?

    A. HMAC

    B. MIC

    C. CBC-MAC

    D. Hash

13. One of the major disadvantages of using threads is a deadlock. What other disadvantage do threads have?

    A. Thrashing

    B. Blocking

    C. Loading

D. Clocking

14. Networks need to be periodically scanned. Which of these is not a valid type of network scanning?

A. Compliance scanning

B. Integrated scanning

C. Vulnerability scanning

D. Discovery scanning

15. Which of the following statements regarding copyrights is true?

A. Copyright law protects the source code, object code as well as the user interface.

B. Copyright law protects only the source code.

C. Copyright law protects the source code and the user interface but not the object code.

D. Copyright law protects the source code and object code, but not the user interface.

16. A credit card company has revamped its internal team structure. Earlier, an informal structure existed, but the new structure now houses an information security department.

Ideally, to whom should this department report?

A. The CEO

B. Corporate Security

C. Administrative Services

D. The CIO

17. Hackers are looking to dial into a Remote Access Server (RAS) and clandestinely access the internal networks of a company. What method will likely be used by them to determine the phone number that provides access to the RAS dial-up modem?

A. Inwarddialing

B. Wardialing

C. Crashdialling

D. Breakdialing

18. If asked to select the fastest Ethernet type between 10Base-2, 10Base-T and 10Base-5, you would choose:

A. 10Base-5

B. 10Base-T

C. All three have the same speed.

D. 10Base-2

19. As a security officer, you are reviewing the security controls on some systems. Which of the following situations may warrant use of fewer security controls?

    A. A proprietary credit card application used across a public network.

    B. A mobile banking application.

    C. A proprietary financial application running in a closed environment.

    D. A banking application delivered across the internet.

20. A company generates large amounts of data every week. Governmental regulations mandate that the company maintain these records for 7 years. Which of the following will help the company maintain this data?

    A. A media library

    B. A data server

    C. A master server

    D. A data library

21. One of the users of an application dealing with confidential data often leaves printouts of such confidential reports on his desk. The user is aware that the information is confidential. What is the procedure to detect such lapses?

    A. Data classification auditing

    B. User training

    C. Data classification assurance

    D. Data classification control

22. Which of these is not a responsibility of the business continuity planning (BCP) team?

    A. Understand the current operational and technical functioning environment.

    B. Provide a solution to protect and restore company data when needed.

    C. Set up and maintain the company's data classification procedures.

    D. Determine the best back-up process so that data can be made available depending on its classification.

23. An administrator would like to ensure that there is absolutely no security breach in accessing very confidential data and decides to implement a system that will capture electrical signals when a person signs a signature. The information from this system will then be used to authenticate users. Such a system would be called:

A. Signature topography

B. Signature control

C. Digital signature

D. Signature dynamics

24. Network Address Translation (NAT) is an effective means to overcome the shortage of IP addresses. NAT enables a network to communicate over the Internet even though it may not internally follow the Internet's addressing scheme. Which of these is not a valid NAT implementation?

A. Port Address Translation (PAT)

B. LDAP

C. Dynamic mapping

D. Static mapping

25. An attacker is trying to gain information about a smart-card.

Which of the following attacks is not a side-channel attack?

A. Fault generation

B. Differential power analysis

C. Electromagnetic analysis

D. Timing analysis

26. Which of the following techniques should be used by programmers while programming using Open Database Connectivity (ODBC) to ensure that the physical location of databases or passwords used to connect to them are not exposed?

A. Use of Data Source Names (DSNs)

B. Encapsulation

C. Use of hashes

D. Use of simple text ciphers

27. The purpose of continuity planning is to minimize the impact of a disaster or an incident. Which of the following is a key metric in the aftermath of a disaster?

A. Compromised customer service

B. Employee turnover

C. Extra expense

D. Revenue loss

28. Business continuity and disaster recovery plans need to be tested to identify their weaknesses. In which of the following tests are specifically identified systems run at the alternate facility and compared with the regular processing that happens at the primary site?

A. Full-interruption testing

B. Parallel testing

C. Structured walk-through testing.

D. Simulation testing

29. Static electricity does not usually cause damage to human beings. However, it can ruin equipment which is sensitive. Which of the following humidity conditions is most conducive for static to develop?

A. Humidity of 35%

B. Humidity of 90%

C. Humidity of 15%

D. Humidity of 60%

30. A company considers that its data is very critical and loss of the data would be disastrous. What is the recommended backup procedure for such critical data?

A. Backup at an onsite location.

B. Backup at an offsite location.

C. Use of a differential backup process.

D. Backup at an onsite location as well as an offsite location.

31. A company has some non-critical work that takes place on its premises. The company does not expect any major threat from domestic terrorists. Normally what kind of material would the company use for its buildings?

A. Heavy timber construction material

B. Fire resistant material

C. Incombustible material

D. Light frame construction material.

32. An individual using an open source software found an important security vulnerability. He contacted the vendor of the software and asked that the vulnerability followed by a fix be released to the public. This is known as:

A. Partial disclosure

B. Full disclosure

C. Interim disclosure

D. Covert disclosure

33. Which of the following situations least warrants the use of an identity management solution?

A. It takes two days to revoke and disable accesses when an employee leaves the company.

B. It takes three days to setup new employees with required accesses to systems.

C. Users have to use five separate IDs and passwords to obtain information from various systems within the company.

D. Login screens are very slow to load and take a long time to authenticate users.

34. A citizen programmer developed an application. As a security administrator, what would you assume about the security of such an application?

A. Its security would exceed that of an application developed by a professional programmer.

B. Its security would compare well with that of an application developed by a professional programmer.

C. It would have a basic level of security.

D. It would lack any security controls and not provide an assurance to security.

35. Which of the following statements is not true about asymmetric algorithms?

A. Keys are usually generated by a cryptographic application without user involvement.

B. Asymmetric algorithms are usually slower than symmetric algorithms.

C. The number of keys required to communicate between 10 people is 45

D. It is simpler to go in one direction (forward) than in the other direction (backward).

36. A computer user was under the impression that he could do little harm with his computer. He sent out a flame email which resulted in his being sued for libel. This type of ethics fallacy is typically labeled as:

A. Shatterproof fallacy

B. Law-abiding citizen fallacy

C. Candy-from-a-baby fallacy

D. Free information fallacy

37. A computer department is in the process of physically labeling all the IT hardware in the company. Which of these would have the least priority to be included on the hardware label/tag?

A. Serial No. of hardware

B. Model of hardware

C. Location of hardware

D. Name of user

38. An attacker tried to launch a replay attack by capturing some data from a session and resubmitting it to the server. Which of these techniques will counter a replay attack?

A. Machine numbers

B. Threshold numbers

C. Packet control

D. Sequence numbers

39. Which of the following is a mathematical model for information flow?

A. Noninterference model

B. Array model

C. Matrix model

D. Lattice model

40. For computer systems, the mean time to repair (MTTR) is likely to be measured in:

A. Seconds

B. Hours

C. Depends on the equipment

D. Minutes

CISSP Mock Exam (LITE) - 14 Answer Key and Explanations

1. C - The gauge of fencing wiring refers to the thickness of the wire used in a fence mesh. The higher the gauge number, the thinner the wire. The mesh size is the distance between the wires. Hence, a 1 inch mesh is more secure than 2 inch mesh and within that, a 9 gauge is stronger than a 11 gauge. [Physical (Environmental) Security]

2. C - System tampering usually indicates an insider attack on a system. When this is noticed, a detailed internal investigation should be conducted to determine if there is a possibility of criminal activity. [Security Operations]

3. B - Authentication can be viewed as a two-step process. The first is the identification step, involving entering of the userID. This is public information. The next step is the authentication step, involving entering of the password. This is private information. [Access Control]

4. D - This is known as Responsive area illumination. This is a feature of the IDS. When an IDS detects suspicious activity in an area the IDS turns on the lights there. However, the possibility of false alarms exists. Hence this should ideally be combined with some form of CCTV monitoring. [Physical (Environmental) Security]

5. B - The Bank for International Settlements came up with a system by which banks could prevent themselves from overextending / becoming insolvent. This is known as Basel II Accord. Information security is a key part of the guidelines. [Legal, Regulations, Compliance and Investigations]

6. B - A screened-subnet architecture provides a high degree of protection compared to a stand-alone or screened host firewall because three devices work together and all three must be compromised before the attacker can gain access. [Telecommunications and Network Security]

7. A - Surges refer to a prolonged rise in the voltage from a power source. These cause a lot of damage and need to be controlled through surge protectors. Although computer power supplies have a basic surge protection, they need to be plugged into larger surge protectors for prolonged protection. [Physical (Environmental) Security]

8. A - Block ciphers operate on blocks of text. Block ciphers usually use a combination of substitution/transposition. As a result, block ciphers are relatively

stronger than stream-based ciphers. [Cryptography]

9. B - Cross-site scripting (XSS) is now considered a key threat in web applications. It refers to an attack where an attacker finds a vulnerability on a website and uses this to inject malicious code into the hosted application. Users accessing the site will then get infected. [Software Development Security]

10. C - Such a situation where a programmer has access to an underlying resource through a program to which he has access can be addressed by adequate granularity of controls. If the security controls are granular enough to address both the program and the user, this is resolved. [Software Development Security]

11. A - At the company level, most companies outline their business company plans to only cover the major threats. Smaller threats are expected to be handled by individual departments through departmental contingency plans. [Business Continuity and Disaster Recovery Planning]

12. D - A hash only offers integrity. If a message has been unintentionally modified, it can be detected. However, it does not offer data origin authentication. HMAC and CBC-

MAC offer data origin authentication. [Cryptography]

13. B - When a thread makes a specific system call (example: an I/O request), the call will not return back until it has completed or the call is interrupted by a signal. If any fault occurs during the call, the call may not even come back, or may take an extended period to return. During this period, the thread cannot execute any other instruction. This is known as blocking. [Security Architecture and Design]

14. B - Integrated scanning is not a valid scanning method used to scan networks. Discovery, compliance and vulnerability scanning are valid methods used to scan networks for specific purposes. [Telecommunications and Network Security]

15. A - Computer programs may be protected by copyright law under the category of literary works. The source code, object code as well as the user interface are covered by this law. [Legal, Regulations, Compliance and Investigations]

16. A - A credit card company has high security needs. Ideally, in such an organization the information security department should report to the CEO directly. This minimizes message filtering and enhances communication. This also sends out a

strong signal that the company values information security. [Information Security and Risk Management]

17. B - Wardialing is used by attackers to find an entry point into a network. Specifically written tools are used to dial a bank of phone numbers. The tools identify lines used for data communication and try to identify the system on the other end of the line. [Telecommunications and Network Security]

18. C - All three offer the same speeds of response, namely 10Mbps. The difference is that 10Base-2 and 10Base-5 use coaxial type of cable whereas 10Base-T uses UTP. [Telecommunications and Network Security]

19. C - A proprietary application running in a closed environment is likely to use fewer security controls since there is already a greater level of control on the users accessing the system. As with all applications, security is always an issue. However, the question here is a relative comparison. [Software Development Security]

20. A - Media libraries are very useful when large amounts of data need to be stored in a protected environment. They allow data to be stored in an orderly manner so that data can be easily retrieved when required. However, a flip side is that they are quite expensive. [Security Operations]

21. C - Data classification assurance is performed to test data classification and assure that the activities are being done. This includes random audits of user areas, information left in open shredding bins, information posted on a public website etc. In contrast, data classification auditing reviews classifications to ensure the accuracy of the information. [Access Control]

22. C - The BCP team is not responsible for setting up / maintaining the company's data classification procedures. However, during their assessment process, they may determine that certain areas are weak or vulnerable and they may make recommendations to management to protect such data. [Business Continuity and Disaster Recovery Planning]

23. D - This is known as signature dynamics. It is based on the fact that when individuals sign, they sign in the same manner each time. This in turn produces a uniform pattern of electrical signatures which can then be fed to a biometric system to distinguish between users. [Access Control]

24. B - LDAP is not a valid NAT implementation. The other three choices Static mapping, Dynamic mapping and Port Address Translation (PAT) are valid NAT implementations.

[Telecommunications and Network Security]

25. A - Fault generation is a method by which an attacker introduces a computation based error into a smart-card. This error could be based on a changed voltage, a clock rate or a change in temperature. The attacker hopes that this will allow him to uncover the encryption process. In contrast, side-channel attacks are nonintrusive and attempt to uncover information without compromising on any flaw or weakness. [Access Control]

26. A - This achieved by the use of Data Source Names (DSNs). These are logical names used to refer to data stores instead of the actual physical location (ex: the drive letter or directory location). This helps the security of the system because the connection strings are variables stored in the registry. Use of DSNs is also a best practice. [Software Development Security]

27. A - Customer service is a key measure in the aftermath of a disaster. It is usually impacted in varying degrees and is reflective of the preparedness of an organization. Compromise in customer service eventually results in revenue loss, but this can be minimized. [Business Continuity and Disaster Recovery Planning]

28. B - Parallel testing is done to make sure that specific, identified systems perform to the required levels at the alternate sites. Their performance is compared to the regular processing and any gaps that exist can then be plugged. [Business Continuity and Disaster Recovery Planning]

29. C - Low humidity conditions (< 20 %) are conducive for static charge to be built up. Hence, it is best to keep the humidity in computer / server rooms between 35 and 60% at all times. Higher humidity causes condensation on the equipment. [Security Operations]

30. D - Critical data should be backed up at an onsite location as well as an offsite location. Onsite copies would be easily accessible in case of non-disasters and day-to-day operations. In case of a disaster, the offsite copy would kick into effect. [Business Continuity and Disaster Recovery Planning]

31. A - Heavy timber construction material is used in constructing office buildings. There are requirements on the thickness and composition of material for protection from fire. The other options of incombustible or fire resistant material may be costly options and need not be used unless the company has critical work on the premises and is concerned about threats due to fire or intrusion. Light frame construction material is only used for homes. [Physical (Environmental) Security]

32. A - Such a model where the individual contacts the vendor of the software and asks for the vulnerability and fix to be published to the public is known as partial disclosure. It could also include release of information about the vulnerability and any possible workarounds. In contrast, full disclosure means that an individual who finds the security vulnerability will disseminate the information to the public at large. [Software Development Security]

33. D - Login screens taking a lot of time to load is not an issue related to access. It may be an issue related to network capacity or the server. An identity management solution will not solve this problem. The other choices are valid reasons why a company would go in for an identity management solution. [Access Control]

34. D - Until proved otherwise, it would be expected that an application developed by a citizen programmer would lack security controls and would not provide assurance to security. This is because citizen programmers are unlikely to have been trained in proper system / application development processes. [Software Development Security]

35. C - Each user requires a pair of keys (a public key and a private key). So, the number of keys required for 10 people to communicate is 10 x 2 = 20. All the other statements about asymmetric algorithms are true. [Cryptography]

36. A - This is known as shatterproof fallacy. Many computer-users believe that they can do little harm by using their computers. They tend to behave in a manner which is inappropriate, although they are aware that behaving in the same manner could lead to trouble in a physical forum not involving a computer. [Information Security and Risk Management]

37. D - The name of the user is the least useful in this list. A hardware tag will not usually include the name of the user. The user details will normally be included in software form. [Security Operations]

38. D - In a replay attack, the attacker hopes to be authenticated again as someone else, by replaying captured data. This type of attack can be countered by timestamps and sequence numbers. Packets contain sequence numbers, so each machine expects a specific number on a packet. If a sequence number repeats itself, it is an indication of a replay attack. [Cryptography]

39. D - The lattice model is a mathematical model that provides a certain basic level of protection if all its rules are followed properly. [Security Architecture and Design]

40. C - The mean time to repair (MTTR) is the time it will take to get a device fixed or repaired and back into action. The lower the MTTR the better. However, it will vary for different types of operations. For example, a disk failure in a server will have a different service level than a disk failure in an end user's workstation. So, the MTTR depends on the equipment. [Security Operations]

CISSP Extended Quiz
Practice Questions

Test Name: CISSP Extended Quiz
Total Questions: 30
Correct Answers Needed to Pass:
25 (83.33%)
Time Allowed: 45 Minutes

Test Description

This CISSP practice test illustrates how the system works by using a small set of questions.

Test Questions

1. Which of the following tools performs a very similar function to that of a password checker?

   A. Password cracker

   B. Password maker

   C. Password dictionary

   D. Password Verifier

2. A secure system maintains a list of a user's last ten passwords and prevents the user from reusing these passwords. This ensures good security and is known as:

   A. Password database

   B. Password match

   C. Password history

   D. Password list

3. A user typed in his username and password into a login screen. The system immediately came back with another screen to enter his username and password again. The user assumed that he had wrongly entered his username / password and re-entered them. He was then logged into the system. What type of attack is this likely to be?

   A. Brute force

   B. Spoofing

   C. Pharming

   D. Farming

4. It is important to identify what information is critical to a company and appropriately classify it. This will help the company protect the data in a cost-effective manner. From the following choices, select a statement which correctly describes a characteristic of a data classification program:

A. Once a data owner is identified, the owner can never be changed.

B. Classification levels should be developed only for data and not software.

C. There should be no overlap in the criteria definitions for classification levels.

D. Procedures for declassifying data should not be created.

5. Voice over IP (VoIP) technology is used to provide advanced voice data transmission with improved bandwidth. What protocol does it employ to setup and break down the call sessions?

A. SS7

B. PSTN

C. SIP

D. PBX

6. A company developed a software product by following a standard software development life cycle (SDLC) and released it into the market. The developers on the project were moved into another development project to develop yet another product. Subsequently, it was found that both products had a

lot of bugs. Which of the following processes was likely missed out, resulting in this situation?

A. Postmortem review

B. Quality assurance

C. Unit testing

D. Regression testing

7. A risk assessment revealed a number of low-level impact and high-level impact risks. The cost of mitigating the low-level impact risks was very high. Which of the following risk management strategies may be used in this scenario?

A. Risk avoidance

B. Risk transference

C. Risk avoidance

D. Risk acceptance

8. Security safeguards are carefully evaluated and a number of parameters related to cost, maintenance, testing, repair etc are taken into consideration before deciding on one. Which of the following is an incorrect statement about safeguards?

A. Safeguards should require minimal amount of human intervention.

B. Safeguards should default to least privilege when installed.

C. Safeguards must be completely concealed.

D. Safeguards should have an override functionality that can be used by an administrator if necessary.

9. Most systems will contain a number of data attributes related to a user. For example, a user could have an email address, a home address, a phone number etc. What is the general rule to be followed with respect to data updates for such profiles?

A. Non-sensitive data can be updated by the user while sensitive data should only be updated by an administrator.

B. The user should be able to access and update all data on his/her profile.

C. All data updates to a user's profile should only be done by an administrator.

D. Sensitive data can be updated by the user while non-sensitive data should only be updated by an administrator.

10. An online photograph company was concerned that photographs from its website were being downloaded and copyright laws were being violated. It decided to insert a digital watermark on the photographs so that illegal users of the photographs could be caught. What is this form of concealing identification data known as?

A. Steganytics

B. Steganography

C. Watermark cryptology

D. Digital copyright

11. Once BCP/DRP plans have been created, they need to be tested. Which of the following will require comparatively more planning and involve a lot of people?

A. Straight-through test

B. Simulation test

C. Checklist test

D. Structured walkthrough test

12. Pretty Good Privacy (PGP) is a well known email security product. Which of the following is another method used for secure email?

   A. S / MIME

   B. TCP / IP

   C. HTTPS

   D. MIME / S

13. The difference between a dictionary attack and a rainbow table attack is:

   A. A dictionary attack is used to match a user's ID whereas a rainbow table attack targets the password.

   B. A dictionary attack and a rainbow table attack are the same.

   C. A dictionary attack uses thousands of words and tries to match them to a user's password whereas a rainbow table attack uses a table with thousands of possible passwords already in hash format.

   D. A rainbow table attack uses thousands of words and tries to match them to a user's password whereas a dictionary attack uses a table with thousands of possible passwords already in hash format.

14. A network administrator found that an internal network was overburdened and decided to divide it into smaller segments for better traffic control and use of bandwidth. What device would she use for this purpose?

   A. A bridge

   B. A divider

   C. A router

   D. A switch

15. Which of the following is a poorly implemented output control?

   A. A heading and trailing banner should indicate who the intended receiver is.

   B. If a report has no information to be reported, it should contain a line saying "no output".

   C. A printout of an authorization email should always be required before releasing sensitive output.

   D. Once output is created, it must always have proper access controls (irrespective of the format in which it exists).

16. Audit trails are used to provide alerts about potentially suspicious activities. They can be used to perform investigations at a later time and to determine how far an attack has gone. Which of these is an incorrect guideline for audit trails?

A. Audit trails of high-privileged accounts such as root or the administrator should not be maintained.

B. Audit logs must be protected from unauthorized changes so that the data is safeguarded.

C. All audit logs should be stored securely.

D. The ability to delete audit logs should be available only to administrators.

17. An operating system needs to be developed such that it works using a ring structure. What can be said about the actual ring structure?

A. The actual ring structure is dependent both on the processor and the operating system.

B. The actual ring structure does not depend either on the processor or on the operating system.

C. The actual ring structure is dependent only on the processor.

D. The actual ring structure is dependent only on the operating system.

18. An intruder was detected in a car parking lot and CCTV footage of the intruder loitering around trying to break into cars was obtained. The intruder was captured by security guards. If the CCTV records are to be presented in court, which of the following needs to be done?

A. The CCTV footage must be displayed in court such that the car number plates and faces of individuals other than the accused need to be blurred out or pixelated.

B. The CCTV footage must be played to the intruder to ask him to confirm that it was his actions that were captured.

C. The CCTV footage must be certified by the CEO before it can be viewed in court.

D. The CCTV footage must be immediately seized and presented in court for public viewing without any changes.

19. An employee emailed the source code of a software algorithm to a friend. As a result, the company decided to terminate the employee. The employee challenged this in court and claimed that he was wrongfully terminated. Given this scenario, which of the following is incorrect?

A. The onus is on the employee to prove that he is innocent.

B. The company needs to show what type of damage has been done or could be done due to the algorithm being leaked out.

C. The company needs to prove what steps it had taken to secure the algorithm

D. The company needs to prove why the algorithm was important to the company.

20. Development on a project involved various modules. A developer on the project wrote a security module with low cohesion. What does this mean?

A. The security module interacts with a lot of other modules to perform its tasks.

B. The security module carries out a single task and that makes it simple to maintain.

C. The security module interacts with very few other modules to perform its tasks.

D. The security module carries out multiple tasks and that makes it difficult to maintain.

21. A company considers that the security of emails is very important and decides to implement e-mail protection. Which of the following is true in such a case?

A. The sender and the recipient can use different encryption schemes but they will need a converter software to convert from one scheme to another.

B. The sender and recipient can use different types of encryption schemes.

C. The sender and the recipient must both use the same type of encryption scheme.

D. The sender and the recipient can use different encryption schemes except in case of PGP and PKI, which are compatible with each other.

22. An organization is heavily dependent on Voice over IP (VoIP) for its day-to-day activities. What implication does this have for the team that is

performing a business impact analysis assessment?

A. The team does not have to do anything specifically to handle this scenario.

B. The team needs to plan to procure additional bandwidth in case a disaster strikes.

C. The team should make a recommendation to avoid use of VoIP systems. This will minimize the risk involved.

D. The team should address the need for redundant voice systems.

23. Companies need to comply with local and national standards in dealing with fire prevention, detection and suppression. How far from electrical equipment should portable extinguishers be placed?

A. At a predefined place in the building.

B. Within 100 ft of electrical equipment

C. Within 50 ft of electrical equipment

D. There is no guideline in this case

24. A retailer decided to create an online shopping website. He registered a domain name and planned to use a static IP address of 192.168.2.15. What would your comment on this be?

A. This is fine as long as the retailer ensures that the static IP address has been uniquely assigned by the Internet service provider.

B. The series of IP addresses from 192.168.0.0 to 192.168.255.255 is reserved as private addresses and may not be used on the Internet

C. The IP address does not matter as long as the website name has been properly registered.

D. The series of IP addresses from 192.168.2.0 to 192.168.2.255 are reserved for governmental purposes.

25. An inexperienced developer on a project wrote code for a security module with high coupling. How would you interpret this statement?

A. This means that the module interacts with very few other modules and is the ideal situation to be in.

B. This means that the module interacts with many other

modules. It is preferable to have low coupling.

C. This means that the module carries out a single task. This makes it easy to maintain.

D. This means that the module carries out multiple tasks. This makes it more difficult to maintain.

26. Individual networks on the Internet are connected with other networks using routing protocols. Which of the following protocols builds an accurate routing table by building a topology database of the network?

    A. Distance-vector routing protocol

    B. Internet-vector routing protocol

    C. Link-state routing protocol

    D. Time-based routing protocol

27. Integrity models map abstract goals of a security policy to information system terms and enforce the security policy. Which of the following is not a goal of an integrity model?

    A. To prevent an unauthorized user from making modifications.

B. To prevent an authorized user from making improper modifications.

C. To ensure that covert channels are available to transfer data.

D. To maintain external as well as internal consistency

28. The European Union takes individual privacy very seriously and has strict laws on what data is considered private. Which of these is not one of the European Union privacy principles?

    A. Only the necessary individuals who are required to accomplish the stated task should have access to the data.

    B. The reason for the gathering of data must be clearly specified at the time of data collection.

    C. Data should only be kept for a maximum of 3 years from the time it was first collected.

    D. Unnecessary data should not be collected

29. A professor in a school shared a time management software with a colleague so that she could check out its features and buy the software if she found it useful. This may have

likely violated the terms under which the software was licensed to the professor. What ethical principle would the professor apply to justify his action?

A. Informed consent

B. User's conservation of ownership

C. Change of scale test

D. Owner's conservation of ownership

30. A safe containing confidential data needs to be protected from potential intruders. Which of the following intrusion detection techniques is least useful for this purpose?

A. Photoelectric systems

B. A proximity detector

C. Wave-pattern motion detectors

D. Standby lighting

CISSP Extended Quiz
Answer Key and Explanations

1. A - A password cracker and a password checker perform almost the same function. When the tool is used by a security professional to test the strength of a password, it is called a password checker whereas it is called a password cracker if used by a hacker. [Access Control]

2. C - This is known as password history. Typically, the last 5 to 10 passwords are maintained by the system and users are not allowed to revert to these while changing their passwords. [Access Control]

3. B - This is likely to be a spoof at logon. In this type of attack, the attacker provides the user with a realistic looking fake logon screen. The user enters his username/password which then is seized by the user. The attacker then passes control back to the operating system so that the actual logon screen is presented back to the user. The user assumes that he mistyped his credentials and re-enters them.. [Access Control]

4. C - While developing data classification procedures, care should be taken to ensure that there is no overlap between the criteria definitions of different classification levels. This ensure proper focus on the data. [Information Security and Risk Management]

5. C - Voice over IP (VoIP) technology uses session initiation protocol (SIP) to set up and break down call sessions. This is an application layer protocol that can work over TCP or UDP. [Telecommunications and Network Security]

6. A - A postmortem review is one in which a completed project is looked at objectively and issues that could be improved upon are identified. It is likely that a postmortem review was missed out on the first project. Hence the bugs seen in the first project were also seen in the second one. Many companies do not see value in postmortem reviews and re-assign developers on a project to new projects to maximize their utilization. [Software Development Security]

7. D - In this scenario, a number of low-level impact risks have been identified. The company is most likely to accept the risks (Risk acceptance) since it is a costlier option to try to mitigate them. The other strategies of risk avoidance, mitigation and transference may not help in this case. [Information Security and Risk Management]

8. C - Safeguards should be highly visible. This announces to potential attackers that the necessary

protection is in place. However, attackers should not be able to discover how the safeguards work, else it will enable them to bypass or get around the protection. [Information Security and Risk Management]

9. A - A typical rule to be followed is that a user can access and update non-sensitive data while sensitive data can only be updated by an administrator. For example, a user may be allowed to update an email address or address information while sensitive data such as the expiry date of the login ID cannot be accessed by the user. [Access Control]

10. B - A method of hiding data in another media type is known as steganography. This technique does not use algorithms or keys to encrypt information. Using a digital watermark to ensure that illegal copies can be detected is also an instance of steganography. [Cryptography]

11. B - A simulation test requires a lot of planning involves more people. In this test, all employees who participate in operational / support functions are brought together to practice executing the disaster recovery plan. It raises the awareness of the people involved. [Business Continuity and Disaster Recovery Planning]

12. A - S/MIME is the security enhancement for the MIME Internet email standard. It provides several features and includes signed and encrypted email messages. [Cryptography]

13. C - A dictionary attack uses thousands of words and tries to match them to a user's password whereas a rainbow table attack uses a table with thousands of possible passwords already in hash format. The other options listed are incorrect. [Access Control]

14. A - The network administrator would use a bridge for this purpose. Bridges are used to divide overburdened networks into smaller segments. A bridge also amplifies signals similar to a repeater, however it has more intelligence built in and is used to extend a LAN. [Telecommunications and Network Security]

15. C - A requirement to have a printout of an email for release of sensitive output is a poor control. The email can easily be spoofed and a printout is no proof that it originated from the person who purports to have sent it. It is better to use a signature based system, which can then be matched against an existing database of signatures. [Security Operations]

16. A - Although administrators may have the necessary access rights to

view logs and delete logs, their activities should also be logged. This will ensure that a trail is available in case of security breaches by administrators or other high-profile accounts. [Access Control]

17. A - The actual ring structure used by a system depends on the processor as well as the operating system. Hardware chips are constructed to provide a certain number of rings, and operating systems work within this structure. [Security Architecture and Design]

18. A - Privacy regulations require that the images of individuals other than the accused, and car number plate information should be blurred. The other choices are not valid. [Physical (Environmental) Security]

19. A - The onus is on the company to prove that the employee was guilty of violating its intellectual property rights by emailing the software algorithm. It must be able to show that it had taken steps to protect the file, had explained to its employees that the file should not be shared or copied, and the type of damage that would be caused as a result of loss of the algorithm. [Legal, Regulations, Compliance and Investigations]

20. D - A module with low cohesion means that it carries out multiple tasks, increasing the complexity of the module. This also makes it

difficult to reuse / maintain. If a module interacts with few other modules, it is said to have low coupling. In general, high cohesion and low coupling are preferred. [Software Development Security]

21. C - When users need to use a security scheme to protect messages from being eavesdropped or modified, both parties (sender and recipient) must use the same encryption scheme. Additionally, if the security administrator or professional wants to ensure that all messages between two points are encrypted and does not want to rely on individual users doing so, he/she can implement a VPN. [Security Operations]

22. D - As more and more organizations move to VoIP, it becomes important for them to plan for redundant voice systems. This is because in case of a disaster, if the network goes down, both network and voice capability are unavailable. The other choices listed are impractical. [Business Continuity and Disaster Recovery Planning]

23. C - As a general guideline, portable fire extinguishers need to be placed within 50 ft of any electrical equipment. They also need to be placed near exits. [Physical (Environmental) Security]

24. B - The series of IP addresses from 192.168.0.0 to 192.168.255.255 are a series of 256 contiguous class C network addresses reserved for private use. They may be used within a company but not on the Internet. [Telecommunications and Network Security]

25. B - If a module interacts with few other modules, it is said to have low coupling. In contrast, a module with low cohesion means that it carries out multiple tasks, increasing the complexity of the module. This also makes it difficult to reuse / maintain. In general, high cohesion and low coupling are preferred. [Software Development Security]

26. C - Link-state routing protocols build accurate routing tables by building a topology database of the network. The protocols look at a number of variables such as packet size, link speed, delay, loading etc as variables in their algorithm to decide on the best routes for packets. [Telecommunications and Network Security]

27. C - A covert channel is a way in which an unauthorized entity can receive information. This is not one of the goals of the integrity models. All the other choices are valid goals.

28. C - The European Union privacy principle does not specify a period for retention of data. It states that data should only be kept for as long as it is needed to accomplish the stated task. [Legal, Regulations, Compliance and Investigations]

29. C - The 'change of scale test' applies in this case. The professor thinks it is okay to let his colleague use the software for evaluation purposes even though specific permission may not have been obtained from the vendor. The other choices do not adequately cover this scenario. [Information Security and Risk Management]

30. D - Standby lighting is the least effective in this case. The other three types of intrusion detection systems listed will detect the presence of an intruder in the vicinity of the safe. Standby lighting does not specifically help once an intruder has broken in. [Physical (Environmental) Security]

CISSP Mock Exam (LITE)15
Practice Questions

Test Name: CISSP Mock Exam (LITE)15
Total Questions: 40
Correct Answers Needed to Pass: 30 (75.00%)
Time Allowed: 60 Minutes

Test Description

This is a cumulative CISSP Mock Exam which used as a baseline score for your CISSP aptitude. This practice test includes questions from all ten domains of the CISSP CBK.

Test Questions

1. A new work area is being setup in the conference room of a small commercial office building. The data cabling is being pulled through the space above the floating tile ceiling from the wiring closet on the same floor. What rating should this cabling have?

    A. Cat6E

    B. UTP

    C. Plenum

    D. 10BaseT

2. Macmillan Aerospace Engineering is installing a perimeter fence. Which of the following will provide the best protection?

    A. A 7-foot solid wall fence with 3-4 strands of barbed wire at the top, tilted outward.

    B. A 7-foot chain link fence with 3-4 strands of barbed wire at the top, tilted inward

    C. A 7-foot chain link fence with 3-4 strands of barbed wire at the top, tilted outward.

    D. A 7-foot solid wall fence with 3-4 strands of barbed wire at the top, tilted outward.

3. Reducing or eliminating risk is accomplished by implementing which of the following?

    A. A quality assurance team

    B. An incident response plan

    C. A risk management policy

D. Countermeasures

B. Parsing

C. ActiveX controls

4. A document mandating a) that all corporate email will comply with HIPAA regulations , and a document mandating b) that a specific email client is to be used are examples of what types of security measures?

D. Parameter validation

A. a) Security Policy and b) Security Guideline

B. Both documents are security policies

C. a) Security Policy and b) Security Standard

D. a) Security Standard and b) Security Policy

6. Marcom Publishers are implementing a new monitoring tool in their data center. Corporate security policy places strong limits on the types of inbound connections that can be made to resources in their network. Which of the following application features might conflict with this policy?

A. Remote desktop control

B. All of the above

C. Out of band management modems

D. Administrative consoles

5. An application module checks the values entered by a user to validate they are within the expected range for the information requested. Once the data is determined to be appropriate, it is passed to another application module for further processing. What is this validation process called?

7. There are many types of cybercriminals. Which of the following would be most likely to deface a corporate website?

A. Virtual machine

A. Script kiddies

B. Disgruntled employees

C. Hactivists

D. Advanced persistent threats

8. Bob wants to implement an authentication system that uses both symmetric and asymmetric key cryptography. Which of the following meet his requirement?

A. AES

B. SESAME

C. Realm

D. Kerberos

9. In which of the following environments would a passive infrared sensor be least effective?

A. An art gallery

B. A climate controlled warehouse

C. A storage shed

D. A gymnasium

10. Matthew is developing a data backup plan for his company. It specifies what data is to be backed up, the frequency, the backup type, and where the backup media is to be stored. What other critical component should this plan cover?

A. Antivirus management

B. How long backups are to be retained

C. Denial of service attacks

D. Network saturation

11. FM-200 is the most effective replacement for which of the following fire suppression chemicals?

A. Inergen

B. FE-200

C. FE-13

D. Argon

12. The management of a mid-sized consulting firm is considering using a qualitative approach to risk management, because it will leverage the experience and expertise of the company's staff. While this approach has a number of benefits, it also has a number of cons, including which of the following?

A. Assessments are subjective.

B. There is not a standard way to compare different vendor's products or processes.

C. All of the above

D. It is difficult or impossible to derive dollar values for cost/benefit determination

13. The security team at Jones Shipping is configuring the company's IDS to send an alert to the team when suspicious activity occurs. The team specifies the activities to be monitored, and the number of times those events can occur before an alert is sent. What is this alarm threshold called?

A. Policing threshold

B. Audit level

C. Clipping level

D. Active log point

14. Auditing is typically set up in an organization to track events and resource access. For auditing to be most useful, however, which of the following should be done?

A. Set appropriate log sizes.

B. Develop an auditing policy and plan.

C. All of the above

D. Audit logs should be reviewed regularly

15. The public library in a small Midwestern city would like to implement a system that will keep a tally of how many users visit the library on a daily basis. Which of the following would be the best choice for this scenario?

A. Turnstile

B. RFID tokens

C. Badge readers

D. Smart cards

16. Mary is a computer forensics consultant who has been called in to testify as an expert witness in a trial. What type of evidence does she provide?

A. Opinion evidence

B. Secondary evidence

C. Corroborative evidence

D. Best evidence

17. Which of the following statements regarding stream and block ciphers is correct?

A. Block ciphers use pseudorandom number generators, stream ciphers do not.

B. Stream ciphers typically execute at a higher speed than block ciphers and have lower hardware complexity

C. Both block and stream ciphers use pseudorandom number generators.

D. Block ciphers typically execute at a higher speed than stream ciphers and have lower hardware complexity

18. Global Manufacturing has establish a policy prohibiting POTS lines in its datacenters in an attempt to prevent what type of attack?

A. Ma Bell

B. Operator

C. Brute force

D. Wardialing

19. A major storm has damaged the headquarters of Brighton Industries. Which of the following processes should be executed first?

A. Damage assessment

B. Business continuity plan activation

C. Critical systems recovery

D. Site relocation

20. SMC Semiconductor has just completed a thorough review of its facilities and operations by a third party to assess its compliance with a particular industry standard. SMC has been declared to be in complete compliance with this standard, and is recognized by the third party as such. What is this recognition called?

A. Qualified

B. Certification

C. Registered

D. Accreditation

21. An organization's security officer should report as high in the organization as possible, to maintain awareness of information security and to ensure accurate translation of security messages in large or extremely hierarchical organizations. Exactly which reporting model an organization

selects depends on its culture. Reporting to which of the following entities is most likely to result in information security being viewed as an enterprise function?

A. CEO

B. CIO

C. CFO

D. COO

22. Western Geology Associates has installed several types of physical security measures at their Dallas, Texas facility. These measures include a perimeter fence with gated access, badge entry system to all buildings, and biometric controls at the entrance to their data center. This is an example of what security model?

A. Layered defense

B. Security zone

C. Restricted access

D. Chinese wall

23. In public key cryptography, public keys are exchanged between two parties that wish to communicate. Which of the following is a key agreement protocol used to share that key over an insecure network?

A. Elliptic curve Diffie Hellman

B. Cipher block chaining

C. Serpent

D. Twofish

24. Jack is suspected of electronically embezzling several thousand dollars from his company. Jack has access the company bank accounts and knows how to setup electronic transfers to other accounts. He has also shared with his co-workers that he is having financial problems. These details are best described by which of the following?

A. Motive, opportunity, and means

B. Circumstantial evidence

C. Chain of custody

D. Criminal intent

25. The triad of information systems security are confidentiality, integrity, and availability. Which access control model provides the best protection for confidentiality?

A. Clark Wilson

B. Biba

C. Bell- LaPadula

D. Non-interference

26. An electrical fire has broken out in a storage room of an accounting firm. What classification of fire is this?

A. Class D

B. Class C

C. Class B

D. Class A

27. An accounting firm wants to use an information security framework that is based on financial reporting and disclosure objectives. Which of the following will meet their needs?

A. Sarbanes- Oxley

B. ISACA

C. COSO

D. COBIT

28. The website of a bank was taken down for several hours by a denial of service attack. A group of loosely organized individuals have claimed responsibility. During the subsequent investigation, the responding law enforcement agency classifies this crime as which of the following?

A. Organizational modification

B. Computer assisted crime

C. Cyber graffiti

D. Computer targeted crime

29. Of which of the following would a Nigerian email scam best be categorized?

A. Computer is incidental crime

B. Computer targeted crime

C. Wire tapping

D. Computer assisted crime

30. A software company sends to a customer a quote for several hundred licenses of one of its products. The customer places an order, claiming that the price quoted was $1 per license. The vendor however, says that the quote they sent priced the product at $5 per license, and believes the customer changed the quote. What function of public key cryptography could prove that recipient altered the message after it was received?

A. Nonrepudiation

B. Authentication

C. Confidentiality

D. Availability

31. Close interaction between IT and facilities is common in many organizations. Which of the following areas of information security would be most affected by environmental issues?

A. Integrity

B. All of the above

C. Availability

D. Confidentiality

32. A large software company discovers one of its applications has a buffer overflow vulnerability, and released a patch as a countermeasure. Which of the following data characteristics is affected by a buffer overflow?

A. Availability

B. Confidentiality

C. Integrity

D. State

33. Bartholomew Systems Inc has implemented a very strong three-factor authentication system. What are the three factors used?

A. Administrative, technical, and logical

B. Something you know, something you have, something you are

C. Confidentiality, integrity, availability

D. Authentication, authorization, and accounting

34. A new badge access system is being piloted at Western Manufacturing. The badges used in this system have an onboard antenna that, when activated by the card reader, powers the chip onboard the card. What type of smart card is this?

A. Contact

B. Contactless

C. RFID

D. Proximity activated

35. What are the key principles, or triad, of information security?

A. Logical, Physical, Administrative

B. Availability, Integrity, Confidentiality

C. Monitoring, Detection, Prevention

D. Content, Privacy, Consistency

36. A government agency has implemented an access control system that regulates access based on the agency's security clearance system: Need to Know, Secret, and Top Secret. What is this type of access control system called?

A. Role-based access control

B. Mandatory access control

C. Discretionary access control

D. Context dependent access control

37. Barnes Manufacturing would like put a fence around their production facility, but they do not own the property and the landlord will not permit the installation of a fence. As an alternative to a physical barrier, the company has installed exterior digital video cameras. This scenario is an example of which of the following?

A. Compensating control

B. Control gap

C. External controls

D. Delay mechanism

38. Mills Manufacturing has used the slogan "You design it, we manufacture it!" on their marketing materials and corporate stationery for the last 15 years. Which of the following would be used to provide protection and redress against another organization using this slogan?

A. Trademark

B. Copyright

C. An intellectual property attorney

D. Patent

39. A semiconductor company has invented a new type of integrated circuit. Which of the following would offer the best protection against another company reverse engineering one of these circuits in order to manufacture and sell a copy of it?

   A. Trademark

   B. Copyright

   C. Trade secret registration

   D. Patent

40. Several companies have deployed their servers in the data center of a managed hosting provider. While these servers are logically segregated by VLANs, there is a management VLAN to which all systems are connected. One of the companies has delayed implementing a critical OS security patch for several weeks because they have not finished testing its interoperability with the applications running on its servers.

While the company is completing its testing, the vulnerability for which the patch is issued was exploited on one of their servers. As a result, the unprotected servers were used to launch a denial of service attack against the hosting provider and some of the other servers connected to the management VLAN. During the course of the incident investigation, it is determined that the company was negligent in delaying the installation of the patch, and that it is responsible for service outages to the service provider and the other companies hosted in the datacenter. Which term best describes this condition?

   A. Criminal trespass

   B. Downstream liability

   C. Civil liability

   D. Criminal negligence

CISSP Mock Exam (LITE)15
Answer Key and Explanations

1.   C - The space above a dropped ceiling and beneath a raised floor is called the plenum. In many facilities the building ventilation systems are placed in these spaces. All wiring, including data cabling, that is placed in these types of spaces must be plenum rated, to ensure they do not release toxic gasses in case of a fire. [Telecommunications and Network Security]

2.   C - Chain link fences provide visibility for security systems and patrols inside the perimeter to identify possible intruders outside of the fence. The barbed wire tilted outward makes it more difficult for an intruder to enter over the top of the fence. [Physical (Environmental) Security]

3.   D - Countermeasures are safeguards that are put in place to reduce or remove a potential risk. Countermeasures include virus scanning software, firewalls, mantraps, and badge readers. [Information Security Governance and Risk Management]

4.   C - Security policies are general statements from an organization's management that dictates the role security plays in an organization, while security standards dictate expected user behavior , or acceptable hardware or software. [Information Security Governance and Risk Management]

5.   D - By using parameter validation, an application's development team can ensure that only the correct type or range of information is submitted to an application for processing. Parameter validation can check data for correct spelling or that only numeric characters are entered in the zip code field, for example. It can also be used as a countermeasure against attacks in which data is maliciously changed prior to processing. [Access Control]

6.   B - All of the above items have the potential to conflict with the company's security policies. Many applications offer features that allow administrators to manage or control devices remotely; the manner in which these tools are implemented either by the application vendor or the purchaser can lower the security

stance of an organization. It is best practice to always examine new applications for obvious or hidden administrative interfaces and disable or harden them as appropriate for organizational policy. [Software Development Security]

7. C - Hactivists are groups or individuals that pursue and promote their social or political agenda by means of disabling or defacing the websites of organizations that support policies or business practices that conflict with the hactivists' agenda. [Legal, Regulations, Compliance and Investigations]

8. B - SESAME, the acronym for Secure European System for Applications in a Multi-vendor Environment, uses both symmetric and asymmetric key technologies. Developed to reduce vulnerabilities in Kerberos, SESAME uses Privileged Attribute Certificates (PACs) to contain user identities, access capabilities, as well as the expiration times and dates of both the PAC itself and object access capabilities. [Access Control]

9. C - Passive infrared (PIR) sensors work by detecting changes in the temperature of the area it is monitoring, which may indicate the presence of an intruder. Because PIR can detect temperature changes as small as 3 degrees Fahrenheit, it is best used in areas where the temperature is well controlled. Outdoor spaces or facilities that are not climate controlled, such as storage sheds, will generate a high level of false positives from PIR; as a result, this type of system is not recommended. [Physical (Environmental) Security]

10. B - A backup plan should specify how long backups should be retained. Defining this parameter is best accomplished by consulting each business department in the organization to discern if there are legal or regulatory requirements that dictate how long company records must be retained. The organization's retention duration should then be set to match the longest requirement identified. [Security Operations]

11. B - Halon, a chlorofluorocarbon harmful to both humans and the ozone, was banned in 1987. It has

not been manufactured since 1992, as per the terms of the Montreal Protocol. The most effective replacement for this fire suppression agent is FE-200. [Physical (Environmental) Security]

12. D - Qualitative risk analysis does not use numerical or monetary values. Rather, it develops rankings of threats and countermeasures, based on opinions, intuition, best practices, experience, and judgment. [Information Security Governance and Risk Management]

13. C - The clipping level is the maximum number of times or threshold a specific activity or event can occur. Activities or events beyond this level are considered suspicious, and alerts are sent to staff so they can respond with the appropriate security posture. [Security Operations]

14. C - A successful auditing program includes all of the above recommendations. An audit policy and plan defines what will be tracked, while regular log reviews can reveal trends indicating possible attacks, a need for

additional capacity, or even a need for additional user training. Additionally, configuring an appropriate log file size- and behavior- is important in order to capture all audit data for the desired duration. If the maximum log size is reached, audit data may be overwritten, the system may shut down, or the log will stop collecting data, depending on how the logging is configured. [Security Operations]

15. A - A turnstile is a cost effective and easy to implement solution for keeping a running tally of visitors. Turnstiles could also be used to limit access to patrons presenting library cards, or to prevent visitors from exiting through portals that are intended for entry only. [Physical (Environmental) Security]

16. A - Expert witnesses provide opinion evidence. Rather than testifying about the facts of the case, expert witnesses educate the jury, judge, and both sides of the case about particular subject matter related to the case. [Legal, Regulations, Compliance and Investigations]

17. B - Block ciphers encrypt blocks of data, while stream ciphers encrypt plaintext data one character at a time. As a result, stream ciphers can execute more quickly than block ciphers, and do not require the complex hardware needed to encrypt entire blocks of data. [Cryptography]

18. D - Wardialing is a form of dictionary attack, in which an attacker uses long list of phone numbers with automated dialing program. The goal is to find one answered by a modem to use as a possible access point to a network or computer. [Access Control]

19. A - Following a major event such as fire, storm, or earthquake, the first process to be executed is the damage assessment. The assessment team will evaluate the extent of the damage, what processes have been impacted, and if they can be restored within the maximum tolerable downtime. Once these things have been determined, the team will decide if the BCP should be activated. [Business Continuity and Disaster Recovery Planning]

20. D - Accreditation is the process by which an organization is assessed for compliance with a standard. Certification is the process by which a product, service, or process meets specific standards. [Security Architecture and Design]

21. D - The COO typically leads the administrative services functions of an organization, including physical security, human resources, employee safety, and facilities management. By having the information security officer report to this executive, there can be a synergistic relationship between these divisions that permits the security officer to focus on the security of both electronic and non-electronic information such as paper and oral communications. [Information Security Governance and Risk Management]

22. A - The layered defense model uses multiple types of tiered physical controls to secure a facility or resource. Each layer in this type of architecture serves as a backup for the layer that precedes it. In this example, the biometric lock serves as backup against badge entry system failure, and the badge entry system protects serves as a backup for any breach of the gated fence. [Physical (Environmental) Security]

23.   A - In public-private key cryptography, both sender and receiver must exchange a shared secret, also known as a key. Elliptic curve Diffie Hellman (ECDH) is a key agreement protocol commonly used to secure keys shared over an insecure link. ECDH is the basis for key exchange in the SSH transport protocol. [Cryptography]

24.   A - Criminal investigators and attorneys must prove that a suspect has motive, opportunity, and means in order to have committed a crime. These three elements describe why a person would have committed a crime, whether the person has a chance to commit the crime, and his or her ability to have committed the crime. [Legal, Regulations, Compliance and Investigations]

25.   C - The Bell- LaPadula model is based on the classification of data and users, with users being permitted to access data only at or below their own level of classification. [Security Architecture and Design]

26.   B - Fires involving electrical equipment and/ or wiring are Class C fires. Fire suppression systems for these types of fires use carbon dioxide (CO_2) or dry power to extinguish the flames. [Physical (Environmental) Security]

27.   C - COSO identifies five areas of internal control that are needed for financial disclosure and reporting. These objectives are: control environment, risk assessment, control activities, information and communication, and monitoring. [Information Security Governance and Risk Management]

28.   D - Computer targeted crimes are those actions that impact a computer or related device. These crimes include installation of malware, denial of service attacks, and buffer overflow attacks. [Legal, Regulations, Compliance and Investigations]

29.   A - A computer is incidental crime is a crime in which a computer is used, but another computer is not attacked, nor is electronic data illegally accessed. In the case of an email scam, the crime that is attempted is fraud. The email is simply the vehicle for the scammers' request for money or banking information. These types of scams were carried out through postal correspondence before the rise of email, and could still be conducted by means of pen, paper, envelope, and stamp; thus the computer is simply an incidental mechanism in the crime. [Legal, Regulations, Compliance and Investigations]

30. A - Nonrepudiation provides assurance that message integrity and origin cannot be contested by sender or recipient. A simple hash of the data sent can be compared to a hash of the data that was received. Hashes that are not identical show that the message was altered. [Cryptography]

31. C - Environmental controls are critical to protect the availability of corporate data. Beyond fire suppression and backup power, facilities staff also work to ensure adequate cooling and conditioning of air in data centers as well as protecting data cabling installed within walls, ceilings, and subfloors. Fluctuations in temperature and humidity can cause component failures that

result in outages, while data cables that are not appropriately protected can be damaged which limits access to data that must be reached by traversing the cables that are damaged. [Security Operations]

32. C - Buffers are temporary storage areas used by applications to store data. If an application is written in such a way that the application attempts to store more data than the buffer can hold, data will overflow into an adjacent buffer. This overflow can potentially corrupt or overwrite data in the buffer where the application is attempting to store the extra data. Anytime data is lost or changed in an unauthorized manner, the integrity of that data is lost. [Security Architecture and Design]

33. B - Three factor authentication uses three "keys" to authenticate a user: something you know, such as a password; something you have, such as a smartcard; and something you are, such as a fingerprint or retina pattern. [Security Architecture and Design]

34. B - Smart cards have micro processing capabilities onboard the card, which are powered when used in conjunction with a reader. The contactless card type has a multipurpose antenna as well. When waved near a reader, the reader's electromagnetic field activates the antenna, generating sufficient power to operate the card's processor. The antenna, once powered, can also broadcast authentication credentials to the reader. [Access Control]

35.   B - Availability, integrity, and confidentiality of data are the key objectives of information security. Availability means data is accessible to authorized individuals in a timely manner. Integrity is the assurance that data has not been altered in an unauthorized manner. Confidentiality means that data has not been accessed by an unauthorized party. [Information Security Governance and Risk Management]

36.   B - Mandatory Access Control bases access to resources on organizational security policy. The security policy is centrally administered and users are not permitted to override policy for resources he or she owns. [Access Control]

37.   A - A compensating control is any control that is implemented in place of another control due to cost, technical, or business reasons. The property owner prohibition on installing a fencing is an example of a business reason for a compensating control. [Access Control]

38.   A - Trademarks are service marks such as slogans, logos, symbols, words, colors or sounds that are used to represent an organization's brand. Registered trademarks cannot be copied or used by a unauthorized organization. [Legal, Regulations, Compliance and Investigations]

39.   D - Patents protect the original inventions of the individuals or companies. In order for the patent to be issued, the invention must be novel, useful, and not obvious. It is important to note that the patent is awarded to the inventor, not to the invention itself. [Legal, Regulations, Compliance and Investigations]

40.   B - The failure of a company to ensure that its actions or inactions do not impact another company is called downstream liability. In this scenario, the company that failed to implement the patch in a timely manner has caused service disruptions for a number of other companies, and could be held liable for their negligence, if one of the impacted companies chose to sue for the damage caused. [Legal, Regulations, Compliance and Investigations]

CISSP Mock Exam (LITE)16
Practice Questions

Test Name: CISSP Mock Exam (LITE)16
Total Questions: 40
Correct Answers Needed to Pass: 30 (75.00%)
Time Allowed: 60 Minutes

Test Description

This is a cumulative CISSP Mock Exam which used as a baseline score for your CISSP aptitude. This practice test includes questions from all ten domains of the CISSP CBK.

Test Questions

1. Stephen wants to email a small portion of a contract to the finance manager at his company for review. He cuts and pastes that text into the body of an email and sends it. It is imperative that the email containing the message be guaranteed to have been sent by Steven. Which of the following will provide this assurance?

   A. Transport encryption

   B. Digital certificate

   C. Digital signature

   D. Link encryption

2. A technology startup company is in the process of building their webserver. The web development team is using server side includes (SSI) to display on every page of their website a banner showing the number of days remaining until their product launch. What should the web team do to ensure their SSI scripts are secure?

   A. Disable port 80

   B. Disable the exec function

   C. Require administrators to log on through a single sign on portal

   D. Install an application level firewall

3. Beth is the administrator of a small network. Several users are reporting that they were unable to log into the finance application just before lunch, but were able to log on when they returned to the office about an hour later. After some investigation, she discovers

an attacker is running a brute force attack on the finance application with known user IDs . Beth had previously implemented a countermeasure against this type of attack. Which of the following might Beth have implemented??

A. Setting password expiration dates

B. Configuring account lockout

C. Disabling user accounts

D. Administratively changing the user passwords

4. World Wide Paint and Pigment estimates the likelihood of a flood damaging its server room is approximately once in 100 years, and the resulting damage would total $150,000. What is the annualized loss expectancy of this scenario?

A. $150,000

B. $75,000

C. $15,000

D. $1,500

5. A critical database server has failed, and the backup server did not come online automatically, causing a three hour outage while the backup server was manually activated. Without the database, the company is unable to look up customer files. Which of the following best describes this scenario?

A. Catastrophe

B. Nondisaster

C. Disaster

D. Failure

6. The promotions manager of Midwest Motors has been made the owner of his department's printers and other resources. The manager is now able to designate who in his department has permission to use a large format printer. This method of access control is known as which of the following?

A. Mandatory

B. Role-based

C. Discretionary

D. Distributed

7. MAC addresses are used to identify systems at the data link layer, while IP addresses identify systems at the network layer. Which of the following protocols provide a mapping between MAC addresses and IP addresses, to enable communication between the network and data link layers?

A. ARP

B. WINS

C. LMHOSTS

D. DNS

8. The network team of a small but rapidly growing company is considering how to rearchitect the network to alleviate some congestion it is seeing. They determine that dividing the network into logical groups by department, thereby keeping interdepartmental traffic grouped together, will improve the overall network performance. What are these logical divisions called?

A. Subnets

B. Domains

C. Port maps

D. Realms

9. For security reasons, two different managers are required to log on to a corporate application in order to launch the quarterly reporting batch process. Each manager uses one half of a single security key. What is this type of security mechanism called?

A. Dual control

B. Separation of duties

C. Collusion

D. Split knowledge

10. Acme Tools is implementing a number of security measures to protect its assets and staff. These measures include badge readers and new remote access policies

and technologies. Acme is performing what type of action?

A. Incident Response

B. Information Protection

C. Due Diligence

D. Due Care

11. In the event the President of the United State is incapacitated, the Vice President will perform the duties of the President. If the Vice President is also incapacitated, the Speaker of the House of Representatives will step in. Many organizations also have some sort of plan that addresses the transfer of leadership and responsibilities to other personnel in the event the head of the organization is incapacitated. What is this business continuity concept called?

A. Organizational modification

B. Delegation of authority

C. Emergency recruitment

D. Executive succession planning

12. Which of the following encryption types offers better protection from inference attacks as data traverses a network?

A. End to end encryption

B. Payload encryption

C. Transport encryption

D. Link encryption

13. Gary is an undercover agent investigating a cybercrime ring. During the course of his investigation, he poses as a student looking to make some quick cash to pay next semester's tuition. Gary is approached by a member of the ring and is recruited to be a mule, handling money laundering tasks. Gary documents everything he learns about the gang's operations during his job orientation. This information, along with the evidence collected by other investigators is used to convict several members of the gang. What is this investigative approach called?

A. Exigent circumstances

B. Enticement

C. Entrapment

D. Collusion

14. When developing an application, programmers must specify how memory is to be managed. Attackers frequently probe applications to determine how memory management is handled and if there are any vulnerabilities that could be exploited. One common memory exploit is a buffer overflow. Which memory management mechanism will alleviate this vulnerability?

    A. Stack registers

    B. E-recycling

    C. Garbage collectors

    D. First In Last Out

15. The security and IT teams at Harvey West Inc. are selecting new electronic door lock mechanisms for a small closet where the company's IT assets are located.

Because the closet is so small, the rack with the servers and other gear is positioned so it can be accessed simply by opening the door. There is no room to close the door with a person inside. Which type of electronic lock will provide the best level of protection for this closet in the event of a power outage?

    A. Badge reader

    B. Fail safe

    C. Pin pad

    D. Fail secure

16. A new R & D facility has been recently built; the facility buildout included redundant UPS systems. The UPS systems are inactive until the power fails, at which time the battery packs are activated. What type of UPS is this?

    A. Standby UPS

    B. Failover

    C. Inline

    D. Passive

D. Reputation

17. Administrative and technical controls often go hand in hand. Which of the following could involve interaction between administrative and technical controls?

   A. Information classification

   B. Password changes

   C. File backup and recovery

   D. Employee terminations

18. Richard is the leader of his company's business continuity planning committee. They are conducting a business impact analysis of the threats to the company and mapping them to critical areas of disruption to the business. Which of the following is an area of potential impact to a business?

   A. All of the above

   B. Financial considerations

   C. Regulatory responsibilities

19. A large real estate firm has recently implemented a configuration management system to track and manage changes to its IT environment. Which of the following items would be a candidate for configuration management?

   A. All of the above

   B. Operating system patches

   C. Firewall changes

   D. New anti-virus software

20. Windows, Linux, and Unix operating systems have the capability to use Kerberos authentication. Which of the following best describes this method of access control?

   A. Enterprise identity management

   B. RBAC

   C. Gated cryptography

D. Single sign on

21. All electronically accessible assets of the mergers and acquisitions department at Wilson Clark Electronics are completely isolated from the rest of the company. This was done to prevent unauthorized access to confidential information about business opportunities the company is working on. What is this this type of separation called?

   A. Chinese Wall

   B. DMZ

   C. VLAN-based security zones

   D. Great Divide

22. Many applications use components called modules to perform specific tasks. This approach, called modular programming, has many benefits, including using a single module to perform the same function in multiple applications. Modules can be measured according to how dependent they are on other modules to perform its tasks. Which of the following indicates a module has very little

need to communicate with other modules?

   A. High cohesion

   B. Low cohesion

   C. High coupling

   D. Low coupling

23. A fire has destroyed the headquarters of Western Data Inc. The company has previously set up a disaster recovery site that can have the company's critical operations back up and running in just a few hours; this facility is owned and managed by Western Data. What is this type facility called?

   A. Warm site

   B. Redundant site

   C. Hot site

   D. Cold site

24. Connection Networks and Provance Semiconductor have each agreed to allow the other

company to use their facilities of in the event of a disaster. What is this type of arrangement called?

A. Tertiary site

B. Reciprocal agreement

C. Alternate facility

D. Hot swap

25. Bill is running data backup program for his company. The type of backup he has selected backs up all files that have changed since the last full backup, and the archive bit of the backed up files is not changed. Which of the following backup types is Bill running?

A. Partial

B. Intermediate

C. Incremental

D. Differential

26. Key stroke logging, shoulder surfing, and social engineering are

methods for thwarting which of the information security principles?

A. Integrity

B. Availability

C. Authorization

D. Confidentiality

27. Every network interface card manufactured has a unique identifying code. What is this code called?

A. IEEE code

B. IANA code

C. MAC address

D. IP address

28. Which of the following enables a device with a private IP to communicate with a device with a public IP?

A. IPv4

B. SIP

C. QoS

D. NAT

29. Which of the following is the most accurate and secure form of biometric recognition?

    A. Iris scanning

    B. Retinal scanning

    C. Vascular patterns

    D. Fingerprints

30. Which enterprise architecture framework is based on a two dimensional matrix?

    A. SABSA

    B. Bell LaPadula

    C. ISO 17001

    D. Zackman Framework

31. When the development process is complete and the code is compiled into its final version, Western Data Corporation stores production ready software in a secure data repository. At that point, the developers have no further interaction with the code. Only the system administration team responsible for the roll out of the application has access to this software. What is this security posture called?

    A. Collusion

    B. Access control

    C. Separation of duties

    D. Job rotation

32. Bob and Alice plan to exchange messages using secret keys. However, they each live in a different country. The most expedient way to exchange secret keys is over a network. However, the key exchange must take place without yet having a secret key to encrypt the data, leaving the key exchange transaction relatively unsecured. Which of the following provides the most secure workaround to this chicken-and-the-egg problem?

    A. Quantum cryptography

B. PKI

C. KDC

D. Digital signature

33. Which of the following can allow unauthorized users to access and alter software code?

   A. Maintenance hooks

   B. Stovepipe implementations

   C. Keystroke logging

   D. Overflow buffers

34. Ethernet is a collision-based LAN technology. If a large number of systems are placed on a single network segment, what a possible result?

   A. All of the above

   B. Latency

   C. Packet loss

   D. Repeated transmissions

35. Bill is reviewing the laws and regulations that apply to his company's use of confidential employee data. Which of the following statements is most true?

   A. Laws are issued by a legislative body, while regulations are issued by a government agency.

   B. Laws are issued by government agencies, while regulations are issued by a legislative body.

   C. Government agencies can issue laws and regulations.

   D. Legislative bodies can issue laws and regulations.

36. A government agency has installed a Class 3 vault to house top secret materials. How long will this type of vault withstand an attack with common mechanical tools?

   A. 1 hour

   B. 30 minutes

   C. 2 hours

   D. 15 minutes

37. Matt has just loaded a computer with the operating system, application, patches, and configuration tweaks that his company uses for all new desktop computer deployments. What is this standard system setup called?

    A. Software inventory

    B. Baseline

    C. Library

    D. Configuration management

38. Bill is testing a newly released operating system update with all supported versions of his company's software products, to ensure operability. What is this type of testing called?

    A. Localization testing

    B. Unit testing

    C. Regression testing

    D. Validation testing

39. Immediately after a significant earthquake, the manager of an IT group begins to assess which of his team members were able to evacuate, to determine if any of his staff may have been trapped in the basement data center. Because the security policy requires employees to badge in and out of the data center, the manager is able to check logs to determine which employees were in the data center at the time of the quake and which ones had badged out prior to that time. What is this system feature called? .

    A. Turnstiling

    B. Anti-passback

    C. Location logging

    D. Badging out

40. Which of the following would provide the most effective tool for reviewing and analyzing data for a security event in progress?

    A. Log management system

    B. Event viewer

C. Incident response plan

D. Security   event   management
   system

CISSP Mock Exam (LITE)16
Answer Key and Explanations

1.   C - Digital signatures provide authentication of the identity of the sender of a message. The digital signature is transformed with a hash function and then both the hashed value- also called a message-digest- and the signature are sent in separate transmissions to the receiver. Using the same hash function as the sender, the receiver derives a message-digest from the signature and compares it with the message-digest it received. Matching message-digests mean the sender is who she or she says she is. [Cryptography]

2.   2.) B - Server side includes can be exploited by an attacker to run malicious commands that could damage a system or its data. By disabling the exec function, attackers are effectively blocked from using this vulnerability to breach a system; some vendor's webserver products have the exec function disabled by default. [Software Development Security]

3.   B - Configuring accounts to be locked out after a set number of incorrect logon attempts is a common way to foil brute force password attacks.   Once the account is locked out, the user will not be able to attempt to logon again until the configured time interval has passed, or the administrator unlocks the account. [Software Development Security]

4.   D - Annualized loss expectancy (ALE) is calculated by multiplying the annualized rate of occurrence (ARO) by the single loss expectancy (SLE).   In this example, the ARO is .01, and the SLE is $150,000, yielding an ALE of $1,500 (.01 x $150, 000= $1,500) [Information Security Governance and Risk Management]

5.   B - A service outage caused by the failure of a device or component, such as hardware or software is categorized as a nondisaster. A disaster is an event that causes an entire facility to be unavailable for a day or longer, and typically involves the use of a backup site while the primary facility is being repaired..   A catastrophe is an event in which an entire facility is destroyed. [Business Continuity and Disaster Recovery Planning]

6. C - Discretionary access control, which is the basis of most mainstream operating systems, is a delegated authority model. The owner of a resource may- at his or her own discretion- specify who may and who may not access that resource, as well as what actions may be taken on that resource. The creator of a file is the owner of that file, but an administrator can assign ownership of resources to other users. [Access Control]

7. A - Address Resolution Protocol (ARP) enables a system to create a mapping of IP addresses to MAC addresses in cache. This mapping is created as the system "learns" which system owns a specific MAC address and IP address the first time it broadcasts for a system with those address. Only the system that has that IP address responds to the broadcast and the initiating system adds this data to its ARP cache, eliminating the need to broadcast for that system again until the ARP cache expires. [Telecommunications and Network Security]

8. A - Subnets break networks into segments. By doing so, traffic can be routed directly between source and destination systems on the same segment, rather than sending the traffic out over the network as a whole. [Telecommunications and Network Security]

9. D - Providing each of two user with one half of the key required to access a resource is called split knowledge. In order for this approach to be completely secure, however, each user must maintain full control over his or her half of the key, and it must be protected by a password known only to the holder of the key half. [Cryptography]

10. D - Due care is the act of developing and implementing security policies, standards, guidelines, and technologies to eliminate or reduce risks to an organization's assets. These risks are identified during the due diligence process. [Information Security Governance and Risk Management]

11. D - Executive succession plans specify the activities to be executed when the head of the organization is incapacitated, killed, retires, or is in some material way unable to fulfill his or her duties for an

extended period of time. These plans may include the terms and conditions under which the leadership changes are required, and which staff will be called upon to step into the head position. [Business Continuity and Disaster Recovery Planning]

12. D - In link encryption, all of the data along a network communication path is encrypted, including routing information. Because it hides the source and destination of the data itself, it is impossible for an eavesdropper to discern which two parties are sending and receiving data. [Cryptography]

13. B - Because Gary was recruited to play a role in a crime that the gang member had already intended to commit, this scenario is best described as enticement. For this to have been entrapment, Gary would have had to manipulate or trick the gang member into committing a crime. Entrapment does not establish that a suspect had prior intent to commit a crime. [Legal, Regulations, Compliance and Investigations]

14. C - Garbage collectors manage memory by reclaiming old and unused objects stored in memory that were not released by an application. Attackers can exploit memory bugs that cause buffer overflows, whereby data exceeds the capacity of its assigned memory space and overwrites data in adjacent spaces. These overflows can cause data loss or application crashes, resulting in loss of data integrity or availability. [Software Development Security]

15. D - In a failure state, devices that fail secure will revert to a most secure stance. In the case of an electronic lock, the lock would remain closed. Devices designed to fail safe will revert to a secure posture, but with built in safety measures; an fail-safe electronic lock would permit some measure of access for life safety purposes. In this scenario, the server closet would benefit from a fail secure device, as the area it is protecting does not require an escape mechanism for staff. [Security Operations]

16. A - A standby UPS offers basic power surge protection and battery backup power. This type of UPS

is not continually powered by utility power, however, so there is a slight delay between the time its sensor detects a power outage and the time the battery packs are activated. [Physical (Environmental) Security]

17. D - Employee terminations. A human resources department has typically developed a set of policies and procedures that deal with employees leaving the company. The policies and procedures are developed collaboratively with several departments to ensure that all appropriate actions are taken, from issuing a final check and an exit interview, to disabling user accounts and remote access and collecting access badges. [Access Control]

18. A - There are a number of areas in which a disaster can impact a business. These include operational disruption and productivity, financial considerations, regulatory responsibilities, and reputation. During a business impact analysis or BIA, the BCP committee identifies of potential threats to the company, and maps them to these areas of impact.. [Business Continuity and Disaster Recovery Planning]

19. A - Any change to a production environment, whether it is hardware, software, or documentation, can be placed under configuration management (CM). The purpose of CM is to formally track what is being changed, who is requesting the change and who approved the change, as well as the testing and implementation of the change. Once a change has been finished, it should be documented and reported as complete, ensuring that there is a record of the complete lifecycle of the change. [Security Operations]

20. D - Kerberos is a single sign on access control mechanism. Upon logging in successfully, users are granted ticket granting tickets (TGTs). TGTs are presented to Kerberos-aware applications such as email, from which these applications acquire service tickets. The service tickets authenticate the user to the application without requiring an additional logon. [Access Control]

21. A - Chinese walls are barriers implemented within an organization to prevent unauthorized access to information by parties who may unduly influence or be influenced by that data. Insider trading is one type of conflict of interest that this is intended to protect against. [Security Architecture and Design]

22. D - Modules with low coupling require very little interaction with other modules to carry out their tasks. Lower cohesion modules are easier to update and reuse than modules that depend more heavily on other modules to complete its task. [Software Development Security]

23. B - A disaster recovery site that is fully configured and ready to operate within a few hours and owned and operated by the organization that will be using it is called a redundant site. A hot site also provides an organization with the ability to be back up and running in just a few hours. However hot sites are not owned by the organization who will be using it; rather they are a rented or leased facility. [Business Continuity and Disaster Recovery Planning]

24. B - Organizations may arrange to allow each company to use the facilities of the other company in the event of a disaster. This is called a reciprocal agreement. If offers cost savings over each company maintaining its own facility, but it may also decrease the efficiency with which each company operates, as the processes, policies, and resource availability of the hosting organization may cause conflicts or constraints for the company that relocates to this site. [Business Continuity and Disaster Recovery Planning]

25. D - In a differential backup, all data that has changed since the last full backup is backed up, without changing the archive bit. [Business Continuity and Disaster Recovery Planning]

26. D - The confidentiality of data is breached when unauthorized parties access it. Confidentiality breaches may be intentional by methods such as shoulder surfing or social engineering to gather passwords, or unintentional such as by failing to encrypt data while it is at rest or in transit.

[Information Security Governance and Risk Management]

27. C - NIC cards are identified by a unique code called a Media Access Control (MAC) address. While this value can be spoofed by hackers, it is typically considered to be a permanent identifying code. [Telecommunications and Network Security]

28. D - Because the available public IPv4 address space is not large enough to support the number of IP devices in use today, private IP address ranges have been implemented. These IP addresses are not routable over the internet, however, so network address translation (NAT) was developed to support communication between devices on private and public networks. [Telecommunications and Network Security]

29. B - Retinal scanning offers low false positive rates, and false negative rates of close to zero. It also has a very small base of outliers, those users who are unable to be enrolled in the system. Further is much more difficult to defeat this type of

system than other types of biometric readers, including iris scanning. [Physical (Environmental) Security]

30. D - The Zackman Framework is based on a matrix consisting of six communications questions and 6 reification transformations. [Security Architecture and Design]

31. C - This division of responsibility is called separation of duties. By restricting access to software code only to the administration group, Western Data has prevented members of the development team from accessing and potentially modifying the code that he or she has written. [Software Development Security]

32. A - Quantum cryptography uses physics rather than mathematics to generate and distribute secret keys. By relying on the unpredictable nature of quantum particles- Heisenberg's Uncertainty Principal states it is impossible to know an object's position and velocity at the same time- keys can be securely transmitted. In quantum cryptography, the spin direction of polarized photons is mapped to binary code that represents the key itself. The sender knows the direction of spin of the photons that are sent; the recipient measures the spin of the photons he receives. Then both sender and recipient have an unencrypted message exchange validating if the spin of each proton sent matches the spin of the proton received. [Cryptography]

33. A - Maintenance hooks are backdoors left in software during the development process to provide an easy way to update software, intentionally bypassing normal security checks. If these maintenance hooks are not removed before deployment, they become a vulnerability that can be exploited by unauthorized users. [Security Architecture and Design]

34. A - In a network that has a large number of workstations or other devices on a single network segment, latency, packet loss, and repeated transmissions are possible. This is because multiple data collisions occur when many devices attempt to send data on same network at the same time. Segmenting the network with subnets , routers, or bridges will decrease the number of systems on

a single segment, reducing the number of collisions occurring on that segment. [Telecommunications and Network Security]

35. A - Laws are issued by legislative bodies such as the US Congress or the British Parliament. Regulations are issued by governmental agencies dictating the manner in which laws will be implemented. For example, the Health Insurance Portability and Accountability Act legislated by the US Congress, but the standards and guidelines governing how it is put into practice are issued and maintained by the US Office for Civil Rights. [Legal, Regulations, Compliance and Investigations]

36. C - Underwriter Laboratories has set forth ratings for vault attack resistance. The lowest rating, Class M, will resist attack for 15 minutes. The highest rating, Class 3, will withstand attack for two hours. [Physical (Environmental) Security]

37. B - A baseline is the list of standard components that make up a system. It includes hardware, software, specific configurations, or other items, such as pre-loaded documentation templates. An organization may have more than one baseline, each one customized for a specific purpose. By only deploying systems with an approved corporate baseline, the IT team can be assured that all systems meet whatever security requirements are in place for that organization, and know which baselines (and systems) need to be updated to be protected against newly discovered security risks.. [Security Operations]

38. C - Regression testing is the process of testing new software components against existing software code, to ensure that all expected and required functionality is preserved upon the addition of the new code. [Software Development Security]

39. B - Anti-passback features require users to provide badges, PINs, or other authentication device every time a user enters and exits specified portals. If an employee fails to badge-out of a restricted area, he or she will be prohibited from re-entering that secured area without administrative intervention. This is a

countermeasure against users sharing badges, PINs, etc. [Physical (Environmental) Security]

40. D - Security event management systems provide a platform for assembling, reviewing, and analyzing log data from multiple sources in real time. Log management systems provide only historical data for review and trending analysis. [Security Operations]

CISSP Mock Exam (LITE)17
Practice Questions

Test Name: CISSP Mock Exam (LITE)17
Total Questions: 40
Correct Answers Needed to Pass: 30 (75.00%)
Time Allowed: 60 Minutes

Test Description

This is a cumulative CISSP Mock Exam which used as a baseline score for your CISSP aptitude. This practice test includes questions from all ten domains of the CISSP CBK.

Test Questions

1. An investment bank reassigns certain of its employees to new positions on a quarterly basis. Further, company policy requires these employees to take 5-business-day vacations every 6 months. What are each of these types of job controls called?

   A. Job rotation and mandatory vacations

   B. Separation of duties and job rotation

   C. Separation of duties and mandatory vacations

   D. Matrix organizations and mandatory vacations

2. ColdFusion and SQL are examples of a class of programming languages that enable developers to rapidly create applications for specific purposes with far fewer lines of code than earlier programming languages. This class of languages was developed with complex business logic in mind. What is this language class known as?

   A. n-tier

   B. 4GL

   C. Middleware

   B. 5GL

3. Johnson Brothers, Inc. has deployed a certain word processor on all of its Windows Vista, Windows 7, and Windows XP workstations,. Which of the following best describes the process that allows the same

application to run on a variety of hardware and operating system configurations?

A. Minimum system requirements

B. Abstraction

C. Standardized field tools

D. Relocation

4. A company has implemented a firewall to reduce the risk of unauthorized access to its network. The risk is not completely eliminated, however. What is the remaining risk called?

A. Transferred risk

B. Mitigated risk

C. Vulnerability

D. Residual risk

5. The network card of an Network Intrusion Detection sensor is set in which mode?

A. M-node

B. Broadcast

C. Analysis

D. Promiscuous

6. Central Coast Farms grows and sells cut flowers to wholesale customers such as grocery stores and florists. The company has decided it is time to start accepting internet orders, and has hired a consultant to design and setup a webstore that integrates with its existing systems. These applications and databases run on disparate hardware and software platforms. To meet the company's integration requirement, the consultant recommends an approach based on which of the following?

A. CORBA

B. Modular programming

C. Multithreading

D. Symmetric processing

7. Castle Enterprises is evaluating the lighting in the parking deck and

other exterior areas of their campus, to ensure the safety of their employees. The consultant they have called in has reviewed the layout of the campus and made a number of recommendations. Which of the following would be the recommendation for the parking deck, which is a light colored structure?

A. More lighting than needed in areas with darker surfaces

B. Less lighting than needed in areas with darker surfaces

C. The same amount of lighting needed in areas with darker surfaces

D. No special lighting is needed

8. A tile manufacturing company has a large warehouse from which they ship their products. Their corporate data center is also located in this warehouse. Which of the following would be used to protect the data center from physical damage resulting from heavy equipment such as forklifts?

A. Motion detectors

B. Bollards

C. Signs indicating the area is off limits for equipment

D. Infrared detectors

9. The IT department at Smith Industries has deployed servers with an estimated lifetime of 33,000 hours. What is this rating called?

A. RPO

B. MTBF

C. MTTR

D. RTO

10. The finance department deployed a very large server with multiple processors to handle a heavy load of database queries. While some of the queries are easily executed, others requires dedicated CPU resources. What is this dedicated state known as?

A. Asymmetric mode

B. Multithreading

C. Symmetric mode

D. Thunking

11. Nancy, the HR manager of WLB, Inc., defines data classification, retention and backup requirements, and access rights for employee data at her company. Dave, the system administrator, implements these controls by performing operational tasks such as setting permissions on files and folders, running backups. Which of the following correctly matches the roles Nancy and Dave play?

A. Nancy is the Data Owner and Dave is the Data User

B. Nancy is the Data Custodian and Dave is the Data User

C. Nancy is the Data User and Dave is the Data Custodian

D. Nancy is the Data Owner and Dave is the Data Custodian

12. The business continuity plan of Ingalls Shipyard includes a large list of resources that must be available in order for the company to continue operating after a disaster. Which of the following items could be included on this list?

A. Network documentation

B. Communications plan

C. Human resources data

D. All of the above

13. Mike is analyzing the traffic on his network to identify the device that is saturating a link with traffic. He is looking at the source address information on a packet. At which network layer are addressing and routing information added, and what is this specific bundle of data called?

A. Network layer; datagram

B. Transport; segment

C. Network layer; frame

D. Transport; datagram

14. Which of the following is best applied to the Biba model?

    A. No read up, no write down

    B. Read up, no read down

    C. No write up, no read down

    D. No read up, write down

15. Nora has embedded a video and photos of her most recent vacation on her social networking page. The video and photos are actually hosted on two other websites. Which of the following allows Nora to share on her social networking page?

    A. XML

    B. OLE

    C. API

    D. HTML

16. Jerry's email application uses SMTP over port 25 to send messages to a mail server. Email applications, regardless of the application vendor, almost always use SMTP over port 25. What is this standardized mapping of a specific port number to a specific protocol called?

    A. Access control lists

    B. Open standards

    C. Well known ports

    D. Sockets

17. A mortgage company is evaluating how secure a new operating system is. The review goes beyond simply checking the default installation configurations; it also includes a complete review of the security and control capabilities and features. Additionally, the company is examining how the operating system was developed. Based on this review, the company deems the operating system to be highly trusted. What are these review points called?

    A. Trusted computing base

    B. Operational and lifecycle assurance

    C. Orange book

D. SDLC

18. The lack of a fire suppression system in a data center is an example of which of the following concepts?

   A. Threat

   B. Risk

   C. OSHA violation

   D. Vulnerability

19. Which of the following leaves a corporate server most vulnerable?

   A. Weak passwords

   B. Out of date virus signatures

   C. No firewall

   D. Installing it in an unlocked closet

20. Over the last 6 months, an IT group has replaced server and network components that have mysteriously failed. These failures

occurred at intervals more frequent than the Mean Time Between Failures rating of the affected components, so the team began to suspect an environmental issue. It was discovered that the HVAC system had not been receiving annual maintenance service. Which of the following could be the result of an HVAC system's faulty performance?

   A. Oxidation and corrosion

   B. Moisture damage

   C. All of the above

   D. Mold growth

21. Wilco Systems has implemented two factor authentication for remote access. A token device is distributed to each employee authorized to have remote access. Token devices are examples of what type of password system?

   A. Password aging

   B. Password clipping

   C. Password hashing

D. One time password

22. A small consulting firm has purchased a new accounting software package. The accounting manager would like to load a copy of the software on her personal computer so that she can work from home occasionally. Which of the following would provide information about where and how many times a given application may be installed?

A. Patent

B. End User License Agreement

C. Copyright

D. Trademark

23. Computer Dynamics is developing an application for one of its customers. They are using the known vulnerabilities of the platform upon which it will be run, as well as the vulnerabilities of other applications that are similar to the application under development, to find potential vulnerabilities in the new

application. What is this approach called?

A. Penetration testing

B. Anomaly based analysis

C. Attack surface analytics

D. Quantum curve analysis

24. Ingalls Electric is developing an incident response policy, and is considering the type of response team that is best for its organization. Ingalls is a very large international corporation, and needs a team that can respond very quickly to incidents as they happen, and supported by staff with particular expertise as needed. Which type of team would be best for this organization?

A. Virtual

B. Hybrid

C. Permanent

D. Role based

25. Global Data Systems has a large IT staff located in various corporate offices throughout the world. Files with data about the organization's network are regularly sent between the staff members. Which of the following should be implemented to protect this data while it is in transit?

A. PKI

B. Transport encryption

C. Digital signatures

D. One-way hashing

26. All computer users at a government agency must meet the following requirements: clearance, documented formal access, and the need to know. This is what type of security operations mode?

A. Privileged security mode

B. Dedicated security mode

C. Directive mode

D. Trusted mode

27. John is pitching his idea for a new software application to some investors. The investors stated explicitly that they are cost sensitive and want this application to his the market as soon as possible, in order to beat out possible competitors as well as reap a quick return on their investment. In which of the following software development phases should security be thoroughly considered, in order to deliver a secure product on time and within budget?

A. Functional design

B. Project initiation

C. Installation and implementation

D. All of the above

28. A municipal courthouse has several self-service kiosks in its lobby. These kiosks have limited access to the court's network because they use a standard internet connection to access the court's web-based applications. However, because the public has physical access to the systems, an attacker can cause damage to the kiosk itself. Which of the following options will prevent a user from accessing the command line?

A. Change the BIOS to enable booting from removable media.

B. Use only wired network connections

C. Implement a constrained user interface

D. Provide only a mouse, no keyboard

29. The business continuity plan team of a regional manufacturing corporation is discussing what constitutes an appropriate interval for testing its plans. Which of the following represents best practices for BCP testing?

A. Every 3 years

B. Every 2 years

C. Annually

D. Quarterly

30. Many systems are configured to acquire an IP address from a remote server rather than using a pre-configured static IP address. What is this remote server called?

A. RADIUS

B. DHCP

C. LDAP

D. RRAS

31. Which of the following RAID options mirrors disks first, then stripes data across the array?

A. RAID 0

B. RAID 1+0

C. RAID 0+1

D. RAID 1

32. Many encryption algorithms mandate the key size, block size, and number of rounds of encryption to be performed. Which of the following do not mandate a fixed value for these elements?

A. RC2

B. RC5

C. AES

D. RC4

33. The DES cipher uses a key of what length?

    A. 16 bits

    B. 64 bits

    C. 256 bits

    D. 56 bits

34. Installation of dual power generators is an example of what element of a business continuity plan?

    A. Reactive measure

    B. Preventive measure

    C. Process automation

D. Operations planning

35. Which of the following is best applied to the Bell-LaPadula model?

    A. No read up, no write down

    B. Read up, no write up

    C. Read up, Write down

    D. Read down, write down

36. Which of the following statements is best applied to quantitative analysis?

    A. Provides realistic cost/ benefit analyses

    B. Relies heavily on subjective information

    C. The opinions of experts are used to identify the highest priority issues and appropriate countermeasures

    D. Requires no calculations

37. Which of the following can be used in conjunction with a CCTV system to eliminate the need for someone to continuously monitor the video feed for intruders?

A. Pan tilt zoom cameras

B. Two-way radios

C. Annunciator system

D. Remote access system

38. Acme Tools has developed a new security policy regarding access to the wireless network. The security committee approved the policy, and documentation has been posted on the company intranet. However the IT group has noticed that compliance is very low. What can be done to increase compliance?

A. Conduct an awareness campaign using non-traditional methods such as prizes to reward compliance.

B. All of the above

C. Require users to sign an acknowledgement that the

have read the policy, understand their responsibilities, and agree to abide by the policy.

D. Conduct user training in the new policy and associated procedures.

39. Developers at Core Graphic Systems are testing the newest version of video card driver, in preparation for release. This code is located on a shared drive, but several engineers have saved a copy to their computers. The team discovers variances in their testing results that are outside the expected range. Upon further investigation it is discovered that, although the revision level of the code the testers are using is identical, there are differences in the code running on each tester's computer. Which of the following would prevent a recurrence of this scenario?

A. Version control system

B. Revision control

C. Rollback

D. Reversion

40. Protection rings are one of the most common architectures implemented to guard system functionality and data from malicious behavior and faults. Which of the following protects the kernel?

   A. Ring 0

   B. Ring 2

   C. Ring 1

   D. Ring 3

CISSP Mock Exam (LITE)17
Answer Key and Explanations

1.   A - Job controls are intended to reduce the risk of internal risks by limiting and or monitoring access to data. Job rotation is the regular cycling of staff through a series of positions, with the goal of uncovering irregularities and preventing collusion between employees. Mandatory vacations allow work to be temporarily reassigned to other staff, during which time irregularities may be discovered through the course of normal business processes. [Information Security Governance and Risk Management]

2.   B - 4GL, also known as fourth generation language, is a programming language that is highly adapted to business logic and abstracts much of the low level complexities of those functions, thus requiring fewer lines of code than earlier 3GL languages. 4GL languages are typically focused on a specific business problem, such as linking a webpage to a database, or extract specific data from a database. [Software Development Security]

3.   B - Abstraction is the process by which a system hides its own processes and hardware from an application, and provides only a simple, high level representation to an application. This allows an application to remain largely agnostic with regards to the specific implementation details of the system on which it is installed. Without abstraction, any given application would have to be rewritten for every single system upon which it is installed, to accommodate for variations in hardware and operating systems. [Security Architecture and Design]

4.   D - Residual risk is the risk that remains after countermeasures have been implemented. It is calculated by this formula: threats x vulnerability x asset value x controls gap = residual risk [Information Security Governance and Risk Management]

5.   D - In order to detect possible attacks, Network Intrusion Detection Systems (NIDS) must examine all network traffic. Promiscuous mode enables a network card to collect, copy, and send to the NIDS devise every packet on that interface. [Access Control]

6. A - The common object request broker architecture, or CORBA, is a standard of interoperability that enables software and hardware from various manufacturers to communicate with each other. CORBA is often called middleware, acting as the agent between a client and a server, retrieving requested data. These transactions are carried out using standard protocols and communications methods which are defined within the CORBA architecture. [Software Development Security]

7. B - Exterior lighting should provide the highest possible contrast between possible intruders and the background surfaces in that area. The best contrast is provided by less light in areas with light colored surfaces and more light in areas with dark colored surfaces. [Physical (Environmental) Security]

8. B - Bollards are concrete or metal pillars that are intended to prevent a vehicle or other conveyance from being driven through a wall.

Typically used to secure the perimeter of a facility, they may also be used inside facilities. In an active warehouse, it is possible for a large piece of equipment to be accidentally or intentionally rammed into a wall, thus permitting unauthorized access to sensitive areas. Bollards provide a physical barrier against this. [Physical (Environmental) Security]

9. B - Mean Time Between Failure (MTBF) is the estimated life of a system or component. The MTBF may be calculated by either the vendor of the device or a third party. [Business Continuity and Disaster Recovery Planning]

10. A - Work that isn't constrained by time or data processing dependencies can typically be handed to an available CPU on an as needed basis. In asymmetric processing, however, CPUs are dedicated to performing specific tasks, and are not available to perform other types of processing. [Security Architecture and Design]

11. D - Nancy is the Data Owner and Dave is the Data Custodian. The Data Owner is typically a manager who has ultimate responsibility for the protection of specific data. However, the Data Owner may delegate some of his or her responsibilities to another person. The Data Custodian is the staff to whom the day-to-day maintenance and security of the data has been delegated. [Information Security Governance and Risk Management]

12.   D - Business continuity plans include any resources an organization needs to continue its essential functions and processes. All of the above items are examples of resources that should be included. Other resources an organization should consider including are spare hardware, equipment and supplies needed to provide a safe environment for staff, and office furniture and supplies for staff housed at alternate work sites. [Business Continuity and Disaster Recovery Planning]

13.   A - As data passes through the layers of the OSI model, different types of information are added at each layer, in a process called encapsulation. The resulting data structure at each layer has a name that identifies it as a product of that layer. Addressing and routing information is applied to a packet at the network layer; the resulting data structure is called a datagram. [Telecommunications and Network Security]

14.   C - The Biba access model focus is integrity. In order to protect data from corruption or unauthorized access, users are prohibited from writing data above their classification label, and from reading data below their classification level. [Security Architecture and Design]

15.   C - APIs, or application programming interfaces, enable two different applications to seamlessly integrate together without either application needing to know much about how the other application works. In this example, APIs enable Nora to share photos and videos on a social networking page, but APIs can also be used to extend functionality or customize off-the-shelf software such as email or finance applications. [Software Development Security]

16.   C - Commonly used port- protocol mappings are called well known

ports. Standardization of these mappings enables interoperability between systems and devices, regardless of vendor. Port numbers between 0 and 1023 constitute the range of well known ports that have fixed protocol mappings. [Telecommunications and Network Security]

17. B - In order for a system to be classified as highly trusted, there must be a way to verify that the system as a whole meets an organization's security requirements. Operational and lifecycle assurances provide guarantees that a given system works only as designed, and was developed within a very secure development and distribution environment. [Security Operations]

18. D - The absence of a protective mechanism, such a as fire suppression system or door locks, is a vulnerability. A threat is the possibility that a vulnerability would be exploited, while a risk is the probability of a threat as well as the loss that could result from the exploit of a vulnerability. [Information Security Governance and Risk Management]

19. D - Physical access to a server is the biggest vulnerability. Once an attacker has physical control or possession of the system, he or she is not subject to time or resource constraints associated with defeating technical access controls such as firewalls, intrusion detection, or access control lists. [Access Control]

20. C - HVAC damage is not limited to systems or component breakdown due to thermal cycling or excessively high heat. Failure to adequately condition the air to control humidity can cause an increase in moisture, resulting in damage to equipment as well as the building infrastructure. [Physical (Environmental) Security]

21. D - Token devices are commonly used in two factor authentication to generate a one time password that is valid for a single use. Token devices provide hashed values to the user for entry along with his or her user ID. The token is synchronized with an authentication service either synchronously or asynchronously. [Access Control]

22. B - End User License Agreements, also known as EULAs, define the acceptable use, terms, limits and conditions associated with a specific application. For instance, EULA may state that an application may be installed on a maximum of two workstations, that it may not be transferred to another party, and that it is intended only for use in an educational environment. [Legal, Regulations, Compliance and Investigations]

23. C - Attack surface analytics are developed by studying known vulnerabilities and flaws inherent in an application's operating environment, and mapping those vulnerabilities to possible points of attack in a new application. These analytics are then used to specify how the application should be developed or modified in order to prevent or eliminate potential vulnerabilities in the new application. [Software Development Security]

24. B - A hybrid incident response team is composed of a core of permanently assigned staff, who can call in other organizational resources as needed to support their investigation. This approach combines the permanent and virtual team types; permanent teams are made up of a dedicated staff, while virtual teams are composed of staff who have other responsibilities in addition to their role responding to incidents. [Legal, Regulations, Compliance and Investigations]

25. B - Encrypting all data as it is sent over the network will protect sensitive data from interception by an attacker. However, it is recommended that all sensitive data be encrypted while at rest and in transit. [Security Operations]

26. B - Dedicated security mode, specified in DOD Directive 5200.28, is an operational mode in which all users have clearance or authorization, documented formal access approval, and a need to know the information stored on the system. Dedicated security mode can be implemented with a single or multiple data classification levels. [Security Architecture and Design]

27. D - Software Development Security should be considered during every phase of the software development lifecycle. By doing so, security mechanisms can be customized for the application as it is developed. Simply bolting-on security controls after the application is complete can result in loss of functionality due to conflicts between the application and the controls. These conflicts can in turn lead to delays and additional costs to test and rewrite the code so the application works with the security mechanisms. [Software Development Security]

28. C - Systems provided for public use can be secured with a constrained UI. By configuring the system to present only the permitted applications, and hiding access to any other applications or operating system functions, users are unable to access the directory structure or command line to view, execute, and/ or delete files. [Security Operations]

29. C - Best practice calls for annual of testing of business continuity plans. However, it is imperative to update the BCP on a regular basis, to ensure it includes the most recent changes in organizational polices, processes, resources, and

goals. [Business Continuity and Disaster Recovery Planning]

30. B - Dynamic Host Configuration Protocol (DHCP) servers assign IP addresses from a set pool. These IP address assignments are called leases. DHCP clients will request the DHCP server to renew its IP assignment when its lease expires. [Telecommunications and Network Security]

31. B - In a disk array using RAID 1+0, data on a drive in the first array is mirrored to a matching drive in the second array, then striped across all disks in each array. In RAID 0+1 data is first striped in an array then mirrored to a second array. The combination of two different types of RAID in a single redundancy mechanisms is called nested RAID. [Security Operations]

32. B - RC5 offers variable parameters that can be configured for encryption with this cipher. Block size may be 32, 64 or 128 bits, key size may be 0 to 2040 bits, and the number of rounds may be 0 to 255. [Cryptography]

33. D - DES, also known as Digital Encryption Standard, uses a 56 bit key. DES was originally introduced as a Federal Information Processing Standard (FIPS) in 1976, but has been replaced in production systems with symmetric encryption algorithms that offer a longer key length.; the short key length of DES is easily cracked by the processing power of modern computers. [Cryptography]

34. B - Implementation of equipment, staff, or processes that fortify a company and protect against a potential loss are preventive measures. In this example, the installation of two power generators is a safeguard against not only a prolonged power outage, but the failure of one of the generators as well. [Business Continuity and Disaster Recovery Planning]

35. A - The Bell- LaPadula access model allows users to read resources at or below their classification level, but they are not permitted to write data in locations below their access level. [Security Architecture and Design]

36. A - Quantitative analysis uses numerical data to measure risks, while qualitative analysis uses a subjective approach to prioritizing risks. Cost/ benefit analyses are more credible when based on numerical data. [Information Security Governance and Risk Management]

37. C - Annunciator systems work in tandem with CCTC systems to alert staff that some sort of movement has been detected, by means of lights, SMS messages, sirens, or other mechanism. [Physical (Environmental) Security]

38. B - Awareness of all security policies is critical to their success. Making announcements via email or company meetings, motivational techniques such as games and prizes, training users in the new policy, and mandating that staff affected by the policy sign an acknowledgement form are all excellent ways to maintain high levels of compliance. [Information Security Governance and Risk Management]

39. A - A version control system provides a formal mechanism or framework for the centralized control of software code or documentation. Going beyond a simple revision numbering scheme, a version control system logs the edits that are made to data stored in the system. By using a version control system as the master source for all code to be tested, application teams can be assured they are all working from identical versions of the same file. [Software Development Security]

40.   A - Protection rings are a form of layered protection to prevent unauthorized access to system resources:

Ring 0 protects the operating system kernel

Ring 1 protects the remainder of the operating system

Ring 2 protects I/O functions and resources

Ring 3 protects applications and user activities [Security Architecture and Design]

CISSP Mock Exam (LITE)18
Practice Questions

Test Name: CISSP Mock Exam (LITE)18
Total Questions: 40
Correct Answers Needed to Pass: 30 (75.00%)
Time Allowed: 60 Minutes

Test Description

This is a cumulative CISSP Mock Exam which used as a baseline score for your CISSP aptitude. This practice test includes questions from all ten domains of the CISSP CBK.

Test Questions

1. Blackstone Realty has been operating at an alternate site following a flood that caused major damage to their corporate offices. The corporate offices have now been repaired and restored to a state of operational readiness, and the company is now preparing to move back into their headquarters. In which phase of the business continuity plan is Blackstone Realty now operating?

    A. Reconstitution phase

    B. Restoration phase

    C. Salvage phase

    D. Recovery phase

2. Richard is the inventory manager at a managed hosting service provider. Some of his company's clients have SLAs with exceptionally high levels of availability. In order to provide this level of service, Richard ensures that there are adequate spares for these customers. For this group, which of the following would be the best sparing strategy for a failed disk in an server attached storage array?

    A. SAN

    B. NAS

    C. RAIT

    D. Hot swappable

3. Jones & Dallas Trucking Co. is developing a business continuity plan. With which of the following corporate initiatives should this plan be most tightly integrated?

Practice Exams and Quizzes

A. Public relations materials

B. OSHA regulations

C. Security policy and program

D. SEC regulations

4. JH Enterprises has implemented a policy mandating that IT staff are to be given only the rights and permissions necessary for a given job description. What is this approach called?

A. Dual controls

B. Job rotation

C. Least privilege

D. Separation of duties

5. Which of the following threats represents a significant threat to data confidentiality

A. Unauthorized disclosure of information by an employee

B. Accidental deletion of critical system files

C. Server side includes

D. Server hardware failure

6. Wilmont Systems has indicated that its data backup systems must support restoring all financial transactions that happened up to 5 minutes before a disaster. What type of goal is this?

A. Service level agreement

B. Restore time objective

C. Maximum tolerable downtime

D. Restore point objective

7. Which of the following standards would apply to equipment a police force deployed as a countermeasure against persons under investigation attempting to intercept law enforcement data transmitted in electrical emissions?

A. SESAME

B. HAMLET

C. TEMPEST

CISSP Mock Exam (LITE) – 18 - Practice Questions

D. WAVES

8.   Tom, a member of Acme Tool's accounting staff downloaded a copy of Microsoft Office 2007 from his corporate intranet to put on his home computer. When asked by his wife where he bought it, Tom said "I just copied it from work. Microsoft is a huge company, and making a copy is not a big deal to their bottom line." This scenario represents which ethical fallacy?

A. Both A and B

B. Shatterproof

C. None of the above

D. Candy From a Baby

9.   An attacker calls a corporate help desk, masquerading as an employee who has lost his password. The help desk staff resets the password to the company default of "password1". The attacker is then able to use this password to access the company

network and information on it. What is this type of attack called?

A. Shoulder surfing

B. Fraud

C. Social engineering

D. Identity theft

10.   What formula is used to calculate total risk?

A. Single loss expectancy x frequency per year

B. Threats x vulnerability x asset value

C. Vulnerability x value x control gap

D. Loss x asset value x threats

11.   Mary has deleted the files on her hard drive prior to donating it to the local library. However, Mary's data may not have been completely deleted, leaving that information subject to access by unknown parties. What is this vulnerability called?

A. Slack space

B. Data mining

C. Data remanence

D. Dumpster diving

12. Application layer protocols interface with applications, ensuring that a given program is able to communicate over a network. Which of the following is an example of an application layer protocol?

A. FTP

B. All of the above

C. HTTP

D. SMTP

13. The IT staff at Finkelstein & Smith Distributing notices unusual activity on a server and discovers the system has been compromised. During the incident response, it becomes apparent that the attack was the result of an exploit that changed the order in which lines of

code that use the same resource are executed. Which of the following is this type of attack?

A. Race condition

B. Time of Check/ Time of Use

C. Smurf

D. Teardrop

14. What tool would a hacker use to obtain a password from a hashed value?

A. Social engineering

B. SAM database

C. Encryption salt

D. Rainbow table

15. Five years ago, Marshall Manufacturing implemented a proprietary ERP system at all 15 of its factories and distribution centers. The software was developed by a company that recently declared bankruptcy and has gone out of business. A critical security vulnerability has

been discovered by Marshall Manufacturing, but because they do not have access to the source code, and the company that wrote the software has closed down, the company is unable to address this problem. Which of the following would have prevented this situation?

A. Software as a service

B. Statement of responsibility

C. Service level agreements

D. Software escrow

16. Which of the following is an example of a cybercrime?

A. All of the above

B. Illegally sharing digital materials

C. Software piracy

D. Disseminating offensive materials

17. Federated Freight is developing a new logistics application in-house.

During a review it is discovered that the way the code was written, it is possible for the authorization process to take place just ahead of the authentication process. What is this type of vulnerability called?

A. Sequence exploit

B. Stack flow

C. Race condition

D. Authentication failure

18. World Wide Paint and Pigment is relocating to a new facility. Melissa, the network architect, is designing the backbone of the new network. Which of the following topologies will provide the best protection from an outage at the core of the network?

A. Bus

B. Star

C. Ring

D. Mesh

19. Smith, Klein & Harper has deployed an IDS that can detect a new type of attack without needing to do regular signature updates. Which of the following IDS types are capable of this?

A. Anomaly-based

B. Stateful matching

C. Rule-based

D. Signature-based

20. Covert intelligence agents Bob and Alice encrypt all their communications with each other. Because of the high level of sensitivity of the information they are sharing, they have implemented a cryptographic mechanism that offers perfect secrecy of their messages. However, the trade-off of this encryption is that it is impossible for Bob or Alice to be 100% sure they are communicating with each other, nor can they be 100% certain of the veracity of the content of the messages. Which of the following types of encryption methods are Bob and Alice using?

A. Stream cipher

B. Blowfish

C. One-time pad

D. RSA

21. Three young boys have formed a club, and use a secret code to communicate with each other. To create the code, they scrambled the 26 letters of the alphabet, and use the resulting order of letters in place of the standard alphabetical order. What type of cipher is this?

A. Transposition cipher

B. Stream cipher

C. Polyalphabetic cipher

D. Substitution cipher

22. The Picket Fence cipher encrypts a plain text message by arranging the letters of the message rows, and then adding dummy characters. The message is essentially scrambled and hidden within other text. What is this type of cipher called?

A. Substitution cipher

B. Transposition cipher

C. Monoalphabetic cipher

D. Homophonic cipher

23. John is replacing a switch and a router in his company's data center. At which layers of the OSI model do each of these devices function?

    A. Switches function at Layer 2, Routers at Layer 3

    B. Switches function at Layer 3, Routers at Layer 2

    C. Switches function at Layer 3, Routers at Layer 4

    D. Switches function at Layer 2, Routers at Layer 4

24. Janet and Steven are using the same encryption software to securely share information between themselves. Both Janet and Steven have a public key that they share with each other, and a private key that is used only by the

owner of that key. The shared key is used to encrypt data, the private is used to decrypt data. By which of the following names is this type of system known?

A. Asymmetric encryption

B. DES encryption

C. AES encryption

D. Symmetric encryption

25. When modems send data, they include a data string that tells the recipient where the data starts and stops. What is this method of communication called?

    A. Asynchronous communication

    B. Baseband

    C. Synchronous communication

    D. Streaming

26. Which of the following are examples of centralized access control technologies?

    A. Diameter

B. All of the above

C. TACACS

D. RADIUS

C. Preserve and strengthen the integrity of the public infrastructure.

D. Take only those jobs you are fully qualified to perform

27. A large hospital has determined that its disaster recovery site must be located far enough away from its primary operations site to avoid potential impacts from a regional disaster. What is the minimum recommended distance from the primary site?

A. 50-200 miles

B. 5 miles

C. 500 miles

D. 15 miles

28. Which of the following is codified in the ISC2 Code of Ethics, to which all CISSPs are bound?

A. Observe and abide by all contracts, expressed or implied

B. All of the above

29. Which of the following protocols would be the best choice for an application that is not dependent on guaranteed packet delivery?

A. IP

B. TCP

C. UDP

D. FTP

30. A common network model uses seven layers to describe network communications. What is the name of this model?

A. DoD model

B. ANSI model

C. OSI reference model

D. TCP/IP stack

31. Smith Manufacturing wants to implement a Computer Incident Response Team (CIRT) to respond to specific types of infosec breaches, evaluate the damage, restore or repair the systems involved, and collect evidence for legal or regulatory actions. What staff should be included on this team?

A. Technical staff

B. Legal and HR staff

C. All of the above

D. Senior and line management

32. A team of hackers has broken the encryption code in use on a law firm's database by monitoring how much CPU power is used during encryption and decryption processes, as well as how long these processes take to execute. What is this type of attack called?

A. Side-channel attack

B. Differential analysis

C. TEMPEST

D. Lands End

33. Which of the following is the most important component of a Kerberos system?

A. PGP

B. KDC

C. Tickets

D. TGT

34. A software development team is reviewing security requirements for a new application the HR department wants. The team is considering the safety needs from both a system and data perspective, and want to design an application that remains secure even when the application has crashed. Which of the following is the best choice for the application design?

A. The application should automatically restart.

B. The design should require the application to be restarted and users to re-logon after restart.

C. A security patch

D. The system must be automatically restarted.

35. Josh's laptop is stolen while he is travelling for work. Some of the data on his computer has been protected with file level encryption, but the majority of the data has not been secured. There is concern that the private keys used by Josh in his daily work could be discovered and used to fraudulently access or attack corporate resources. What should be done to ensure the key is not used by an unauthorized person?

A. The laptop disk should be formatted remotely

B. Josh should be terminated

C. Josh's password should be reset

D. The key should be revoked

36. Best practices for the organization of information technology specify which of the following reporting structures?

A. The security administrator should be in the same chain of command as other administrators.

B. Security administrative functions are part of the executive team.

C. Security administrative functions should be absorbed by other administrators.

D. The security administrator should be in a separate chain of command from other administrators.

37. In order to send a message from an email application running on a Windows workstation to another user receiving email through a browser on a Linux workstation, the data must be packaged in a way that permits each layer and intermediary link to direct the data appropriately. What is the process called?

A. Transfers

B. Encapsulation

C. Ethernet

D. Store and forward

38. The legal counsel of Marbury Enterprises has advised that its incident response procedures should be well documented in order to stand up in court. As a result, the team developing the process has decided to base its policy on the six phases of incidence response identified by ISC2. Which of the following is not one of theses phases?

A. Tracking

B. Containment

C. Restitution

D. Triage

39. Due to budget cuts, several developers at a small company have been laid off. Before their access rights were terminated, one of the developers, angry at the

company for his job loss, plants a script intended to delete certain files on a date approximately 6 weeks in the future. What is this type of attack called?

A. Logic bomb

B. Social engineering

C. Trojan horse

D. Counterclockwise

40. Which of the following accurately represents the state of a trusted computing base?

A. Trusted but not trustworthy

B. Trusted and trustworthy

C. Two way trust

D. Transitive trust

CISSP Mock Exam (LITE)18
Answer Key and Explanations

1. A - Once an organization is able to move from an alternate recovery location to its original facility, or to the facility that is the permanent replacement for the original facility, it is considered to be in the reconstitution phase. Until this time, the company is considered to be operating in an emergency state. [Business Continuity and Disaster Recovery Planning]

2. D - Hot swappable drives will provide the fastest repair path for these customers. In the event a disk in an external attached drive array failed, it could be replaced without powering down the system it serves. [Security Operations]

3. C - A business continuity plan is a set of policies, procedures, guidelines, and standards that are intended to ensure the survival and continued operation of a business following a disaster. It should be tightly coupled with the corporate security policy and program for reasons of operational efficiency, cost savings, as well as providing an overarching framework protecting the business and its

assets from threats to its survival and well being. [Business Continuity and Disaster Recovery Planning]

4. C - Providing a user only the minimum rights and permissions required for his or her job is known as least privilege. This approach prevents control of or access to critical resources from being distributed too broadly within an organization. [Security Operations]

5. A - Many organizations focus significant resources on preventing attacks from external parties. However, the unauthorized release of data by company employees is also a significant threat to data confidentiality. Such a release can cause harm to an organization in many ways: loss of reputation, fines for violation of regulations regarding the secure storage and use of certain data, and trade secrets falling into the hands of competitors are all potential outcomes. [Security Operations]

6. D - A recovery point objective is a goal mandating that functionality or data access must be restored to a specific moment in time or level

of capacity. It differs from a recovery time objective in that it does not mandate how quickly this goal must be achieved. [Business Continuity and Disaster Recovery Planning]

7. C - TEMPEST is a set of technical requirements for the reduction of electromagnetic waves for the purpose of making it very difficult for an attacker to gather information from those waves. [Access Control]

8. A - Software piracy is an example of both the Candy From A Baby Fallacy and the Shatterproof Fallacy. The Candy From A Baby Fallacy is the belief that because something is easy to do with a computer, it can't be wrong. The Shatterproof Fallacy is the belief that actions taken with a computer only affect a few files, without considering the harm that can be caused to others through those actions. [Information Security Governance and Risk Management]

9. C - Social engineering is any attempt by a hacker to use non-technical means to acquire sensitive information such as

passwords or PINs, in order to gain access to secured information.. The best countermeasure for this kind of attack is a strong security awareness and training program. [Security Architecture and Design]

10. B - To determine total risk, one must first identify and quantify threats and vulnerabilities, as well as the value of assets, and then apply the following formula: threats x vulnerability x asset value. [Information Security Governance and Risk Management]

11. C - Data remanence refers to data that remains on a disk or in memory even after attempts have been made to remove it. [Security Architecture and Design]

12. B - All of the above protocols are used by applications to transmit data over the network. Each of these protocols interfaces with a specific type of application to ensure that data it sends or receives is constructed in a format usable by the application and the adjacent presentation Layer [Telecommunications and Network Security]

13. A - In a race condition, two different processes need to use one resource to perform their tasks, and the processes must follow a specific sequence. In this type of attack, the order in which code is processed is changed, thereby allowing an attacker to control the outcome. For example, an attacker could force an application to process a request for data access first, circumventing the process for authentication. [Security Architecture and Design]

14. D - A rainbow table is a precalculated list of possible passwords based on the hashed value of a password. Rather than using a dictionary or brute force attack to crack a password, an attacker can use a previously generated list of possible passwords that have been hashed. The hashed value of the password is compared to the rainbow table in an attempt to find a matching value. [Access Control]

15. D - Contracting with a 3rd party to hold source code, documentation, user manuals, and other supporting data owned by one company but implemented by another company is called a software escrow. The interests of both companies are protected by this type of agreement. The intellectual property of the software owner is held securely by a 3rd party, and a contract defines the conditions under which the implementing company may access it. In this scenario, software escrow would have permitted Marshall Manufacturing to legally access the source code in order to develop necessary patches, despite the fact the developing company is defunct. [Business Continuity and Disaster Recovery Planning]

16. A - The types of activities classified as cybercrimes extends beyond the theft of credit card numbers, denial of service attacks, or vandalizing a corporate website. A cybercrime is any act where digital property such as software or digital music is used in a manner not authorized by the owner, or where the type of information disseminated violates local ordinances. Distribution of unlicensed software, copyrighted movies or music, or pornographic materials in violation of local laws are all examples of cybercrimes. [Legal, Regulations, Compliance and Investigations]

17.   C - A race condition results when an application attempts to complete two steps at the same time, and the completion of one process is dependent on the output of another process. It is possible that an attacker could exploit the Federated Freight application by forcing the authorization process to take place first, bypassing the authentication process. [Access Control]

18.   D - Meshed networks provide multiple pathways between devices in a network, ensuring that if one path fails, all devices will still be able to communicate with each other over the remaining pathways. [Telecommunications and Network Security]

19.   A - Anomaly-based IDS systems monitor system activity to classify it as either normal or anomalous. Because it is able to determine from its own analysis if an attack is underway, it is not dependent on signature updates. [Access Control]

20.   C - Encryption using one-time pads offers perfect security or confidentiality of messages. Because the key is never reused,

never shared, and is randomly generated, messages encrypted in this manner cannot be broken. However, this type of mechanism does not offer any sort of authentication of the sender's identity, nor does it offer any data integrity mechanism. Therefore, a 3rd party could pose as a legitimate sender, or intercept and modify the message in some way. [Cryptography]

21.   D - Substitution ciphers are based on the simple substitution of cipher characters for plaintext characters. The code is created by rearranging the order of the alphabet, and mapping the "real" alphabet to the re-ordered alphabetic characters. Because of the simplicity of this type of cipher, it is easily cracked, often by simple frequency analysis of character usage. [Cryptography]

22.   B - Transposition ciphers are created by rearranging, or scrambling, the order of a plaintext message. A numerical key is generated based on the relative location of the rearranged characters. While this is similar to a substitution cipher where one letter is used in place of another, a substitution cipher bases the order of characters in an encrypted message on a separate cipher key, not the plaintext itself. [Cryptography]

23. A - Switches are Layer 2 (Data link Layer) devices that are intended to simply transmit data from device to device, while routers are Layer 3 (Network Layer) devices that are intended to transmit data from network to network. [Telecommunications and Network Security]

24. A - A public/ private key system is an asymmetric encryption mechanism. Public keys are shared between users of the same encryption software, while the private keys are known only by the owner of that key. The sender uses the public key of the recipient to encrypt the message, while the private key of the recipient is used to decrypt the message. Asymmetric encryption is more computationally intensive than symmetric cryptography, and is best used for small data payloads. [Cryptography]

25. A - When two systems communicate, they must be able to

determine where data starts and stops for processing purposes. Asynchronous communication, used by modems, terminal services, and serial communication devices, uses data strings to denote that information. Because these start and stop delimiters add additional overhead, it is best for communications that involve sending small amounts of data at one time. [Telecommunications and Network Security]

26. B - In the centralized access control model all authentication, authorization, and accounting functions are handled by a single entity. RADIUS, TACACS, and Diameter are all remote access control technologies that are managed by a single entity. The advantage of a centralized model is consistently applied access policies. The disadvantage, however, is this model tends to be slower to respond to requests for changes, adds, or deletes. [Access Control]

27. A - Industry best practices recommend disaster recovery sites be located a minimum distance of 50-200 miles from the primary site to avoid potential impact from regional disasters such as storms or

earthquakes. [Business Continuity and Disaster Recovery Planning]

28. B - All of the above responsibilities are part of the ISC2 Code of Ethics. The Code is composed of 4 major canons, which are intended to guide CISSPs and information security professionals when ethical dilemmas are encountered. [Legal, Regulations, Compliance and Investigations]

29. C - UDP is a transport protocol that offers very fast speed with very low overhead. However, it is a connectionless protocol, meaning it does not establish a communications channel with the system with which is communicating, nor does it offer any sort of guaranteed packet delivery or sequencing. [Telecommunications and Network Security]

30. C - The OSI reference model compartmentalizes network functions into seven layers: physical, data link, network, transport, session, presentation, and application. [Telecommunications and Network Security]

31. C - Computer Incident Response Teams (CIRT)are composed of staff with a range of roles, responsibilities, and skills both technical and non-technical. Depending on the organization and the types of incidents to which the CIRT is chartered to respond to, these teams include members of legal, human resources, finance, IT, and senior management. [Information Security Governance and Risk Management]

32. A - A side-channel attack uses data gathered from the physical infrastructure upon which an encryption algorithm runs to crack an encryption key, rather than brute force or exploiting weaknesses. This can include monitoring CPU cycles and usage, electromagnetic patterns, power usage, or even the sounds a device makes as it executes computational functions. [Cryptography]

33. B - The Key Distribution Center (KDC) is the most critical component of a Kerberos system. Besides containing the secret keys of all users and services, the KDC provides key distribution and authentication services. [Access Control]

34.   B - When an application fails it should enter a mode called a failed state. Once an application enters a failed state, it must be restarted and user credentials presented again. By designing this as the default failure recovery mechanism, application teams do not have to develop solutions for every possible reason an application may fail. [Software Development Security]

35.   D - When a private key is lost, it must be revoked to prevent unauthorized persons from using it. Revocation is performed within the key management system. [Cryptography]

36.   D - Best practice calls for security administrative tasks to be handled by dedicated staff, and these staff report to a different chain of command than the other administrative staff. This prevents conflicting priorities between daily operations management tasks and security management functions, which can result in a lowered security stance. [Security Operations]

37.   B - Encapsulation is the process by which destination and control information is added to or removed from data as it is passed from layer to layer in a network model. [Telecommunications and Network Security]

38.   C - ISC2 subdivides incident response into 6 distinct phases: triage, investigation, containment, analysis, tracking, and recovery. [Legal, Regulations, Compliance and Investigations]

39.   A - A logic bomb is a piece of malicious code that is intended to perform one or more processes at such time as specific criteria are met. Planting code that is set to execute a file deletion script on a certain date is an example of this type of attack. [Security Architecture and Design]

40.   A - A trusted computing base (TCB) is the set of all the hardware, software, and firmware components that are critical to a system's security. The TCB is trusted to provide system security within practical limits, but it is understood the TCB is not trustworthy, can be compromised by defects such as faulty code or

physical failure of the hardware.
[Security Architecture and Design]

CISSP Mock Exam (LITE)19
Practice Questions

Test Name: CISSP Mock Exam (LITE)19
Total Questions: 40
Correct Answers Needed to Pass: 30 (75.00%)
Time Allowed: 60 Minutes

Test Description

This is a cumulative CISSP Mock Exam which used as a baseline score for your CISSP aptitude. This practice test includes questions from all ten domains of the CISSP CBK.

Test Questions

1. The security department at Global Storage Technologies is evaluating fingerprint readers for biometric access to its facilities. They are particularly interested in systems that have a minimum rate of false errors. Which factor should the security team scrutinize most closely?

    A. Crossover error rate

    B. Type II errors

    C. Ejection rate

    D. Type I errors

2. A development team is designing an application that is dependent on reliable data delivery. Which transport protocol will best serve their needs?

    A. UDP

    B. HTTPS

    C. FTP

    B. TCP

3. Drafting software in use at an architecture firm is a very CPU intensive application due to the amount of resources required to support the graphics. This type of application would run in which mode?

    A. User

    B. I/O

    C. Privileged

    D. Protected

4. Fairfield Bay Semiconductor has implemented a backup mechanism that provides redundancy for database transactions. What is this type of backup called?

A. Journaling

B. Vaulting

C. Incremental

D. Full

5. Mills Trucking has implemented a special zone to house its corporate network. This zone is logically situated between two firewalls. One firewall is between the webserver and the Internet, the other firewall is between the webserver and the corporate network. What is this zone called?

A. Gateway

B. Subnet

C. VLAN

D. DMZ

6. ActiveX is used to provide extended functionality and interactive content for websites . The controls are downloaded onto the system of the user visiting the website. In which of the following would ActiveX download settings be configured?

A. IDS

B. Firewall

C. Web server

D. Web browser

7. A user enters a www.acme.com into a web browser, and the request is sent over the internet to the webserver that hosts that website. Because network traffic is directed across the internet by means of a destination address, what service is necessary to translate www.acme.com to its IP address?

A. ARP

B. DNS

C. WIINS

D. Cache

8. The law firm of Ross, Huff, and Wilson is remodeling its single story office building. The renovation work includes replacing all exterior windows and doors. Which of the following types of glass is recommended for this scenario?

   A. Bullet resistant glass

   B. Tempered glass

   C. Laminated glass

   D. Wired glass

9. Which of the following is not a type of malware?

   A. Trojan horse

   B. Virus

   C. Worm

   D. Mobile code

10. Which of the Rainbow Series books defines the requirements for

testing the security of a computer system?

   A. Blue Book

   B. Yellow Book

   C. Orange Book

   D. Red Book

11. The customer credit card data of PCC Industries has been stolen by hackers who then used this information to make hundreds of fraudulent credit card purchases . Several affected customers decide to sue PCC. During the trial their attorney provides evidence that PCC had a legally recognized obligation to protect it's customers' data but failed to do so, and the customers' damages were the result of this failure. What has the plaintiff's attorney established?

   A. Criminal intent

   B. Malfeasance

   C. Negligence

   D. Risk

12. What types of risk management are representing in the following scenarios? a) Implementing an enterprise backup system to reduce the likelihood of data loss is an example of what type of risk management, and b) acquiring insurance for the data center in which the backup system resides.

A. Risk Acceptance and Risk Transference

B. Risk avoidance and Risk Transference

C. Risk Transference and Risk Avoidance

D. Risk Mitigation and Risk Transference

13. Planning for a disaster must include more than just a plan for replacement facilities and infrastructure. Which of the following is another critical area of analysis and business continuity planning?

A. Business process recovery

B. Role evaluation

C. Responsibility matrix

D. Resource accountability

14. The city library of Pine Branch would like to provide a computer for the public to use for internet access. However, the staff wants to prevent users from accessing critical system files or changing configuration parameters like screen savers, desktop background, and so forth.   Which of the following access controls would best meet their needs?

A. Discretionary

B. Role-based

C. None of the above

D. Access control lists

15. Joan and Mary each work for a different company, but often collaborate on projects.   Both companies have setup PKI infrastructure, and their employees have been given certificates authenticating their identities. Joan needs to access resources in

Mary's network, and Mary needs to access resources in Joan's network. Which of the following would allow Joan and Mary to be authenticated to access the resources they need?

A. Key distribution server

B. Cross- certification

C. Root certificate

D. Access control list

16. The administrator of a small office LAN is investigating the cause of slow performance on the network. It appears that a broadcast storm from a faulty network card is the cause of the latency. Which of the following devices would pass this broadcast traffic from one LAN segment to another?

A. Bridges

B. Concentrator

C. Router

D. Repeater

17. Carl wants to send a file securely to Bob. It is important that the encryption mechanism be fast and provide a high level of confidentiality. Message integrity, authentication, and non-repudiation are not as important to Carl. Which of the following encryption mechanisms best meets Carl's needs?

A. El Gamal

B. RSA

C. AES

D. Diffie-Hellman

18. The database administrator at a mid-sized insurance company is implementing a way to grant different levels of access rights and permissions to different employees, without assigning those access rights and permissions on a user by user basis. What is this approach called?

A. Role-based access

B. Group policy

C. Rule-based access

A. Data diddling

B. Embezzlement

D. Access control list

C. Superman attack

D. Salami attack

19. A New York-based company is acquiring the assets of a company based in London. They will be sharing sensitive and personally identifiable information about employees and customers. Which of the following is a framework that these two companies could use when determining how to secure the data being shared?

21. Following an information security breach, the incident response team at Lloyd & Grace, LLP gathers evidence of the attack. The team documents who gathered the evidence, how it was gathered, to whom the evidence was given for safe storage, where the storage site is located, and every person that has accessed the evidence following its collection. What is this documentation called?

A. Safe Harbor

B. SAFER Barrier

C. PKI

A. Chain of custody

D. X.509

B. Logging

C. Incident report

20. Ted is a sales rep for a health club. Once he has closed a sale, he takes payment for the $80 joining fee. Every so often, Ted tells the new member the joining fee is $100, charges the customer this amount, but enters $80 into the club's accounting system and keeps the extra $20 for himself. What is type of data attack called?

D. Protocol

22. Tim is a system administrator at his company. In addition to managing the servers, his duties include non-admin tasks such as creating system documentation and script development. Which of the following is the most secure method for Tim to conduct these additional duties?

A. Logging into his workstation with an ordinary user account.

B. Adding admin privileges to his user account.

C. Logging into his workstation with an admin account

D. Disabling his admin account when not in use

23. The property manager of an office building is installing a new video surveillance system in all public areas. What is the best type of camera lens to be used in the building's lobby area?

A. Telephoto

B. Auto iris lens

C. Long focal length

D. Short focal length

24. A company has taken out an insurance policy as a countermeasure against loss due to a material breach in its network. What type of loss could be incurred from a data breach?

A. Losses related to the cost of recovery from the breach

B. Loss of revenue due to interruption of business

C. Loss of reputation

D. All of the above

25. Zoey is performing penetration testing on her company's network. What is the purpose of this type of testing?

A. Vulnerability identification

B. Intrusion prevention

C. Intrusion detection

D. Malware prevention

26. A small business has implemented a security policy mandating the use of 2-factor authentication to log on

to their network, and the encryption of all data sent into or out of the network. However, limiting their security policies to just these two protective mechanisms will leave the business exposed to what type of threat?

A. Man in the middle

B. Spoofing

C. DoS

D. Replay attacks

27. John swipes his badge to open the door to the warehouse of Wilson Lumber and holds the door for Jane to pass through without swiping her badge. What is this type of access control circumvention called?

A. Carpooling

B. Proximity access

C. Piggybacking

D. Man in the middle

28. The Capability Maturity Model (CMM) provides a framework to assist organizations standardize their approach to software development. There are five maturity ratings within this framework. Which of the following levels indicates an organization has budgeted and integrated plans for continuous process improvement?

A. Managed

B. Optimizing

C. Defined

D. Repeatable

29. The lock on a storage facility uses an electronic keypad for access code entry. What additional security components should be implemented with this?

A. Solenoid mechanism and adequate area lighting

B. Entry delay and badge reader

C. Mantrap and egress control

D. Keypad shield and battery backup

30. Because of the computational capacities of modern computers, the DES standard was replaced by the National Institute of Standards and Technologies by a more cryptographically secure standard. Which of the following algorithms is the basis for the new standard?

A. Twofish

B. RC6

C. Rijndael

D. MARS

31. Jan is calculating the maximum tolerable downtime (MTD) for financial reporting capabilities for her company's business continuity plan. After interviewing the company's senior and executive management team, it is determined that, because the company operates on a global basis and a disaster at one location would not necessarily impact operations at another location, the ability to run these reports should be restored

within 24 hours. Which of the following MTD estimates would apply to reporting capabilities

A. Critical

B. Normal

C. Urgent

D. Important

32. The most recent inventory at McCall's Fixtures shows the level of certain types of products in storage is lower than expected. In response, management decides to change the types of locks in use on its storage facilities. They have selected a type of lock that is resistant to attack for 30 minutes. Which of the following locks have they selected?

A. Security container key lock

B. Rim Lock

C. Deadbolt lock

D. Cylinder lock

33. Currently, when a sales person at MPC Systems wants to know which customers purchased a specific product, he or she must run the same query on each of several databases that contain information from each of the company's divisions. This approach takes several minutes, and the sales person must then consolidate the data into a single report before analyzing the data. Which of the following could streamline this process?

A. Relational database

B. Data warehousing

C. Object oriented database

D. Data mining

34. McDonald Engineering is developing a physical security plan that incorporates multiple types of protective elements, including lighting, landscaping, alarms, badge access systems, and patrols. Which of the following best describes this approach?

A. Deter-detect-delay-respond

B. Crime Prevention Through Environmental Design (CPTED)

C. All of the above

D. Defense in depth

35. Dan is reviewing account usage logs and sees that Jan has not logged in for several weeks. He contacts Jan's supervisor to investigate this inactivity, and learns that Jan is on maternity leave for the next 60 days. What should Dan's next step be?

A. Disable Jan's account

B. Change the password on Jan's account

C. Delete Jan's account

D. Rename Jan's account

36. What type of risk assessment includes likelihood determination?

A. OCTAVE

B. PUSH

C. All of the above

D. Delphi

37. A small company has posted links to several files on its public website. Rather than using a sanitized version of a URL that points to a virtual directory, however, the URLs for these files reveal the actual file and folder structure of the server where the files are housed. Which of the following attacks exploits this particular vulnerability?

A. Denial of service

B. Spoofing

C. Rainbow tables

D. Directory traversal

38. The Payment Card Industry Security Standards Council has mandated various security standards for ATM hardware, software, and keypads. Which of the following encryption algorithms is the PCI standard for ATMs?

A. 3DES

B. Blowfish

C. SSL

D. DES

39. Backing up to tape or other removable media can take a significant amount of time to complete. Which of the following backup types take the least amount of time to perform?

A. Partial

B. Incremental

C. Intermediate

D. Differential

40. As an alternative to removable media backups, some organizations opt to use online backups. Which type of online backup provides faster IO access to files?

A. Journaling

B. Electronic vaulting

C. Differential

D. Disk shadowing

CISSP Mock Exam (LITE)19 Answer Key and Explanations

1. A - The crossover error rate (CER) provides the best insight into a biometric system's accuracy. It is the point at which Type I errors (false rejection rate) equal Type II errors (false acceptance rate). When comparing the CER of two systems, the system with a lower rate is the more accurate of the two. [Access Control]

2. D - TCP is a connection oriented protocol that sets up a virtual connection between two systems. This connection, also known as a socket, is built and taken down when no longer needed by means of a three-way handshake between the two systems. Additionally, TCP ensures that all data has been received, and the packets that have been received are assembled in the correct order. [Telecommunications and Network Security]

3. C - CPU-intensive applications typically run in privileged or kernel mode; this processing mode allows code to have direct access to all hardware and memory in the system, including the CPU. [Security Architecture and Design]

4. A - Journaling provides the ability to recover a database by means of transaction replay. When a transaction is conducted in the primary database, the completed transaction is stored on a redundant database system. If the primary database fails, the transactions stored on the backup system can be replayed, thus rebuilding the database. This type of backup allows rapid recovery up to the point of the last completed transaction; a tape backup solution provides a restore point only as recent as the last tape backup. [Security Operations]

5. D - A DMZ, or demilitarized zone, is a buffer zone between the Internet and a private network. Firewalls are used to delineate the boundaries of this zone. Devices and servers placed in the DMZ are vulnerable to attack, so they are typically hardened and further protected by an intrusion detection system (IDS). [Telecommunications and Network Security]

6.   D - ActiveX download settings are configured at the user level, within the browser. Users may opt to download ActiveX components automatically (less secure) or manually (more secure). [Software Development Security]

7.   B - DNS, or domain name service, is used to map friendly names, called domain names, to IP addresses. When a user enters www.acme.com into a web browser, a name request is forwarded to a DNS server, where the name is mapped to a corresponding IP address. The IP address is returned to the requester, and the system then sends the original web request to the IP address of the webserver. [Telecommunications and Network Security]

8.   C - Laminated glass is recommended for use in street level windows and doors. It is composed of two sheets of glass bonded to a middle layer of plastic. When laminated glass is struck with enough force to break the glass, the plastic layer prevents the glass from shattering and displacement onto surrounding surfaces. [Physical (Environmental) Security]

9.   D - Mobile code is any application that has a remote source but is executed locally. Examples of this type of threat include java scripts hidden on website, or applications on removable media that launch and run automatically upon insertion into a system. Because there is no need for user intervention to launch these code attacks, it is easy for attackers exploit remote systems that do not have appropriate countermeasures. [Access Control]

10.   C - The Rainbow Books are a series of security guidelines and standards published by various US government agencies. They are known as the Rainbow Books because each book has a different color cover. The Orange Book is called the Trusted Computer System Evaluation Criteria (TCSEC) and sets forth the requirements for assessing the security of a given computer system. [Security Architecture and Design]

11.   C - An individual or organization that does not take adequate precautions against a risk and a 3rd party is injured because of this failure can be held liable for the damages caused. To prove liability, there must be a legally recognized obligation to protect the 3rd party, the person or organization must have failed to implement protective measures, and the injury or damages must be the direct result, also called proximate causation, of the failure to implement protective measures. [Legal, Regulations, Compliance and Investigations]

12. D - Risk mitigation and risk transference is the correct response. Risk mitigation is the reduction or elimination of a risk by implementing countermeasures against a threat. Countermeasures include such safeguards as backup systems, firewalls, or badge readers. Risk transference is the practice of passing the risk to another party, such as an insurance company or a managed service provider. [Information Security Governance and Risk Management]

13. A - Business process recovery is a very important element of a business continuity plan. The BCP

team must identify critical business processes and analyze the steps in those processes, as well as the staff and resources required to execute the process. This information is used to create a contingency plan for recovery in the event of the loss of staff or resources needed to execute the processes. [Business Continuity and Disaster Recovery Planning]

14. C - None of the above is the correct answer. The access control technique the library staff should implement is called a constrained user interface. This control prevents or limits access to functions or files by not allowing users to request prohibited resources. This can be accomplished by providing a menu that contains limited choices. In the case of the library, the menu could present only the web browser. [Access Control]

15. B - Multiple organizations that have a need for its users to be recognized by each of the other organizations can sign each other's public key or root certificate. This is called cross-certification, and establishes a trust relationship based on the controls negotiated

by the organizations. Cross-certifications can be peer to peer or hierarchical. [Cryptography]

16. A - Bridges are used to subdivide networks into smaller segments. Because they have more intelligence than hubs, they are able to forward traffic between network segments. However, this capability also allows broadcast storms that occur on one segment to be forwarded to all other segments, potentially impacting an entire LAN. [Telecommunications and Network Security]

17. C - AES offers the highest level of encryption among the cryptographic mechanisms listed. It is a symmetric algorithm, and encrypts data very quickly. However, it does not offer authentication, integrity, or proof of origin controls. The remaining algorithms are asymmetric algorithms used for exchanging keys, not the encryption of data. [Cryptography]

18. A - Rather than granting permissions and access rights to individual users, database administrators can assign these rights and permissions to a role,

then add the user to that role. By managing security at the role level, administrators can avoid situations whereby individual accounts may, over time, accumulate more access rights and permissions than required for their specific job within the organization. [Software Development Security]

19. A - Safe Harbor is a set of principles that provide guidance on acceptable levels of security for personal data transmitted between organizations in Europe and the US. This framework allows each country to adhere to its own laws, regulations, and organizational policies, while still providing a meaningful level of security trusted by other countries. [Legal, Regulations, Compliance and Investigations]

20. A - Data diddling refers to an attack that alters existing data in some way. In this scenario, the data was altered between the new member's approval of the $100 fee and Ted entering it as $80 in the accounting application. [Legal, Regulations, Compliance and Investigations]

21. A - When evidence is collected during an investigation, documentation is created to log what was collected, who collected it, to whom it was transferred, and its current disposition. This paper trail is called the chain of custody, and it is used in court to prove that the evidence has not been altered or tampered with. [Legal, Regulations, Compliance and Investigations]

22. A - Adhering to the principle of least privilege, Tim should have two accounts: a privileged admin level account for performing systems work, and a non-privileged account such as an ordinary user or power user to perform non-administrative tasks. [Security Operations]

23. D - Short focal length lenses provide a wide angle view of an area, which is ideal in an open area such as a lobby. Long focal length lenses provide a very narrow view, which is more appropriate for small areas such as entry/ exit points. [Physical (Environmental) Security]

24. D - When the security of an organization's data is breached, both direct and indirect losses can occur. Direct losses include loss of trade secrets and intellectual property, while indirect losses can include loss of reputation, lost productivity during an outage caused by the breach, and the cost of fines and restitution related to the loss of confidential customer or employee information. [Legal, Regulations, Compliance and Investigations]

25. A - Penetration testing can identify vulnerabilities that may be exploited by an attacker. By proactively discovering these vulnerabilities, an organization can implement countermeasures to reduce the risk of a successful attack. [Security Operations]

26. D - Strong authentication and encryption will thwart most man in the middle and spoofing attacks. However, the data packets in transit may be intercepted and used in a replay attack, where the data is resent to the destination at a later time. Using some sort of timestamp on the packets being sent are an effective countermeasure to this threat. [Cryptography]

27. C - Piggybacking is the term for two or more persons passing through an access point on a single access method, such as one card swipe or PIN entry. This isn't always a malicious intrusion; many times one employee simply holds the door open for the employee behind him or her. However, this could allow users without proper authorization to enter highly sensitive or secure areas. A security awareness program reminding users that every staff member must use their access control mechanism (e.g. swiping their badge or entering their PIN) every time they pass through a controlled portal is a company policy is a countermeasure for this. [Physical (Environmental) Security]

28. B - Optimizing is the highest level of maturity in the CMM framework. Organizations reaching this level have reached a point in their development processes where continuous improvement of existing processes is the focus. Less mature levels in the framework place the focus on developing, implementing, and managing standard, repeatable processes. [Software Development Security]

29. D - When using electronic cipher locks, it is highly recommended that the keypad be shielded from view by anyone but the immediate user, to prevent unauthorized users from shoulder surfing key codes. These types of locks should also be connected to a battery backup to ensure continuous operation of the lock during power outages. [Physical (Environmental) Security]

30. C - NIST selected the Rijndael algorithm as the replacement standard for DES. Also known as the Advanced Encryption Standard or AES, it is a symmetric block cipher that supports key sizes of 128, 192, and 256 bits. [Cryptography]

31. C - ISC2 provides the following MTD estimates for business continuity planning: nonessential: 30 days; normal: seven days; important: 72 hours; urgent: 24 hours; critical: minutes to hours. It is important to note that more than one estimate will be used within an organization, as various functions and capabilities much each be MTD-rated. [Business Continuity and Disaster Recovery Planning]

32. A - Underwriter Laboratories standard 437 requires that security container key locks withstand 30 minutes of attack by various means, including picking, drilling, sawing, prying, and punching. [Physical (Environmental) Security]

33. B - Data warehousing could streamline data gathering and reporting for this organization. A data warehouse consolidates data from different databases and provides it in a user friendly format. It is important to note the warehouse contains copies of the data from each source it services; when a user executes a query, the results returned are from the warehouse's data store. [Software Development Security]

34. C - A robust physical security plan includes multiple elements that are layered in such a way as to act as failsafe measures. Defense in depth, CPTED, and deter-detect-delay-respond all address this layered approach to security. [Physical (Environmental) Security]

35. A - Personnel policies should be implemented requiring managers to notify IT of an employee's extended leave or termination. However, as a backup to this policy, user account activity should also be regularly monitored by IT. In the event an account is discovered to be inactive for an extended period of time, best practices dictate the account be temporarily disabled if the account owner will be returning, or deleted if the account owner has left the organization. Unused accounts are susceptible to fraudulent use, as the identity of the perpetrator of such use would not be easily discovered by simple auditing. [Security Operations]

36. C - OCTAVE, Delphi, and PUSH are qualitative risk assessment methodologies that use subjective measurements, including likelihood determination and determination of impact, to determine risk. Quantitative risk assessment methodologies use numerical values to determine risk. [Information Security Governance and Risk Management]

37. D - When an attacker can see the true file path as part of a URL, he or she can execute a directory traversal attack to navigate into other folders and files. This is accomplished by inserting a standard comandline directory navigation command, "../" , into the URL to move upward in the directory structure, then running other commands to view and change directories at will. This attack is also known as the "dot slash" attack, named after the characters used to initiate the directory traversal. [Software Development Security]

38.   A - 3DES, also known as Triple DES is an encryption algorithm that applies the DES cipher 3 times to each data block, with either 2 or 3 different keys. This is a very strong cryptographic algorithm, but the tradeoff is that it is also very computationally intensive. [Cryptography]

39.   B - Incremental backups take less time to complete than either full or differential backups, as only the files with changed archived bits are backed up. However, incremental backups are more complicated and take more time to restore, because they must be restored in the precise order in which they were backed up to avoid missing a file. [Business Continuity and Disaster Recovery Planning]

40.   D - Disk shadowing uses two complete and identical sets of data on two or more disks that appear as a single drive to the system. In the event that one of the disks fails, the data on the remaining set is still available to users. Because identical data are available on two separate disks, IO performance is improved when a multiple users attempt to simultaneously access a file. [Business Continuity and Disaster Recovery Planning]

ADDITIONAL RESOURCES

Exam Taking Tips

Studying for a multiple choice exam entails preparing in a unique way as opposed to other types of tests. The CISSP exam asks one to recognize correct answers among a set of four options. The extra options that are not the correct answer are called the "distracters"; and their purpose, unsurprisingly, is to distract the test taker from the actual correct answer among the bunch.

Students usually consider multiple choice exams as much easier than other types of exams; this is not necessarily true with the CISSP exam. Among these reasons are:

- Most multiple choice exams ask for simple, factual information; unlike the CISSP exam which often requires the student to apply knowledge and make a best judgment.

- The majority of multiple choice exams involve a large quantity of different questions – so even if you get a few incorrect, it's still okay. The CISSP exam covers a broad set of material, often times in greater depth than other certification exams.

Regardless of whether or not multiple choice testing is more forgiving; in reality, one must study immensely because of the sheer volume of information that is covered.

Although 6 hours may seem like more than enough time for a multiple choice exam; time management remains a crucial factor in succeeding and doing well. You should always try and answer all of the questions you are confident about first, and then go back to those items you are not sure about afterwards. Always read *carefully* through the entire test as well, and do your best to not leave any question blank upon submission—even if you do not readily know the answer.

Many people do very well with reading through each question and not looking at the options before trying to answer. This way, they can steer clear (usually) of being fooled by one of the "distracter" options or get into a tug-of-war between two choices that both have a good chance of being the actual answer.

Never assume that "all of the above" or "none of the above" answers are the actual choice. Many times they are, but in recent years they have been used much more frequently as distracter options on standardized tests. Typically this is done in an effort to get people to stop believing the myth that they are always the correct answer.

You should be careful of negative answers as well. These answers contain words such as "none", "not", "neither", and the like. Despite often times being very confusing, if you read these types of questions and answers carefully, then you should be able to piece together which is the correct answer. Just take your time!

Never try to overanalyze a question, or try and think about how the test givers are trying to lead astray potential test takers. Keep it simple and stay with what you know.

If you ever narrow down a question to two possible answers, then try and slow down your thinking and think about how the two different options/answers differ. Look at the question again and try to apply how this difference between the two potential answers relates to the question. If you are convinced there is literally no difference between the two potential answers (you'll more than likely be wrong in assuming this), then take another look at the answers that you've already eliminated. Perhaps one of them is actually the correct one and you'd made a previously unforeseen mistake.

On occasion, over-generalizations are used within response options to mislead test takers. To help guard against this, always be wary of responses/answers that use absolute words like "always", or "never". These are less likely to actually be the answer than phrases like "probably" or "usually" are. Funny or witty responses are also, most of the time, incorrect – so steer clear of those as much as possible.

Although you should always take each question individually, "none of the above" answers are usually less likely to be the correct selection than "all of the above" is. Keep this in mind with the understanding that it is not an absolute rule, and should be analyzed on a case-by-case (or "question-by-question") basis.

Looking for grammatical errors can also be a huge clue. If the stem ends with an indefinite article such as "an" then you'll probably do well to look for an answer that begins with a vowel instead of a consonant. Also, the longest response is also oftentimes the correct one, since whoever wrote the question item may have tended to load the answer with qualifying adjectives or phrases in an effort to make it correct. Again though, always deal with these on a question-by-question basis, because you could very easily be getting a question where this does not apply.

Verbal associations are oftentimes critical because a response may repeat a key word that was in the question. Always be on the alert for this. Playing the old Sesame Street game "Which of these things is not like the other" is also a very solid strategy, if a bit preschool. Sometimes many of a question's distracters will be very similar to try to trick you into thinking that one choice is related to the other. The answer very well could be completely unrelated however, so stay alert.

Just because you have finished a practice test, be aware that you are not done working. After you have graded your test with all of the necessary corrections, review it and try to recognize what happened in the answers that you got wrong. Did you simply not know the qualifying correct information? Perhaps you were led astray by a solid distracter answer? Going back through your corrected test will give you a leg up on your next one by revealing your tendencies as to what you may be vulnerable with, in terms of multiple choice tests.

It may be a lot of extra work, but in the long run, going through your corrected multiple choice tests will work wonders for you in preparation for the real exam. See if you perhaps misread the question or even missed it because you were unprepared. Think of it like instant replays in professional sports. You are going back and looking at what you did on the big stage in the past so you can help fix and remedy any errors that could pose problems for you on the real exam.

Made in the USA
Lexington, KY
10 September 2014